I hope yc

— Remy

9-16-15

PRAISE FOR

THE SEA IS WIDE: A MEMOIR OF CAREGIVING

"It is a must-read for those taking care of loved ones suffering from Alzheimer's and for those in the medical and nursing profession. I will definitely recommend this book to my patients and nursing students."

—Louise O'Keefe, PhD, CRNP

"A real insight into the depth, love and reality of a caregiver and a victim of Alzheimer's"

—Debbie Rombach, RN

"[A]n honest look at what daily care looks like through the eyes of a loving care-giver. I laughed, I cried, but most of all, I observed how it is possible to care for a loved one through the very bad days that are inevitable while also being grateful for every respite. [...] I want to thank you for showing me that beyond all the heartache this can be a journey of love and dignity."

—Cynthia Phillips, Caregiver

"*The Sea is Wide* gives healthcare professionals an inside look at the struggles that families of those effected by Alzheimer's face on a daily basis"

—Nicole Wayman, LPN

"I highly recommend this book"

—Wilmer Estevez, RN

"I laughed and cried my way through [...] it echoed things I went through with my mother and her dementia."

"[T]he book also teaches allowing the victims of Alzheimer's as much dignity and independence as possible at each stage keeps him from being less than the person he is capable of being and even triggers joyful moments.

"Alzheimer's is ultimately a death sentence. Like life, however, it's not the destination that should be the focus, it's the journey—like the journey you recounted in *The Sea is Wide*."

—Alice Janick, Caregiver

"I would recommend this story to anyone, and not only to those touched by Alzheimer's. *The Sea is Wide* is an incredibly enlightening and informative read."

—Christina Reap, LPN

THE SEA IS WIDE
A MEMOIR OF CAREGIVING

Rundy Purdy

Wild Jot Press
Oxford, NY

THE SEA IS WIDE: A MEMOIR OF CAREGIVING

Published by Wild Jot Press
565 Moran Road
Oxford NY, 13830
Wildjot.com

For information about special discounts for bulk purchases please contact
editor@wildjot.com

The author of this book is available to speak at events. If you would like more
information, or to schedule an event, contact the author at
rundy@caregivingreality.com.

Additional support and resources for caregivers is available at
CaregivingReality.com/

Cover design by Justin Purdy

Text set in 11pt MgOpen Canonica

Library of Congress Control Number: 2015901392
ISBN: 978-0-9864469-0-0 (paperback)
ISBN: 978-0-9864469-1-7 (Kindle)
ISBN: 978-0-9864469-2-4 (epub)

Publisher's Cataloging-in-Publication Data

    Purdy, Rundy.
      The sea is wide : a memoir of caregiving / Rundy
    Purdy.
      LCCN 2015901392
      ISBN 978-0-9864469-0-0 (paperback)
      ISBN 978-0-9864469-1-7 (Kindle)
      ISBN 978-0-9864469-2-4 (ePub)

    1. Purdy, Rundy--Family. 2. Purdy, Ivan D., Sr.,
1927-2009. 3. Alzheimer's disease--Patients--United
States--Biography. 4. Alzheimer's disease--Patients--
Care--United States--Biography. 5. Caregivers--United
States--Biography. I. Title.

RC523.2.P87 2015   362.1968'3100922
                  QBI15-600029

This one is in memory of Grandpa,
who took the Alzheimer's journey.
And for all of you,
who have known the touch of that disease.

Also by Rundy Purdy

Fiction:

The Stuttering Bard of York
The Stuttering Duke of York
The Vishkalli Conspiracy (forthcoming)

I wish I was in Carrighfergus
Only for nights in Ballygrant.
I would swim over the deepest ocean,
The deepest ocean to be by your side,
But the sea is wide and I can't swim over
And neither have I wings to fly.
If I could find me a handsome boatsman
To carry me over to my love and die.

—Old Irish folk song

CONTENTS

- 2006 -

FULL CIRCLE

It's strange how life travels in full circles. The years roll past, and what once was is now reversed.

When I was growing up, my grandparents kept a camper in an RV campground called Slumber Valley, down in Pennsylvania. For a few summers around the time I was twelve, they invited the three oldest boys in our family for a week's vacation. It was a time of swimming in the park pool, eating meals outside at the picnic table behind the camper, and playing board games.

Grandpa wasn't a socializer and *was* a homebody, so he didn't care for these vacations. Why go live in a tiny camping trailer for a week when your own home was good enough? It was all foolishness to him. He stayed in the background, or disappeared entirely, so I have no recollection of what he did those summer days. Only a few memories stand out.

This first memory stays with me clearly. I'm a worrier, and as a child I worried obsessively about the most foolish things. The incident is among a thousand like it in my life, but this one stuck in my mind because I *realized* I was worrying in a foolishly obsessive manner. The self-recognition made the memory stick.

Before we left for Slumber Valley, Grandma was loading the car and doing other preparations. While Grandma kept herself occupied, Grandpa decided to take a walk in the woods until she was ready to leave. We three boys tagged along.

Almost as soon as we walked into the woods I began worrying.

"How much time do we have?" I asked.

"When should we go back?" I wondered. "What if Grandma is waiting for us?"

"What if we don't hear when Grandma calls us?" I fretted.

Then, "Maybe it's time we go back," I said.

On and on I went. I obsessed over the idea of Grandma waiting for us, and I'm sure I wearied Grandpa. As he answered every one one of my questions and not-so-subtle suggestions, I realized I was being unreasonable. Didn't I trust my own grandfather? Was I really afraid that Grandma might leave without us? If I was in such a hurry to get back, why on earth did I go on the walk in the first place? I recognized my foolishness, but I couldn't shake the nagging thought that Grandma could have called for us and we hadn't heard. I felt we really *ought* to go hurrying back. Something bad might happen. The feeling defied all reason.

Finally, Grandpa gave in to my pestering, and we went back. Of course, Grandma hadn't called for us.

My worrying habits were always with me. While at Slumber Valley, Grandpa told us that if a high wind came when the camper canopy was extended, the wind could rip the canopy right off the trailer. If we woke up in the middle of the night during a windy storm we were instructed to wake him to close the canopy.

Wind ripping the canopy off the trailer—scary thought. Warning Grandpa before it happened—big responsibility. So I obsessed over the possibilities while I lay in bed that night. How would I know when it was a bad enough storm to wake Grandpa? Would he be mad if I woke him and it wasn't really necessary? I didn't want to make Grandpa mad. But equally scary was imagining the damaged camper if I didn't wake him when it *was* necessary. Two bad possibilities weren't enough, so my mind fretted over a third: What if I accidentally slept through such a storm and didn't have the chance to wake Grandpa?

That night we had a terrific thunderstorm. The lightning flashed in brilliant white, the thunder crashed like an artillery barrage falling all around us, and the rain beat on the roof by the bucket-fulls. It sounded like a storm to end all storms, but any mature person listening realized that for all the crashing and booming and drumming, the rain was coming straight down. There was very little wind and not much reason to go out in the middle of the night and get completely soaked just to retract the canopy. But all I could think about was the violent storm, and my moral duty to save the trailer from permanent damage.

I scrambled out of bed and nervously hurried to the back of the trailer, pounding on the bedroom door.

"Grandpa! Grandpa!" I called. "There is a storm! It's—"

"Yes, I can hear it," he said (who couldn't, with it booming loud enough to rattle the windows). "Go back to bed. Don't worry about it."

I went back to bed, feeling relieved that I had done my duty. And when we all got up in the morning, the canopy was still attached to the trailer.

Grandpa was a reticent fellow. In part he simply didn't have as much to say as an outgoing and vivacious person, but there was also a part to his silence and stillness that was a shield and defense. If he didn't speak, and didn't act, he couldn't say or do something that would leave him open to emotional wounding, humiliation, or regret.

Growing up, I never really saw much into his life. He was that smiling and laughing man, always happy to see his grandchildren. He would read us a story, or make peanut butter brittle, or maybe go on a walk and we could come along. But that was as deep as it went, and the older I became the more I realized that most of Grandpa was hiding behind that wrinkled face—stories and thoughts locked up behind those watery blue eyes.

Sometimes, a little more of him would show through, brief flashes of a larger man. Once, we went for a walk with Grandpa at Slumber Valley. There was a waterfall on the creek that ran beside the camp and he took us to look at it. I don't remember how the conversation went as we walked along, but he must have been in a playful mood. Somehow we got on the topic of running, and it came to Grandpa and running—and how he couldn't.

"What, you think I can't run?" he said. "You think I'm too old? I'll show you!"

Next thing I knew we had a race, and Grandpa was running down the forest trail.

We were flabbergasted. At first we tried to give chase but we were so surprised, amazed, and amused that it was hard to not stop and watch him—just to laugh for the fun of it all. Grandpa was racing us! He was already in his mid-sixties, but for that brief moment the years fell away and we saw a much younger man, a *different* man, sprinting down the trail ahead of us, light on his feet, finishing with a quick leap over a branch laying across the trail.

I think that was the only time I have ever seen my grandfather run, the only time I have ever seen him so fully take leave of all care and thought, and act like someone who truly remembered what it was to be a boy once.

The years have swung past now, the summers flashing by like moments of bright light in the quickly spinning orb of life. Grandma and Grandpa took their camper out of Slumber Valley, and the summer trips stopped. The years have passed, one to another, and I've grown up, becoming, perhaps, just a little less of a worrier. And Grandpa—well, time has worn at him. It hasn't strengthened him in the vigor of life, as when the dew of youth is still fresh. For him that was a long time ago. Instead, time has ground youth and health from him and brought disease instead. The years have milled him fine and thin, and now Alzheimer's is grinding him away. Will anything remain?

Once, Grandpa drove me and my siblings around, as he took the extra kids that couldn't fit in my dad's car to the family gatherings. Now I take Grandpa to family gatherings.

Once, I followed Grandpa on walks in the woods and worried about being away from home too long. Now I take him out of the house, and he worries and wants to go home as soon as we've reached where we're going.

Once, I worried about the weather, and things that didn't need to be worried about. Now Grandpa stands at the window and looks at the gray sky, the rain, or the snow, and frets and worries. "I don't like it," he says. "Something doesn't feel right." The unease hangs over him, an unease no rational thought can chase away.

Today is the last day of December 2006, the day when the old year gives way to the new. My grandfather was born this day, many years ago. He is turning seventy-nine, and he is sick with Alzheimer's. We don't know what to do.

Grandpa struggles to show affection. I know it is there; I have seen it in him. It comes out in the backward way of words that say "I love you," without being so embarrassing as to actually say it. I don't recall him ever directly commenting on how my father raised us, or directly complimenting me any further than perhaps a rare "You're a good lad," that might escape as if by accident. But in spite of that scarcity of words, I still knew. For him, you didn't say those sort of things, but I knew he loved us because when I was little his face lit up with a smile when we came to visit. He would read a story when we asked, pop out his false teeth to surprise and maybe even scare us, and then hug us goodbye when it was time to leave. I knew what he thought of our character when we grew older because then, when he needed help, he asked us for help—whether it was help with the roofing project or help with the moving project.

He never talked much, but he made things. He was an artist, a tinkerer, and a man of his hands. He would draw and paint, carve, whittle, and build whatever came to his fancy and satisfied his muse. He could tune a piano, and play it some, a mandolin, too. He could even sing, I was told. His house was filled with the things he made. And yet, he was his own worst critic. Nothing he made was good enough in his eyes. Even if others wanted to buy what he created, he was ashamed to sell what he had made.

He grew up in the heart of the Depression, and that marked him. All his life he was certain poverty was at hand, and destitution waited around every corner. Born on the last day of a fading year, a middle child of ten, he became a quiet country man. Sometimes temperamental, his mood could range from melancholy to bouts of fierce anger. Short and slim to the point of being scrawny, he worked hard, smoked hard, and drank copious amounts of coffee. He raised a family with his wife, held a number of respectable jobs through the course of his life, and retired early from a job at IBM creating prototype circuit boards. He never thought he amounted to much.

Now he is losing all that he once had. Those hands which once controlled the sharp tools of the woodworker now struggle to use a light switch or button his shirt. The things he knew and the things he learned are deserting him. His past creations haunt him as reminders of skills lost and what he is becoming. His tools sit on shelves and in boxes and bins, unused. The last remaining drawings and carvings sit in corners of the house like forgotten markers of a fading past. Except not forgotten—not exactly. No, they are put away in the hopes that the loss they represent might be forgotten, and the pain of loss with them. The mandolin given to him for Christmas a few years ago is hidden under his bed at his request. To be kept safe, he said. And now he lays on that bed in restless slumber.

Alzheimer's takes even the smallest things. Grandpa curses himself now when he stumbles and cannot walk, or struggles to turn on a faucet. He knows he could. He remembers, and he struggles, determined to do what he once did. But it is a struggle he cannot win. It is a thing painful to think about, a thing I try to put from my mind. Otherwise, it will break my heart as I daily watch him lose his fight—as I see ever more clearly what he had, what he has lost, and what he still has and is daily losing. I feel the urge to laugh with a bitter-sad laugh because the echo in my mind is a cry of tears when he acts the fool because he had forgotten how, and calls himself a stupid filthy man because he urinates on the floor, spills his coffee, and can't remember how to dress himself.

The days are hard, but worse for him, the nights. Restless nights, and with each one he seems anxious for the dawn. One morning Grandma came into the kitchen while I was helping Grandpa with his morning routine.

"How was last night, Papa?" she asked.

"Terrible," he said.

"Well," she answered, leaning over to give him a kiss. "Maybe the next one will be better."

"Awww, shit," he said. "You know that isn't so. The next one is going to be worse than the last, and the next and the next and the next after that..." Then he trails off before continuing, as if to himself (and perhaps only I heard it), "I never thought I would be, but I'm scared."

I hold out my arms now, ready to catch him when he totters and falls. I tuck him into bed at night and give him a goodnight kiss. He is losing his life one bit at a time. He knows it, and I know it. He is scared, and I am sad.

§§§

NOBODY HERE

This week I found Grandma sitting in her chair, crying," my brother Arlan informed me. "She said, 'I can't take it anymore. I can't handle Grandpa. Tell Rundy I need him now.'"

Arlan brought Grandma's plea on September 24th, 2006, and I left the same day. I was twenty-four, and I was going to live with my grandparents and care for them. Alzheimer's had frayed their lives until everything began unraveling. I had decided I would help, and that decision changed my life.

When did it start? I think all of us asked that question. Maybe the answer is "At the very beginning"—the seed of sickness sown in DNA, growing through childhood and adulthood like some hidden monster until it couldn't escape notice anymore. That is speculation. I have read that the human brain has an amazing ability to compensate for losses. In one article it was suggested that cognitive function may begin altering years, if not decades, before the brain's coping ability fails in ways we notice. I suspect this is true.

But there is another question whose answer is not speculation: *When did we notice?* When did this disease begin affecting Grandpa's life in ways we could not miss? When did we get the first hints that something was wrong, even terribly wrong?

The realization was progressive. The signs were at first excused, denied, or minimized. Grandpa was growing old. Old people were forgetful. They made mistakes. It was okay. Really, it was. At least, it wasn't too bad, right? Nothing that would amount to anything.

Except it did.

I remember one incident that occurred years before anyone realized Grandpa had a problem. It surely wasn't the first sign, but it was one that lodged in my memory, an occurrence remembered, and reflected upon.

At the time we all laughed, even Grandpa, though he was sheepish with embarrassment. Grandma told the story on Grandpa at a birthday party.

"We were in a gas station convenience store," Grandma said, almost breaking down in laughter before she could finish the tale. "We were picking up a few things. Pa takes them to the check-out girl to have them rung up. And the girl says to him, 'Do you have gas, sir?'"

Grandma started laughing and had to regain control of herself before continuing.

"He looked at her completely serious," Grandma said, "and put a hand to his stomach and answered, 'No, not right now. But sometimes I do after supper.'"

We all had a good laugh at Grandpa's mistake in the cashier's meaning. Afterward, a few people privately wondered if it was a sign that Grandpa wasn't quite as sharp as he used to be—but in the end, so what? It was a little mistake, we told ourselves. Embarrassing, yes, but he was in his seventies and mental slowness was expected.

But it was only the beginning.

When Arlan moved in with Grandma and Grandpa in 2003 to attend college we began to hear more firsthand stories. During Arlan's early college years they were stories of little oddities which confirmed that Grandpa was no longer the sharp man he had been. But those little signs grew into something more. At first, the incidents were more frustrating than ominous. Grandpa disassembled the kitchen faucet to fix a drip, and then couldn't put it back together. (Who hasn't been in that situation once?) Driving out to social engagements, he would suddenly turn onto a different road, which no one else thought was the way to go. There would be an argument about why this way had been taken, with Grandpa sometimes stubbornly insisting that, "This was the way to go." Eventually they would reach their destination. Maybe Grandpa had known what he was doing. (Anyhow, who hasn't taken the wrong way once?)

The mistakes grew worse, and the events became harder to explain away. Grandpa was involved in a car accident, pulling out in front of a vehicle he didn't see. Then, on a very normal trip back from picking up his car from the repair shop, Arlan observed Grandpa in the other vehicle, driving in a highly irregular fashion, quickly switching lanes, inexplicably taking turns down side streets, then disappearing into the unknown. Grandpa eventually returned home, uninjured—but with no explanation for what he had done, or why.

It was indisputable that it was no longer safe for Grandpa to drive. He hated, even feared, the act of driving—but he didn't want to give up the right to drive. Giving up that symbol of competence and independence was a sign of a frailty he refused to admit. Grudgingly, he allowed someone to chauffeur him on longer trips. Mercifully, before a disaster occurred or a confrontation developed over the possession of keys, outside events intervened. After an incident where Grandpa drove erratically down the highway, declaring that the car was acting "strange," Grandma had the vehicle traded in for a new model. Grandpa insisted on checking the car out, but once seated in the vehicle, he couldn't decipher how it worked. A little change, a little different look, and everything was incomprehensible.

Grandpa couldn't drive.

He continued to grow worse.

He began to act strangely. He would get lost in stores and Grandma would have to find him. He sometimes failed to recognize a grandchild at family gatherings. He wanted to go home shortly after arriving to visit. He began to agitate, even at home, and follow Grandma around, shadowing her constantly. He sometimes spent the night on the couch instead of going to bed. He began to have trouble remembering how to use the TV remote, and sometimes confused it with the telephone. He began to forget how to turn on lights and turn off faucets. He forgot where he was going, what he was doing, and what he wanted. He made odd requests and strange demands.

Nobody was laughing now.

But we hoped, or perhaps pretended, that it wasn't so bad. Some days Grandpa acted like his old self, as if nothing was wrong. Some days, he *was* his old self. But then there were the other days, the days when he did things which shouted, "Something is not right!"

A dramatic turning point came when Grandpa was scheduled for a routine colonoscopy. He was given a solution to take home and drink, which would clean out his colon for the upcoming procedure. But instead of having several bowel movements, Grandpa vomited throughout the evening, and into the night.

That night he became a different man, a crazy man. He wandered around the house, mumbling to himself, poking at little LED lights on electronic devices, trying to make them go out. In the middle of the night he entered Arlan's bedroom, waking him from a sound sleep.

"Is something the matter?" Arlan asked, startled. "Can I get you something, Grandpa?"

Like a mute, Grandpa bumbled about the darkened room, pawing at things, his hands finally coming to rest on Arlan's printer, which he then attempted to put in the garbage.

"What are you doing, Grandpa?" Arlan said.

Muttering something about taking out the garbage, Grandpa struggled a little while longer then said, "Oh, never mind," and left as he had come.

Life in the house suddenly had an entirely different feeling.

That night of sickness gave a glimpse into Grandpa's future. What was coming could no longer be denied.

Grandpa recovered from his vomiting, but it seemed that things were permanently different. I remember when Grandpa came over for a birthday party some time later. He was noticeably impaired—not enough for an inattentive stranger to detect, but I noticed. He appeared even more withdrawn than usual, as if his world had shrunk to a little circle around him. He hunched at the dinner table as I brought him his coffee for supper, looking harried and uncertain at the prospect of eating in the boisterous atmosphere. During the meal he acted disconnected, one minute present for the conversation the next minute distant, as if a synapse broke somewhere, leaving him to wander off in his own thoughts.

The evening became even more strange.

After supper Grandpa got up from the table to use the bathroom but instead headed for the laundry room. When I intercepted him he explained in the most reasonable manner that he wanted to "Go piss in the corner over there."

Once he was redirected, and his business completed (properly in the bathroom!), Grandpa went out to sit on the porch. Apparently he found the chair too uncomfortable, because he went back in the house, took a soft dinner roll from a basket on the table, carefully wrapped it up in a paper towel, and brought it outside. There he placed the roll on his chair, and sat on it.

Both events went beyond odd. They were bizarre, surreal, and so unlike the Grandpa I had known. This was only the beginning of the Grandpa I would come to know.

He was taken in for tests. A brain scan, and many questions later, he was diagnosed: Alzheimer's, a sentence given with finality. The doctor labeled him with the mental ability of a two-year-old (quite unfairly, I think), and pronounced that soon he would be unable to recognize even his wife. There we had it—Alzheimer's, and no escaping it.

The disease was a bit of a secret at first, at least for Grandma. And to her it remained a shame long after it wasn't a secret. This wasn't supposed to happen. It was an embarrassment. Other people went senile, lost their minds, and acted crazy—but not her man. It couldn't be happening.

Yet it was happening, no matter who wanted to deny it. What was to be done? Something had to be done.

Arlan graduated from college and began to look for a job in the spring of 2006 while at the same time trying to help Grandma and Grandpa as much as he could. But once he had a job there would be no extra person home all day. That left the question of what would happen next.

When the call came to inform Arlan that he was accepted for an employment position, Grandpa was the only one around to answer the phone. The conversation that followed was later related to Arlan by his new employer, on whom it had made an impression.

"Hello?" Grandpa said, picking up the phone.

The man said he wished to speak with Arlan.

"Okay, let me go find him," Grandpa said.

There followed a long wait. Then Grandpa returned and picked up the phone again.

"Hello?" he said.

The man stated his request again.

"Okay, hang on," Grandpa said again, and left for the second time.

There followed yet another period of silence during Grandpa's absence. Finally, he finished wandering around and picked up the phone yet again.

"Hello," he said. "I can't help you, and apparently there is nobody here who can."

§§§

SORRY

I'm sorry it's come to this." Grandma spoke from the darkness, her voice croaky and wretched.

"It's okay." I tried to reassure her, uncomfortable and slightly embarrassed. "I'm glad to do this."

"I know, but..." she said.

"It's okay," I insisted. "Don't worry about it."

That was the first night.

It was late when Arlan and I arrived. The house was wrapped in darkness, and everyone had gone to bed. Grandma and Grandpa hadn't shared a bedroom in years, so the plan was for me to share Grandpa's small bedroom, our beds no more than two feet apart. I would—quite literally—be very close for any night time needs. Grandma used the large master bedroom suite for her personal belongings, but because her heart condition made it difficult to lie in bed, she rarely slept there. Nights for Grandma were spent propped up in her recliner in the living room, and it was from there she greeted us with her sad apology.

Grandma was proud, and didn't want to inconvenience anyone else. She hadn't wanted to imagine that Grandpa would ever get bad. Not this bad. Not bad enough to make her ask for help. She wanted to provide everything Grandpa needed, all by herself. When Arlan conveyed to her my willingness to come and assist them she only grudgingly granted that if—and only if—it came to the dire end where Grandpa required physical lifting would she accept my offer. She painted such an end as only a faint possibility. We hadn't argued. Reality had its own way of forcing itself upon Grandma. In time, the reality of Grandpa's increasing needs broke Grandma's pride. It came more quickly than she dreamed, more quickly than even we expected.

Bag in hand, I made my way down the hall. I didn't want to wake Grandpa, and so left the bedroom light off as I entered, trying to bumble my way through the dark to the second bed. In spite of my efforts Grandpa woke briefly, but in reply to his mumbled question I said, "Everything is okay, go back to sleep." Apparently satisfied, he complied.

I crawled into the other bed and tried to sleep. Rest was not easy in coming. When plans had first been made for me to eventually come and care for Grandpa, I had worried about him being so lost in his disease that he wouldn't remember me. Events had proved that worry needless. Instead of Grandma caring for Grandpa up to the end, I was called on to help relatively early in Alzheimer's progression. Grandpa was still mostly in his faculties. He was a bit forgetful, confused at times, and needy. But he certainly still remembered me. He still remembered his own place in life, that he was a Grandpa, and my relation to him. So I found myself facing a different immediate problem. Did he know why I was there?

Everyone knew Grandpa didn't want to admit he needed help, just as everyone knew that he would rather die than go to a nursing home. The fact that those two realities were contradictory didn't need discussion. Grandpa was proud in his own way, and he was stubborn. Exactly how well could he understand the situation created by his disease? Could he cognizantly take part in a discussion about his needs? If his mind was able to grasp his condition, was he emotionally able to face the reality? Was he willing to accept help?

I didn't know the answers to those questions.

I had never faced Grandpa's anger personally before, but stories of his temper were well known. I had seen a few flares of that anger, briefly, from the sidelines. I knew he could be unreasonable, and even cruel with words in his anger. The idea of facing Grandpa in that state filled me with apprehension.

I don't think anyone discussed how the matter of my care would be presented to Grandpa. I don't know that the matter *was* discussed with him explicitly. My dad attempted to obliquely broach the topic with Grandpa to see how he felt about having another person come live with them and "help." Grandpa had answered to the effect that he didn't mind having people in the house, but he didn't want someone to come and boss him around, telling him what to do. That response was open to interpretation.

I got the sense that the default reaction by everyone was to let Grandma present the matter to Grandpa as she thought best. I heard nothing, so it seemed that presenting a *fait accompli* was Grandma's method, along with a blind hope that all the details would work themselves out.

I felt pretty sure Grandma had mentioned *something* about my coming, but I knew that if the situation suited her Grandma was not above being less than forthright. If she had felt Grandpa would react badly to the news that I was there to take care of him, she might have told a story about how I had come to "help." Grandpa would have been a lot more agreeable to the idea that Grandma needed help, and it would have been convenient to leave the reality of the situation without clarification.

Convenient for Grandma, anyhow. I wasn't sure how aware Grandpa was that he would be sharing his room with someone else, or how he felt about that whole arrangement, much less the larger issue of caregiving. I did not look forward to caring for someone who was resentful of my presence, not to mention unaware of the true reason and goal of my residence. Uncertain did not begin to describe how I felt that first night, lying in the darkness, staring up at the ceiling.

It felt like an improper beginning. In some cosmic irony, Arlan's visit home that weekend was originally to celebrate his birthday. Grandma's tears changed everything and his day became a mission to bring news of the immediate need for me. We had known it was coming. It had been discussed, and I had volunteered to go. I had agreed. And yet...we thought we had more time. I thought we had more time. Then it came so suddenly, not even a day of advance notice. It felt like my arrival had begun on the wrong foot. There was the subdued birthday party, the hasty packing, awkward goodbyes, and now all of this stumbling into the bedroom in the dark, telling Grandpa to go back to sleep without so much as a "How are you?" And all of this without any knowledge if he understood or was agreeable to my moving in.

What had I gotten myself into? Uncertainty swirled though my thoughts, thick as the night darkness around me. Arlan had recently started his first post-college job and though he still lived with Grandma and Grandpa he was making a lengthy commute to work. That summer my younger cousin Melinda had also been sent to live with Grandma while she finished out her last year of high school. Between them and myself, it was a full house. While on the one hand this meant there were several people who could pitch in and help from time to time, it also meant that there were as many differing expectations, opinions, and feelings about everything that went on.

There was much to learn—an overwhelming new reality. I needed to discover where Grandpa was at in his disease, and also learn the flow of life (and interpersonal politics) in the new house. The complex relationship between Grandpa's Alzheimer's disease and how it related to everything else would become increasingly apparent with time, but even from the beginning the situation was clearly not simple.

But as badly done as this start felt, it was the beginning I had and so I had to make the best of it.

Eventually I fell asleep.

§§§

Grandpa didn't seem surprised to find me in the other bed the next morning, though I wasn't sure what to make of that. It left me wondering—did he understand more than he was letting on, or was he so far gone that the sudden appearance of a roommate didn't raise any questions?

I began gingerly feeling out my new life.

The first day with Grandpa went well. I had read enough about Alzheimer's disease to know where this journey would end—with Grandpa incontinent, immobile, incoherent, and helpless. It was a dreadful frightening future to know, but when he got up that first morning and only needed a little help buttoning his shirt and someone to microwave his coffee it didn't seem so bad.

The day passed with a certain degree of normalcy. That evening we all sat around the kitchen table and talked. Grandpa was able to join in, after a fashion. He was articulate enough and cognizant in spite of his failing abilities. He managed to follow perhaps half of the conversation, and even added some commentary of his own. But I watched him carefully and I could tell he mentally struggled.

Half of the problem in conversation with Grandpa was that Alzheimer's made his mind slow, and Grandma (and other people) simply rode over him, taking the conversation on to the next topic before he had a chance to speak. It wasn't that anyone was deliberately being rude—they just acted like it was a normal conversation where everyone naturally goes on to a new topic which then suddenly doubles back to old topics. In conversation our minds leap about with a mental agility we don't even realize we're using. We interrupt each other without even thinking about it because a thought (for us) can easily be picked back up. But poor Grandpa could only handle one thought at a time, and that one thought very slowly. To be interrupted (or even for someone to speak to a different person when he was trying to speak), derailed Grandpa entirely. For him to talk, everyone else had to be silent. There had to be one single, orderly, and slow train of conversation. That isn't how people naturally speak in relaxed conversation, but in watching Grandpa I could see his great frustration when attempting to participate.

But if a bit slow and halting, he certainly didn't come across like some demented person reduced to the capabilities of a two-year-old, as the doctor had so recently pronounced. As that first day drew to a close it seemed that perhaps things were not quite so bad. Maybe it would be okay.

I had been warned by Arlan that nights were worse than days for Grandpa, and some nights were very bad. This was partly because Grandpa was tired at the end of the day, and thus not able to make his mind work as clearly. But an issue contributing to the nighttime confusion was that with Melinda's recent arrival Grandpa had been moved out of his old bedroom. That had changed his normal bedtime routine.

The house was a split level, and Grandpa's sleeping quarters had at first been moved to the finished basement. Arlan then realized Grandpa walking downstairs every night to go to bed was not working, so he swapped his small bedroom on the upper floor with Grandpa. Having now used three different bedrooms in the space of nearly as many months, Grandpa struggled to remember what bedroom belonged to him. Going to bed in the right room at night was a problem.

Contributing to the bedtime tension was a new habit Grandpa developed, a desire for Grandma to put him to bed at night. Grandma was exhausted by 10:00 PM and playing nursemaid to Grandpa (telling him how to take off every piece of clothing if he was having a bad night, then tucking him in and kissing him goodnight) was too much for her. So one of the first things Grandma did that first day was make it clear—repeatedly—to Grandpa that I would be putting him to bed, not her. Grandpa was indignant at the suggestion that he needed *my* help (the pretense being that he *liked* her to put him to bed, not that it was needed). I cringed at Grandma's blatant heavy-handedness.

But so it was that when bedtime came around it was my job to make sure Grandpa got ready for bed—and into bed in the right room—all while pretending as much as possible that I was *not* helping him.

The bedtime routine started out well enough. I discovered the key was to keep Grandpa from becoming mentally derailed from the task at hand, or else helping him get back on track when he became derailed. Nonetheless, I tried to be very careful how I gave that help.

He was capable of doing everything himself, but brushing his dentures at the sink could quickly turn into cleaning the sink, which could turn into washing the counter and by that point going to bed was completely forgotten. It was a tricky and delicate task for me to keep him on course because he was very sensitive to the presence of someone breathing down his neck. I felt bad that he could perceive that he was being kept under constant surveillance. I had been thrown into the situation to learn to sink or swim on my own, and I managed as best I could by hanging far enough back so as to seem engaged in something else, and then just "happen" to wander by and suggest that maybe he could stop washing the dishes with his denture brush and put his dentures in their container.

All things considered, Grandpa didn't really need help that first night. He acted completely sane, if slightly forgetful. As I walked with him to his bedroom I felt both awkward and a little unneeded.

It was at this point that he became mixed up and the situation rapidly deteriorated. We went into the bedroom and I think he concluded he was seeing *me* to bed. We both stood there in the room—uncomfortable pause—then Grandpa turned and took the door handle saying, "You need anything?"

I figured he had forgot something and was going out to get it, so I said, "No, I'm fine."

"Okay," he said, and left, closing the door behind him.

What followed was a moment wherein I wasn't exactly sure what I was supposed to do. I heard a little commotion out in the hall so I decided I had better go check. Grandpa was fiddling around in the entrance to Melinda's room (his old room). He finally started walking into her darkened room (she wasn't home at the time), so I turned on the light hoping he would recognize it wasn't his room anymore. He was trying to articulate something, but was incoherent as he pointed at various objects. I managed to direct him back out of the room, reminding him that this was where Melinda slept. Thus redirected, he started peering in Grandma's room. At this point Grandma intervened.

"You're not going in that room, and you're not going in my room either, Pa," she said. "You're sleeping in that room and Rundy is going to put you to bed and that's the way its going to be. I'm sorry."

I don't know how much he understood, but she briskly directed him back into the bedroom he was supposed to be in, and left.

In retrospect I realized he had thought he was seeing me to bed and had confused himself because he couldn't figure out which bedroom *he* was supposed to sleep in. Because he had been moved around so many times some part of him thought he wasn't supposed to sleep in any of the rooms, but he knew he was supposed to sleep *somewhere*—and it all became a jumbled mess in his mind. Grandma didn't try to straighten him out. One could say her solution was "effective." She told Grandpa what he would do, but didn't answer his questions, or resolve his confusion. On top of that, she had hurt his feelings.

When Grandma left Grandpa said something that seemed to have the tenor of "She wasn't very nice" or "She wasn't very clear" to which I shrugged in response because with his dentures out he was slurring and I couldn't tell for certain what he said. Then he said, "Well, at least I thought so."

He didn't need me to put him to bed. He managed to get out of his pants all by himself. I turned on the CD player because Arlan had told me Grandpa liked listening to the audio Bible when he went to bed. Then I tucked him in and gave him a kiss goodnight. After that, I went to bed.

A half hour later the bedroom light came on. Grandpa was poking around the room like he was looking for something. Squinting through the light, I had a pretty good guess. He had asked me to turn up the CD volume when I put him to bed, which I had found a little odd because I knew it had been left at the volume at which he had last used it. So I said, "You looking to adjust the volume?"

He turned around and said, "Oh, I didn't know you were in here. Yeah, I'm trying to turn it down." So I pulled out the remote and turned the volume on the CD player down a few notches. "That good?" I asked. He cocked his head, listening. "A little more," he said. I suspected as much (but had wanted to test him) and now set it down to *exactly where* it had been before I had adjusted the volume. "Yeah," he said as soon as I hit where it had been. "That's good."

Clearly his ears were still functioning very well.

Grandpa turned off the light and went back to bed. "It isn't too loud for you is it?" he asked.

"It's fine, Grandpa," I said. "I'm okay."

It was a little peculiar, that second night. He sometimes expressed concern about how I would feel about the noise, or some other thing related to being in the same room with him. Then at other times I spoke up and his reaction was, "Oh, I didn't know you were in the room."

I don't know how he resolved the reality of me in the room. Perhaps since he knew I was family he didn't find it worth bothering with the particulars. He was, at least, very agreeable and for that I was thankful.

I found it wisest to go to bed at the same time as Grandpa to make sure he got up without trouble for his regular bathroom trips, and also so that I was present to adjust the volume or turn off his CD player for him. I didn't always follow this wise course, but if I wasn't there he tried to deal with things himself, with disastrous results. From day one of my arrival Grandpa couldn't adjust the volume on the CD player to save his life. The machine was a mystery to him, and his end result was futility at best and more likely things knocked off shelves, and shelves knocked down as he pawed around in the dark. I wondered (and felt bad in considering) how many frustrating nights he had suffered when he couldn't adjust the volume for himself and there had been no one else to do it.

While Grandpa was quite agreeable to my presence, and on occasion seemed even oblivious to my existence in the room, this was not usual in the early days. At that time he typically was very sensitive to the obligations of sharing a room and he constantly fretted about bothering me, which made me feel bad for him. I tried to put him at ease about bedroom disturbances. He liked to have the bedroom door open for the first half of the night—I think until after the TV had gone silent and Grandma had settled down. With the door open he felt more connected to the activity outside. After the house went completely silent he sometimes shut the door. He liked to have the door open, but always asked, "Is that going to bother you?" To which I said, "I'm fine, Grandpa. I'm fine. Don't worry about me." Deep down I would have preferred the door shut, but having it open was obviously important to him.

Even after the first few nights he remained concerned about his CDs disturbing me. When it came to volume adjusting—which happened almost every night—he would tell me to either turn it up or down (depending) and then say, "Is it okay? If it's bothering you—" and I would say, "If it's good with you, I'm fine."

After a while I put him at ease and we got to the point where—if he remembered—he simply told me what he wanted done with the volume and didn't get out of bed and didn't fret about if it was bothering me. This meant that I would be sort of dozing and he would say into the dark, "Okay, you can turn it down now." Then maybe a half hour later, "Okay, you can turn it off," and I'd grab the remote control and comply.

I tried to accommodate him as much as possible, but I had my limits. One thing I quickly decided was that I couldn't let the Bible

CDs play all night, even if Grandpa didn't ask me to turn it off. The first night I put it on for him he didn't ask for the player to be turned off, and I felt bad about shutting it off on him. So I spent the entire night in a state of semi-dozing, listening to the New Testament from Romans chapter three to Hebrews...twice. Never again. During my waking hours I found it pleasant to listen to the CDs, but it was impossible for me to sleep at all when I could hear a voice droning on. Ear plugs didn't help, and after that first night I knew I would quickly lose my mind if I didn't draw the line somewhere. After that night if Grandpa didn't ask for me to turn the CD player off, I always did anyhow when I thought he had fallen asleep.

If there had been no CD player then the issue of noise and volume adjustment would have been removed, and with it a big source of trouble for me. But Grandpa dearly loved the CDs, so I was inclined to suffer a lot on their account. Still, sometimes I found the CD playing quite trying. Sometimes he got up to go to the bathroom after it was turned off and then asked for it on (perhaps forgetting that it had been on once already). At such times I was sorely tempted to admonish him that it had already been on and turned off for the night, but then I reminded myself that he had few pleasures left in life and held my tongue.

Even without the CD playing it was hard to sleep deep and restfully. I was constantly primed for Grandpa to do something. I was normally a light and somewhat fitful sleeper so typically Grandpa needed to do little more than sit up in bed and I was awake. But there was a part of my mind that feared I would slip up, and wouldn't wake when something important happened. At first I didn't realize how much that impacted my sleep. Then one morning Arlan dropped something in the kitchen as he was getting ready for work. I heard the clatter and was out of bed and into the hall, frantically looking and saying "Where is Grandpa?" before I was even completely awake. I did a quick search of the house and didn't find him anywhere—moment of panic—before going back to the bedroom to find him still there, sleeping peacefully.

I realized then how much I was unable to rest, even when I was sleeping. It really was being on the job twenty-four hours, every day.

§§§

Grandpa's situation grew progressively more clear to me over the first days and weeks. There was a bizarre disjunct in his life and that was hard to explain to someone who wasn't present and living with him. His short term memory was compromised and he increasingly struggled to accurately comprehend the world around him. But at the same time his *senses* still worked with a surprising acuity for a man of his age. The connection between mind and body was coming unglued, and in that reality he could quickly alternate between seeming perfectly sane and utterly bonkers. Between the two extremes his days became fraught with nonsensical incongruities.

He never talked much about his Alzheimer's and when I first came I wondered if he knew about his problem. But as time passed he let enough words slip so that I knew that he knew, and I could guess— like a faint shadow—some of what passed through his mind in the long hours of the day. In spite of all the uncertainties and questions that plagued everyday life, it soon became evident that there was one thing Grandpa did understand: He knew why I was there.

Grandpa's older brother Doug lived just up the street and shortly after I arrived Doug began to make regular weekly visits. For a man already into his eighties he was still hale and hearty of both mind and body. I presumed he had been informed of Grandpa's situation and that the visits were his gesture of support. But one day the three of us were sitting around the kitchen table and Doug looked at me curiously and asked, "So...what are you doing here? Are you just visiting for a while, going to school..."

I was caught by surprise—and was a little shocked—that Doug had no idea why I was there. He lived just up the street, so I figured if anyone knew what was going on it would be him. My surprise gave way to embarrassment. For a moment I wasn't sure what I was supposed to say. If the whole situation was Grandma and Grandpa's dirty little secret, how much should I say?

I was saved by Grandpa speaking up.

"No, it's me," he said bitterly. "I'm screwing everything up. I'm making a mess out of things and he has to come here to—"

"Oh, no, no, you're not making a mess of things! Don't say that," Doug said hastily. "You're doing fine. It's not your fault."

I found out later that Doug had been told something vague about Grandpa having "troubles" but from that statement hadn't realized how serious the situation was, nor connected Grandpa's problems to my appearance. He clearly regretted having accidentally humiliated Grandpa. Doug had known other people with dementia, and in the coming years he would be very supportive of Grandpa, as best he knew how. Doug and I both tried to assure Grandpa that the problems weren't his fault, it was okay, and nobody blamed him.

Still, the situation bothered Grandpa deeply.

One night I woke up to find Grandpa fumbling around in the dark. I suspected he wanted the CD player turned off, which he confirmed. After I turned the CD player off he said, "I'm going to the bathroom," but trying to deal with the CD player had put him mentally off track. Instead of walking to the door he walked into the corner of the room and started fumbling around for a handle that wasn't there. I tried to open the door for him, but he simply walked into the door, clueless and uncomprehending of his surroundings. I had to turn on the light, reorient him, and then direct him on his way.

He finally made it to the bathroom and back. As I was helping him into bed he gave a sad kind of laugh and said, "You're getting more than you thought you signed up for, aren't you?"

The words slipped out, a raw admission of what he was, and what he was becoming. I looked at him, sitting quietly sad and ashamed, and I wished for an instant that he could have been ignorant of why I was there, so he could have been spared the shame.

"No, Grandpa," I said softly. "This is exactly what I expected."

"Well, I'm sorry," he said. I'm sorry, but this is just the way it is."

We were all sorry.

§§§

KEEPING THE ROUTINE

Going to the mailbox was a habit for Grandpa. Formerly an active man, it was one of the few productive things he could still do—though by the time I arrived on the scene his ability to go to the mailbox unsupervised was dubious at best. Still, it was something he could "do" and he liked having something to do. For this reason he was often given the duty of bringing something out to the mailbox, or else took it upon himself to go out and check the mail.

For him this trip was a great undertaking, and sometimes he would gird himself like a man preparing for an expedition. Once he left the house (however oddly attired) I might peer from the window to watch him trundle down to the edge of the road, glance about, check the mailbox, and then return. The idea of Grandpa wandering off occurred to me, but it never happened. It was never even attempted during all the time I cared for him.

Grandpa's problems with checking the mailbox occurred in other ways.

One afternoon a few weeks after I moved in I looked over my shoulder to see Grandpa with one shoe on. He was standing in the hall studiously putting a tissue box on his other bare foot. Seeing trouble in the works I got up from my computer and went to investigate further. Grandpa was walking down the hall toward the bedroom with one shoe on, and one tissue box on the other foot, looking lost.

"Grandpa," I said. "Are you going out to check the mail?"

"Yeah, I was," he admitted. "But I think I won't."

"Would you like some help?" I asked.

"Yes, I do," he said.

I very much didn't want to embarrass him, but seeing him walking down the hall going *clump, clump, clump* with a tissue box on one bare foot looked funny, and the situation was so absurd, so completely unreal, that the laughter came bubbling up. The prospect of saying, "Grandpa, you're wearing a tissue box," was too silly. The ideal solution was to obliquely help him correct the situation without directly pointing out that he had done such a ridiculous thing as putting a tissue box on his foot instead of a shoe.

"Come here and I'll give you a hand," I managed in a very normal voice. Then watching him became too much. As he *clumped* down the hall I had to turn away and laugh as quietly as I could under my breath. It was utterly sad, and funny at the same time. When he reached me I managed to regain control and with nearly straight-faced seriousness I offered him his second shoe.

"Here is your shoe," I said. "I think you'll find this will work better."

"I wondered where that thing went," he said. (It had been right beside where he had retrieved his first shoe.)

When he took off the tissue box I quietly removed it and left him to put the shoe on by himself.

That wasn't the end of the shoe troubles for the day. A little later I checked on him again and discovered he was trying to put a different shoe *inside* the shoe I had given him.

"I don't think you want to do that," I prompted. "You don't need that shoe."

"But there isn't a shoe inside it," he said, sounding as if this were a quite reasonable requirement.

"There doesn't need to be a shoe inside that shoe," I said. "You put your foot inside the shoe." After I took the extra pair of shoes away and guided him through the process he managed to put his foot inside the shoe and I laced it up. Then I helped him into his coat and he went out to fetch the mail.

This wasn't the end of his troubles. About fifteen minutes later I heard him muttering and complaining to himself and I went into the kitchen to check on him. He had taken off his pants and was trying to put his coat on his legs instead. He had already successfully put one leg through an arm hole, but at that point became stymied.

"Looks like you need some help there," I said. "How about we swap. I give you these—" I picked up his discarded pants, "and you give me that." I pointed to the coat.

"Okay," he agreed, and then looked confused over how he might get rid of the coat now that he had his leg through one armhole.

I managed to keep from laughing, but this time Grandpa laughed. It wasn't a happy laugh—more like a sad laugh, as he realized his complete confusion. With my guiding he got out of the coat and back into his pants.

Some people might think he didn't realize that he had made so many mistakes that afternoon. He was clueless, right? But no, after I got him back into his pants I asked him if he wanted me to turn on the TV and he said, "Yeah, I guess so. Maybe then I won't get into any more trouble."

Faced with Grandpa's many problems there was always the temptation to become frustrated or angry. Watching his decline, bleak feelings often came. Humor was my antidote. Imperfect though it was, it meant surviving in an at least somewhat healthy state of mind. If I just forgot for a moment what everything meant, a lot of it was really funny in an absurd sort of way. If I could see cause for a good-natured laugh, kindness and patience came easier. I could either get mad when Grandpa came walking down the hall without any pants on, or I could fetch a pair of pants and ask him (like a salesman) if he was interested in the fine pair of pants I had. If I became mad and lectured him about not wearing pants he would become humiliated or angry. If I, in good humor, suggested I had a fine pair of pants he might be interested in he might stop a moment and say, gee, he supposed he could use some pants. Then he would put them on and nobody would be bent out of shape, or worse for it. On a good day sometimes even he would appreciate the ridiculousness of the situation. Then, in appreciating the humor, he could feel a little less ashamed.

But I had to be careful. There was a thin line between laughing *with* Grandpa, and laughing *at* him. Sometimes it was hard to know where one stopped and the other began. Sometimes it just depended on how Grandpa took it. Sometimes the important thing was to *not* laugh, even if it was funny. It is very difficult to face the realization of failing abilities. It's even worse when someone laughs *at* you. There were times I had to try very hard to not laugh, even when it was funny.

§§§

A trip to the mailbox could wander into all sorts of diversions. One day, as best I can reconstruct it, he went down to the mailbox to put out some bills Grandma wanted mailed. While down there he saw the empty garbage can beside the mailbox. (It was garbage day.) Then he checked the mailbox and saw the mail had already come. So he took the garbage can back up to the garage without doing anything with the bills in his hand that he had intended to mail. Then, since he couldn't figure out how to open the garage from the outside he went back into the house by the front door and went down to the garage. But now in the garage he couldn't remember what he was doing, so he took something out of the garage into the house in the hopes it would randomly be what he had initially intended to do. I heard all of the door opening and shutting and went down to check on him. I found him in the garage with the out-going bills still clutched in one hand, randomly moving a jug of windshield washer fluid around.

"Need any help?" I asked.

"I don't think so," he said.

Since he declined the offer of help and wasn't getting into any dangerous trouble, I let him be. Later he came up and asked me where he should put the bills. After a little questioning I managed to determine that because the mail had already come he didn't see any point in putting the bills out until tomorrow. Or perhaps he had a brain freeze at the mailbox and couldn't figure out how to take the delivered mail out and put the bills in at the same time. Or he was afraid someone might steal the bills if they stayed in the box overnight. In any case I told him he could put the bills by the telephone to go out later. Satisfied, Grandpa decided he would get the mail that *had* arrived.

When he came back inside with the mail he saw some specks of dirt on the carpet. So he put the mail on the floor and got on his hands and knees to pick up the flecks of dirt. I sorted the mail and Grandpa went to take his little flecks of dirt down to the trash can in the garage.

This was a very convoluted and meandering process, and some days were worse. Another day Grandma was suffering from heart pain and was laid up in bed for most of the day, leaving Grandpa with me as his only company. We were both a little off from our normal selves because of Grandma's condition. He went to check the mail three times that afternoon. The first time he brought the mail in. The second two trips were sparked by his latent agitation over Grandma and feeling like he needed to do something.

The first and second time he went out to check the mail he got himself together pretty well. The third time I caught him walking toward the stairs wearing only one shoe—on the wrong foot—and carrying a large couch cushion under his arm, while clutching a second pair of shoes. He looked like a man valiantly preparing for a great journey.

I had a rule of seeking to maintain his dignity and minimizing humiliating events when possible. This meant that I avoided pointing out his mistakes unless he expressed a desire for help. However, this was a delicate balance because if he discovered for himself that he was being a fool and realized that I *hadn't* pointed it out and had let him carry on like a fool then he would *still* feel humiliated, and indignant besides. Sometimes I couldn't win.

"Where are you going?" I asked as he walked by, cushion under arm, clumping along in his one shoe. "You going on a trip?"

Sometimes a general question would make Grandpa stop and consider what he was doing. If he stopped and had a second thought sometimes he realized his mistakes. Or, at least a few of them. Sometimes. But not this time.

"Yep," Grandpa said, brimming with confidence, and continued toward the stairs.

His carrying a couch cushion under one arm and wearing the one shoe on the wrong foot made navigating the stairs hard. I watched him carefully as he went down the stairs, tensed and ready to lunge after him should he start to fall.

"Where is he going?" Melinda asked, coming out of her bedroom and stopping in the hall.

"He's going outside carrying a couch cushion and a pair of shoes, and wearing only one shoe," I said.

"You're going to let him go?" She looked slightly appalled.

I shrugged. "He won't get far." I was confident that he wouldn't take more than a few steps out in the cold weather before realizing he hadn't attired himself correctly. He would realize his error for himself without me harassing him about how he was doing things wrong.

As I talked with Melinda, Grandpa stepped outside and shut the door firmly behind himself. I started down the stairs after him and by the time I reached the front door the latch was already rattling. I opened the door.

"You want to come back in?" I inquired.

"Yeah," Grandpa said, sounding equal parts surprised and perplexed. "I can't be out here like this. I only have one sock on."

And then I couldn't help it. His tone of bewildered surprise and shock was too much. I started laughing. Fortunately, Grandpa must have seen some of the humor in it because he looked at me and started laughing as well. But he was embarrassed too, because as funny as it was he also realized that it was funny *because* he had done a very silly thing. Who would go outside with only one sock (shoe) on?

"Well," he said, "you think I should sneak in the back way to escape the humiliation? I'm sorry—"

He started his usual apologizing, but I told him it was no problem, and he wasn't stupid. I just thought it was funny, that was all. Trying to choke back my laughter I helped him up to the top of the stairs. I relieved him of his couch cushion and his extra pair of shoes, switched his one shoe to the proper foot and helped him put the shoe's mate on. Then I gave him his cane and let him go check the mail again.

Such were the adventures of Grandpa's life. He had the routines of his old life, and he was trying to keep them. It was important to let him try. In his faltering routines his old life was crumbling, and with that dissolution he saw an uncertain future before him. What he could hold onto was very important to him. It gave him some comfort, and some normalcy.

Being with him in these halting steps and small moments I saw how my old life had also ended and the new was just beginning. For me, adjusting to my new life encompassed more than just helping Grandpa in his daily routines and constant struggle with Alzheimer's. I wanted to pretend that my adjustment wasn't a struggle, but the change in life took its toll on me as well. Several weeks after I had moved in I was beginning to settle, but it would be several months, and more, before I was truly settled. After a few weeks I had learned the basic necessities of daily life and was beginning to have a feel for the rhythm and flow of the house.

For all of the big changes in my life, sometimes it was the small mundane bits that stood out. Things were different. Where I had lived before the nearest small town store was ten minutes away, the nearest chain grocery store was twenty minutes, and downtown thirty or so minutes. Now the nearest chain grocery store might have been three minutes away, and downtown ten minutes, or less. Before, back at home there were so many people that dinner required ten pounds of potatoes. Now dinner required maybe two pounds of potatoes. In the beginning when I made supper for Grandma and Grandpa I always thought the amount of food I prepared wasn't enough. There was too little meat, I was sure of it. There were too few potatoes. Then, much to my surprise, such a small amount was more than enough. But, of course. I eat one piece of chicken. Everyone else in this house ate only one piece of chicken. That meant we only need five pieces of chicken, not fifteen. I kept doing the math to reassure myself that the meals were not about to come up woefully short.

The change wasn't just the food and the environment. It was the people, too. There was no bunch of growing boys seated around the table anymore. There were no loud rambunctious conversations, or rowdy jokes. Absence can speak louder than words, and the quiet spaces reminded me of things gone and things changed. It was a different life in more ways than just caring for Grandpa.

There was the struggle of adjusting my thinking to the new environment, but there was also the struggle of adjusting the environment to me. A few weeks into my journey, neither of these adjustments had been completed. Growing up in a large family, I was accustomed to structure and a certain type of routine. Meals were planned in advance, and care was taken to make sure enough food was on hand. In contrast, Grandma and Grandpa were used to a much less structured environment. Grandma bought food on a whim, and made supper based on what she could find in the house. So I added structure—especially meal and grocery shopping structure. But I also accepted that there wouldn't be as much structure as I was accustomed to back home.

In my personal life I was also still seeking a balance—and over the next three years that would be an ever moving target. In my old routine certain things happened certain days, and certain things at certain times in each day. This type of structure in my life kept me focused so that I didn't feel as though I were floundering around, lost, and with no idea of where I was going or what I was trying to accomplish each day. It also kept me accountable to myself. If I had a schedule I knew when I was supposed to do what, and if I wasn't doing it.

Alzheimer's didn't fit into such a neat little schedule. I couldn't write on my list that Grandpa would need help at 9:00 AM and noon, and the space between was free for me to use as I wished. There was no such routine. Sometimes Grandpa went to bed late, and got up early. Sometimes because of him we were up half the night. It was futile to attempt a rigid schedule, but what structure and schedule I did manage in life was helpful. A bit of structure kept a sometimes tenuous shred of sanity to the day, and my life, on the days when all sanity felt like it had taken flight. Making sure I had some time to exercise, and some food in the refrigerator for supper, could be the difference between coming emotionally and mentally unglued, or making it through another day. I needed my small routines.

Mixed in with all of this new life was something else, another feeling that sprung from the knowledge of why my help was needed. One could say the mortal pall hangs over all of this life, but it existed with particularly visibility in my present situation. Alzheimer's at the end is a fatal disease, and though it wouldn't kill Grandpa today or tomorrow there was a very real way in which I felt called to a long death watch. It wasn't something I thought about in every moment of every day, but it was always there. It wasn't something that we really talked about, but we all knew I was there because of what was happening to Grandpa. I had come to help him, yes, but then another voice echoed in the silence that I had come to watch him slowly die, his dignity and his mind stripped from him by inches, day by day. I knew it. We all knew it. It was like a monster that lived in the house with us, which nobody wanted to talk about.

But sometimes we did, a little.

§§§

Hugs, Too

Is everything all right in there?" I called through the bathroom door, answering a shout from within.

"Yeah, you can come on in," Grandpa said.

This was during the early months of my time caring for Grandpa. He was still somewhat capable so I had started a shower for him and adjusted the temperature, then left him—on his insistence—to wash in privacy. The shout had called me back to the bathroom minutes later. On entering I found him standing in the shower stall with the door open.

"What would you like?" I asked. "Need some help?"

"Yeah," he said. "The water, over there. Can you—" he waggled his finger at the toilet. "Is that thing over there—check it. Is it cold?"

I discerned that he wanted me to check some water somewhere, but for what cause, and what water he wanted checked, wasn't clear. He pointed to the toilet, but I couldn't understand how that had anything to do with his shower.

"Is your shower too cold?" I asked. "You need it adjusted a little more?"

"No, it's fine. Just check it," he insisted.

"Well..." I hesitated. At this point *I* was confused, no longer able to guess the nature of his concern. I wasn't going to check the toilet water, so I hazarded a guess that his concern had something to do with the sink faucet. I turned it on and checked the water.

"Is it cold?" Grandpa asked.

"I can make it cold," I said. "Right now it is hot."

At this point Grandpa became flustered and mumbled that he guessed everything was all right. I left thinking that maybe he had been concerned that he was stealing all the hot water from everyone else in the house and wanted me to check.

Later I found out otherwise.

Loss of short term memory meant Grandpa was often distracted from his initial goal, but sometimes a thought would stay with him over a surprising period of time. That same evening after supper he left the table and went to the bathroom. In reconstructing the situation afterward, I figured out he had gone to move his bowels. But I didn't know that at the time, and he didn't remember why he had gone to the bathroom after he got there.

Grandpa usually took off his over-shirt before he sat down on the toilet out of a fear that his shirt might somehow drop in the toilet or otherwise get wet. However, he also took off his over-shirt when he was preparing to take a shower, wash his face, or shave. All of these projects involved taking off his shirt, and so this point was often where he became derailed from his intended activity. What started out as one activity turned into another. Such was the case this evening. He took off his shirt and forgot about the toilet.

A little later he came tottering back out of the bathroom naked to the waist, requesting something which he was unable to articulate. I took a good guess and asked him if he wanted a washcloth.

"Yes, that's it," Grandpa said. "I want a washcloth."

I got him a washcloth and checked in on the situation in the bathroom. Up until that point I wasn't sure if he intended to wash his face or take a shower. I saw a towel laid out on the floor and concluded that he was preparing to take yet another shower. He had already taken one that morning, he didn't need to take another, but I wasn't going to argue him out of it. Taking a shower would cause him no harm, and it would cause him less agitation if I let him do what he wanted instead of arguing.

By this time Grandma joined the show, which I was trying to avoid because she often argued when he did something foolish. Soon as she understood what he was trying to do, she tried to stop him. "Why are you doing that?" she demanded. "You already took a shower this morning, Papa. You don't need a shower. You don't need anything in there." By the time she finished Grandpa was sputtering, defensive, humiliated, and even more confused.

Grandma left him simmering in the bathroom doorway.

"I can still help you take your shower," I said after she had left.

"Never mind that," he said angrily. "I'm not going to take one. I'm not going to do *nothing*."

"What would you like to do?" I asked.

He looked at me. "Can you take those things off?" he asked. "Those socks and stuff." He gestured to my socks and pants.

"Yes, I can take them off," I said, not sure where this was going.

"Well, take them off and come in here and stick your leg in this water and test it for me," he said.

I went over to the tub and stuck my hand under the faucet. "You want me to get some water the right temperature?" I said.

"No, stick your hand in that water." He pointed at the toilet. "It's veeerry cold."

I paused. Whenever possible I tried to fulfill whatever requests Grandpa made, no matter how strange they might seem. His requests had meaning to him, and as such they were important to him. I tried very hard to not brush him off. But there was a big problem with this request.

"Grandpa," I said, "that has piss in it."

"Oh, come on," he said. "It's got to have been flushed a half a dozen times."

The water in the bowel was yellow with urine.

Feeling a confrontation coming, and not exactly sure how to deal with his request that I stick my hand in the toilet water, I decided to stall by flushing the toilet.

"Um, Grandpa," I said after clean water had come in fresh. "Why do you want me to check the water?"

He flustered a bit, then turned away and said, "Never mind. I'm not as stupid as you guys think."

He was angry because Grandma had made him feel a fool, he was angry because he couldn't convey his desire, and I think he was angry and humiliated because some part of him realized that in trying to convey his wishes he had asked me to do something really stupid. But even so another irrational part of him was annoyed because I hadn't understood what he wanted, and I hadn't done what he wanted.

Dressed in nothing but his undershorts he tottered toward the kitchen, grumbling about how everyone thought he was stupid and no one was any help. "And you most of all," he said, catching sight of Grandma.

I wanted to let it go. Grandpa was humiliated, confused, and angry. I was willing to let him chew out the world, and me included, if it made him feel better and if it would lay the matter to rest. But Grandma heard his final "And especially you," and she took it as being aimed at me. "Don't you go talking to your help that way, Pa," she said.

Great, I thought. *We don't need another argument now.*

But it didn't become an argument. Instead, now on top of everything else Grandpa felt guilty about his attitude and actions—as well as angry, frustrated, and confused. "I know I shouldn't," he said, shamefaced. At this point I tried to intervene again, saying it was all right. Still trying to mollify him, and honestly fix whatever was bothering him if I could, I asked if there was anything he wanted me to do. I said I would try to do it.

This launched him into a long rambling aggrieved discourse through which I finally managed to understand that since it was cold outside he was concerned about the water line to the toilet freezing. The events of the day, with all the bizarre requests surrounding the toilet, finally clicked into place.

"Okay," I said. "I understand what you are concerned about. You are worried about the pipes freezing. What would you like me to do to take care of the problem?" It was important to restate Grandpa's concerns and requests to make it clear I understood him. It was also always better to offer a pro-active solution to Grandpa rather than soliciting whatever idea he might imagine. He could imagine some very wild things. But in that instant I couldn't think of what I could do to alleviate the perceived danger of the toilet water line freezing since there really was no danger.

"Well," Grandpa said, sounding offended, "someone could at least open the door to the closet under the stairs to let some warm air in. But nobody wants to—"

"Okay," I said. "I'll go do that. I can open the door under the stairs."

"Never mind, never mind," Grandpa said. "I'm not in charge here. I don't have any say. You guys do what you want."

So we came back to doing nothing. Grandpa got back into his clothes and combed his hair. Afterward he apologized and I said I forgave him and I didn't think he was stupid.

But I still wondered how he knew the toilet water was veeery cold.

§§§

So life went on, the every day small troubles punctuated with the occasional bigger problem. Sometimes the issue was not what Grandpa wanted stuck in the toilet, but rather what was supposed to go in the toilet and *wasn't* making it there. Grandpa developed a problem where he would urinate in the wastebasket beside the toilet instead of in the toilet. The distinction between receptacles was growing fuzzy. Other distinctions were blurring too.

One evening Grandpa came into the living room and handed Grandma a plate and fork. "I need to take a crap," he told her.

"Okay, go," she said. "You hurry along."

"Why?" he asked.

"Because I want you to hurry up and go to the bathroom," she said.

"Oh," he said in a vague sort of way, and started back toward the kitchen.

I got up and followed. At this point in his decline I realized that for Grandpa everything was starting to become the toilet. It had begun as the rare slip up, but more and more it happened. I came into the kitchen behind Grandpa in time to observe him dropping his trousers and preparing to sit in his chair.

"Grandpa," I said, trying to be as gentle as possible. "Don't you want to do that in the bathroom?"

"What?" he said blankly. Then he looked down at himself. He gathered that I objected to something he was doing, but couldn't figure out what. I guess he caught on that he wasn't doing it properly and then realized that if he wanted to take a proper crap he needed to drop his undershorts as well. He promptly began attempting to pull down his undershorts.

"No, Grandpa," I said, stopping him. "You don't want to do that here. You want to do that in the bathroom."

"What?" he said.

"The bathroom," I prompted. "Remember? This is the kitchen and your chair. You don't want to take your crap here."

It took repeated prompting before he grasped his situation. Once he realized his error he said, "Well, gee, why are you trying to get me to do it in here for?" as if going to the bathroom in the kitchen was *my* idea.

I let it be. Sometimes, the protestation that it was my idea was the best he could manage in a feeble attempt to save his dignity.

It was so hard for him.

Another day that week he was having a bad evening and needed to "take a leak," as he put it, and couldn't find the bathroom. I directed him to the bathroom but I saw he was very confused (indicated in part by the fact that he didn't shut the bathroom door as he did when he was in his right senses). I hesitated before leaving him to his own devices and in that moment of hesitation I saw him beginning to undo his pants in front of the garbage can.

"You're not quite there, Grandpa," I said.

"Uh-huh," he agreed, and continued to work at his pants.

"No, Grandpa," I said. "A little further. The toilet is there," I added, pointing.

"Yep," he said, taking maybe a teeny step forward and not taking his attention off his pants and the garbage can.

"Keep going," I said, more urgently. "You're going to miss it."

"Mmmm," he mumbled, finally getting his pants open.

"Grandpa—"

It was no good. He didn't properly understand a word I said even as he blandly agreed with every statement. Getting him to take a leak in the toilet would have required physically pushing him the rest of the way and doing the proper aiming for him. I wasn't ready to violate his personal dignity to that extent so I watched helplessly as he finally managed to get a stream of urine going and peed inside the garbage bag and all down the side and across the floor.

"Am I doing it right?" Grandpa asked. "Is this right? Is this how you want it?"

I couldn't stand to keep watching. He was trying so hard to do it right, and I didn't have the heart to tell him he was urinating all over the floor. I didn't want him to feel the utter fool when he finally understood my words and realized he had done a completely stupid thing right in front of me. So I left. Let him finish and leave, I figured. I would go back after he left and clean it up, and maybe he would be spared yet another realization of what he was becoming.

I went into the living room to wait but it was little more than a minute later when Grandpa stuck his head out the bathroom doorway. "Hey," he said in a miserable voice. "I need help. I made a mess in here. I screwed up."

"It's okay, Grandpa," I said, seeing his crushed expression and trying to soothe him. "Don't worry about it. I'll clean it up. You don't worry about it and just go back and sit down on the couch and rest."

"I'm terribly sorry," he said, still sounding wretched. "I don't know how—I shouldn't have done it. It's all over the place. You shouldn't have to clean it up. I'm such a dirty, filthy, old man. I—"

"It's all right, Grandpa," I said. Sometimes words are not enough. This was one of those times. I came over and gave him a hug. "It's okay. Don't worry about it."

The hug seemed to make him feel better because he immediately stopped apologizing. After a minute he gave a little laugh. "Well," he said. "My foot is soaked."

Since Grandpa was often completely aware of being foolish—even when he was incapable and incoherent—issues of dignity were paramount unless it was a matter of life and death. It hurt him badly to be the fool. All his life he had been a neat and fastidious man, orderly, independent, and desiring to be respectable. Alzheimer's was taking all of those things from him. There were times, especially in the early days, when the confusion would clear from his mind for a moment and he would realize what utterly foolish things he had done and the shame he felt was painful to witness. When I think back on the years I cared for him, those moments can still make me choke up. It is horrible to see someone overwhelmed with a sense of degraded humiliation at themselves.

I tried to keep him from feeling that shame.

At the beginning whenever Grandpa needed to do things I shadowed him to make up for his deficiencies. How much I shadowed or intervened was a delicate issue which I handled somewhat by instinct. He had not lost his self-awareness so I tried to manage a careful balance of respecting him while at the same time dealing with the reality that he could not function with true independence. There were a lot of things that would have turned out better if Grandpa had allowed someone else to do it for him. But as much as possible I tried to allow him the dignity of choice (or at the very least the appearance of choice), even if his choices meant he was somewhat frustrated or things did not turn out ideally. I would ask him if he would like help going to bed. He would say no (because it is shameful to need help), but then would add, "But if I have trouble I will holler." If he became really stuck he would go back out for help—to Grandma. So my usual routine in the early days was to ask him if he needed help going to bed, he would say no, and I then waited a short amount of time before going into the bedroom after him. He was often by that point in the middle of some confused attempt at something—sometimes having to do with going to bed, sometimes not. Having just "happened" to walk in the room at that moment I would suggest the way forward and help him along. Since he hadn't asked for help, it was okay. Eventually, the idea of my help with the bedtime routine became expected and accepted.

But the acceptance took time. Everything took time.

Each day was full of activities that gave Grandpa trouble. It was difficult to know how much and how far to let him go in his frustration before helping. I had the choice of pandering and pampering him (a natural first instinct) or letting him live as much as possible in attempted independence—that frustrated, failing, and sometimes humiliating life of his dissolution.

He wanted to live his own life, and I tried to let him. But it was hard. Very hard. Hard for him to live, and hard for me to watch.

§§§

SMART PEOPLE AND BIG CHIEFS

One day after lunch Grandpa came into the kitchen with a washcloth, making some request. Arlan, sitting in the kitchen (not having to work that day) thought Grandpa wanted to shave. Working on that presumption, Grandma went off to gather shaving equipment. I wasn't sure Arlan had presumed correctly, but since Grandma was pursuing that idea I didn't intervene to figure out what he wanted. I thought Grandpa had been misunderstood, and I was proven correct when he became very mad when Grandma set everything up and told him he could start shaving.

After his blow-up, Grandma suggested he might want to go for a walk to "clear his head."

Grandpa decided he would take a walk up toward Doug's house. I decided I had better go with him. It was a nice autumn day, warm and sunny. Grandpa was feeling fairly well so we made it to the top of the hill where Grippen Road met Glenwood before he decided to turn around.

When we turned around Grandpa seemed to collect himself and then said, "I do hope and pray that this curse would be taken away."

I said nothing at first. I wasn't certain if he was talking about the general state of things in his out-of-the-blue comment. I thought not. I guessed his recent blow-up at Grandma was on his mind. "Well, Pa," she had said after his angry words, "You're not very clear." "I'm sorry I'm not clear," he had said. That fast failing clarity was on his mind and the way he had gathered himself before making the statement about praying indicated he wasn't making an off-hand comment about the condition of the world in general. It was something much more personal, something difficult to say.

He said nothing more after a few steps, so I said, "It's hard, isn't it?"

"Yes," he said. "It's very hard. I think..." Then he stopped. Finally, he said, "I don't know what I think."

He spoke no more on that subject and a little later when he spoke again it was on a different topic.

I wasn't sure he would ever speak so openly about his condition again, but about a week later we had another exchange.

On this occasion Grandpa had gone to bed for the night. I needed to finish some stuff I was doing, so I tucked him in but didn't go to bed at the same time. I went to check in on him a little later and found him sitting up in bed. I took care of his minor problem and was starting to put him back to bed when he paused and said, "Do you believe that?"

"What?" I asked.

"What he said." Grandpa gestured toward the CD player. "Do you believe it applies to this age?"

I had left the Bible on CD playing and the section being read was from the gospel of Mark where Jesus spoke about faith saying, "If a man has faith he can say to the mountain 'throw yourself into the sea' and it will be done."

"Yes," I said. "I believe it."

"Well, some people say there are two ages," he said.

"It says elsewhere in scripture, Grandpa, that all scripture was written for our instruction. So I believe it, yes."

"But some people say, 'Well, then, why are you sick?'" Grandpa said.

Ah. Now we were getting to the heart of what was bothering him.

I answered, "Jesus' disciples asked him why a man was born blind: 'because of his own sin or his parents sin?' Jesus told them 'Neither, but that the glory of God might be revealed in his life.' We can say the same for your situation, Grandpa."

He gave a little chuckle and said something to the effect, "I don't understand why."

I said, "I know. The situation of Job is a good example. He suffered very much and God didn't give him an explanation. God wouldn't explain himself to Job—Job had to accept it because God was God. We have to believe by faith that God is a loving and compassionate God."

"Yeah. It certainly gives you something to ponder," Grandpa agreed.

Then, in alluding back to the issue of faith, he said, "I sure would like to be healed from this...or whatever comes down the pike."

I said, "He will, Grandpa. He will heal you...if not by making this body well, then by taking you out of this body."

He gave another little chuckle and said something about hitting him over the head with a board. I smiled. Earlier, as I had put him to bed, he had expressed distress about waking up so much in the night. I had jokingly suggested he hit himself over the head with a board to go back to sleep. Now he furthered the joke by suggesting we hurry God's job along by dispatching him by the same method.

Grandpa could joke about it, but his disease bothered him profoundly. On a spiritual level, he struggled with questions of guilt. The thought nagged that God had done this to him in recompense for some past deeds. A few times he openly wondered what he had done to bring the sickness on himself. I tried to comfort and encourage him as best I could, but often he seemed unreachable when faced with his own private guilt and shame.

On the practical level, he was both deeply frustrated and afraid.

One evening while I was in the bathroom I heard Grandpa trying to communicate with Arlan. I came out and asked Arlan what Grandpa had wanted and Arlan said he hadn't been able to figure out. So I went to investigate.

I found Grandpa coming up from the basement.

"What would you like, Grandpa?" I asked, meeting him on the stairs.

"I don't know," he said absently, picking up a bit of lint from the carpet as he finished ascending the stairs. "I can't remember. I know it was something, but I can't remember. I wish..." he trailed off as he walked into the kitchen. I followed.

"...Typewriters, shorthand, and all that stuff. You know," he said, taking his chair.

"I know what shorthand is, and I know what typewriters are," I said, not sure where he was going or what he was getting at.

"Is that my coffee?" He pointed at the mostly finished cup.

"Yes, that's your cup," I said.

"Well, I think about it," Grandpa said. "...I think about it to myself and I wonder 'couldn't all the smart people and big chiefs get together with the stuff and come up with something down the pike for people who can't talk?'"

"Well..." I paused, now understanding what he was getting at. Grandpa's failing ability to communicate was one of the biggest sources of grief for him. I think sometimes he imagined that everything would be fixed if only he could communicate better. I didn't have a nice pat answer to what I knew was the heart of his problem, but since he stated his question in a general way I decide to continue the conversation in the same manner.

"For someone who couldn't talk," I said, "they could learn how to type and they could communicate that way."

"Yeah," he said, and rubbed at his eyebrow. "But for someone with Alzheimer's...they need something. When you try to say something you can't and then you lose it, but it's still there and you know it. People...Grandma is the worst."

"She just stares at you like she doesn't understand anything," I said.

"That's right." He adjusted his glasses and mimicked Grandma's blank blinking stare. "They say 'What? What? What do you want? What's coming down the pike?' And you can't say it. It's lost."

"I know," I said. I didn't know what else to say.

Grandma's reaction to Grandpa's failing ability to communicate hurt him deeply. When she just said, "I don't understand what you're saying," and didn't make any attempt to interact with Grandpa, he felt rejected and brushed off. To lose the ability to communicate with your family is to feel both trapped and abandoned.

"I know a little bit what it is like, Grandpa," I said. "Sometimes I lose my words too and I can't figure out how to say it."

"That's right," he said, sounding vindicated. "It happens to everyone sometimes." Then he laughed a little and said, "Well, if you come up with something I'll sing your praises."

And that was the end of it.

The above doesn't communicate all the nuance of our exchange. In our conversations sometimes half of the communication took place on the unspoken level, where context and situation were crucial, nuance and interpretation, key. When I write it out it seems so clear and easy to follow, but the reality was that it took all of my attention to follow and piece together what he was trying to say. Grandpa struggled so much to hang on to his thoughts and keep them in an organized fashion that he often only spoke half of them, spoke unclearly, and on top of that often used the wrong words. It could take all of the attention, and mental dexterity I had to comprehend what he was trying to say through the veil of Alzheimer's.

Grandma's inability to understand Grandpa was only half her fault. She could have been more long-suffering and patient with him and taken more time to listen, more time to try to understand. But interpreting his words and his non-verbal communication did require quick thinking and an agile mind—things Grandma didn't have anymore. I managed to decipher what "Shorthand, typewriters, smart people, and big chiefs" meant, but it would have been meaningless babble to Grandma. It wasn't fair to fault her for the fact that she wasn't young, and no longer mentally agile enough to interpret an associative conversation on the fly. But it was more than just that. Grandpa was also very sensitive to her attitude, and it hurt him because it seemed to him that she didn't really care. Her terse replies gave the appearance of simply attempting to appease him or brush him off without trying to understand.

Very rarely did anyone understand immediately what Grandpa was talking about, but simply saying, "I don't know what you're talking about," was like shutting the door on him. He felt that statement meant, "I don't understand, I don't care, and I wish you would leave me alone." I discovered that some amount of effective communication could be managed if I got very close to him and made eye contact. Then I clearly reiterated whatever he had said (even if it didn't make much sense), and often he would clarify or correct himself, stating, "That wasn't the right word. What I meant was..." or else he would continue his line of thought and sometimes the continuing thought would make it clear what he meant.

Conversation required constant effort, attention, and patience. In the previous example, I responded to his first statement about shorthand and typewriters by telling him I knew what they were. This gave him the confidence to feel like he was really communicating with me. When he went on to talk about smart people and big chiefs getting together with all the stuff to get something down the pike to help people who couldn't talk, the context was set and I was able to interpret the idea he was trying to convey without flustering him or confusing him by trying to *make* him explain everything.

Understanding what he meant even when he couldn't say it right was my goal, but it became harder to achieve as his Alzheimer's grew worse. It reached the point where educated guesswork about what he meant was often the best I could manage, and sometimes I was completely stumped. Perhaps paradoxically, it reached the point where Grandpa was *also* stumped when trying to figure out what he meant. The progression was quite visible when six months later in the spring of 2007 we had a similar conversation.

Again, it was after supper and Grandpa wanted to talk.

I was sitting next to him, keeping him company while he drank his coffee. As we sat, some type of problem came to his mind because he set down his coffee, made an attempt to straighten out the shredded tissue on his place mat, and then pointed at the cloth and said, "How do we get this thing working?"

"It's a place mat, Grandpa," I said.

"Okay, it's a place mat," he agreed. "But how do we get things to... to...line up. Say we have one thing here and another thing here and we want to..." he pointed at different spots on the place mat as he described but he eventually trailed off, probably having not known where he was going with his thought to begin with, and now realizing he couldn't reach a conclusion.

Something was bothering him, even if it was just the sensation that something might not be right. He tried several more times to articulate some idea about getting things to work, continuing to use his place mat as a demonstration piece. It did nothing to clarify the matter for me.

"I'm sorry, Grandpa," I said, "but you haven't got it quite far enough along for me to guess."

"Yeah, I haven't got it quite far along enough for me to even understand either," he admitted.

So we sat in silence a little longer.

After a bit he smoothed out his place mat again and said, "Okay, I'll try again. So," he put his finger on one spot on the place mat. "Let's say we have ca...ca...coyotes. Yeah. Okay, coyotes. So they go over this way—" He moved his finger across the place mat to another location. "And they check out this place over here and find that it isn't commodious. So they say, 'yeah, okay, whatever,' and then they go over here to the ca...ca...caaannnn...canvas. So they go to this canvas and they're laughing at them, but even so they're trying to help as much as they can and then they go over here..." he moved his finger yet again tracing the continuing route of the coyotes then looked up at me and trailed off.

"Anyway, getting back to the main point..." he fumbled around with the stuff on the table, separating out the nearby silverware.

"So," he picked up a knife and drew an imaginary box around the head of a spoon. "So you have a block there and it is a good one and you can use it," he said.

I still wasn't making any headway. I knew the story about the coyotes was only language imagery, trying to convey a thought indirectly that he couldn't grasp with explicit words. I knew he was concerned about something. It had to do with getting something accomplished or done, but beyond that I couldn't make sense of it. He kept reaching for words, saying something only to immediately throw it aside, shuffling phrases and stuttering in-between his short parabolic utterances. He gave up multiple times, only to make another attempt a little bit later.

"Ahhh, I can't describe it," he said.

"Would you like a pencil and piece of paper to draw it?" I asked.

"No, I guess not," he said. "I can't draw very well, and in any case half the time I don't understand what I just drew anyhow." He laughed. "If you know what I mean."

I knew what he meant.

After another lapse into frustrated silence he said, "So, what do you think? What do you think about anything?"

I talked a bit about the weather and how spring had finally come, and next week was going to be nice.

Some more silence, then Grandpa spoke up again, seeming to have returned to whatever thought he was wrestling with. "Is there any law about...if you have some problem and you need to go to a doctor..." he couldn't finish the thought, but this time he was hitting close enough to reality that I could make some educated guesses.

"And the emergency room," I supplied.

"Yeah, the emergency room," he agreed. "And if...and if you have the doctor and..." but he couldn't get any further along in the thought. At that moment had to go to the bathroom so he got up from the table, saying, "I'll be back."

That was the end of the conversation. I don't know if there was a fixed event or question behind Grandpa's desperate attempt at communication. He may have simply felt generally ill at ease and wanted to make sure "everything" was being properly handled. Or, perhaps, his thoughts had drifted back to Grandma's recent trip to the emergency room for her heart problems and he was trying to articulate some concern about handling the insurance bill. That would have been like him, so I suspect that thought was in his mind somewhere, trying to get out.

Alzheimer's crept further and further into his life, but with all that he had lost he still tried to communicate. He was trying to think, and communicate. He *did* communicate, in his own way. He was still there, and he still had concerns, thoughts, and worries that needed addressing. They deserved addressing.

I tried to deal with Grandpa's concerns and requests because I wanted him to feel like he had received a hearing, and that both his feelings and his person were valued. Since I was far more effective at communicating with him, I increasingly functioned as Grandma and Grandpa's go-between. Grandpa asked Grandma a question and Grandma gave him a blank stare. I interpreted what Grandpa was trying to say and then Grandma understood and answered me. I then conveyed what Grandma had said to Grandpa in terms he could understand. It was effective, but also made the growing divide between them plainly evident. Once Grandpa said in a mildly hurt voice, "Why does she always answer you and not me?"

I couldn't give him a good explanation.

With all the problems that Grandpa had it was easy to think he "wasn't there" or somehow not able to appreciate the depths of his situation. But in the rare times he did talk about it he revealed a man who was much more aware of his problems than most people would have given him credit.

Many times he demonstrated quite clearly that he was painfully aware that he couldn't communicate, and that he made a "fool" out of himself by doing stupid things. The inability to communicate frustrated Grandpa, but I think the larger issue of the reason for his Alzheimer's bothered him on a deeper level. He knew he was doing these things because he was succumbing to Alzheimer's. Why had God allowed this to happen? Of all the questions Grandpa had, that bothered him the worst.

A person can say, "I hope and pray" in a very flippant manner, but that was not the way in which Grandpa spoke that autumn afternoon when we went on a walk. He spoke quietly, but in an earnest way that told of what was deep within him. I felt it was a rare moment where he opened up to express his recognition of his condition, and I didn't know what to say.

Sometimes I wonder if I can comprehend Grandpa's loss of ability sufficiently to have real empathy. Can I understand what it is like to wrestle every day with a disease which is slowly stripping a person of everything, and their ability to communicate first? I can say, and believe, that God is still there—but how well do I understand the loneliness of alienation that came to Grandpa when it felt like God had abandoned him to his sickness?

I don't know.

§§§

THE LITTLE DOG

Bright light. My eyes snap open. I had come to the edge of wakefulness with the creak of bed springs which signaled Grandpa rising for his first night trip to the bathroom. The hope that he would (this time) make it out of the bedroom without turning on the light ended with the click of the switch.

Squinting through the bright light, I saw Grandpa pawing around in a befuddled manner, hunting for the door knob. He knew he was looking for something to let him out of the bedroom, and had turned on the light to help his search, but he still wasn't recognizing the door knob in front of him. Finally he latched onto one of the bed-post knobs on the foot of his bed and began determinedly attempting to turn it.

"Grandpa, that's not going to open the door," I said, tiredly.

"I'm trying, the bugger isn't working," he said, giving the bed-post knob his best effort, nearly dancing in his desperation to go to the bathroom.

Sighing, I rolled out of bed and went to open the door. After edging Grandpa out of the way to open the door I ushered him from the room and watched him totter down the hall toward the bathroom. The oddity was, half the time he could get out of the bedroom without even turning on the light. The other half of the time—such as this—he couldn't even find the door knob with the light turned on.

Once he was free of the bedroom confines I could only wait until he came back, and hope he would agreeably return to bed.

Every night had its own variation. Another night he *did* make it out of the room without turning on the light, but on returning switched it on. Again, I jerked up, eyes squinting. I could make out Grandpa at the foot of his bed, hand on the light switch, surveying the room like a man in search of something. His gaze fell on a sweater lying at the foot of his bed. A pause, then he picked it up and began putting it on.

"Grandpa," I said, "do you really want to put the sweater on?"

"I might get cold," he explained. It certainly was the thought prompted in his mind by seeing the sweater, but in reality he wouldn't get cold in bed—he would end up too hot.

"All right," I said, feeling groggy and tired.

He was halfway through putting on the sweater when he stopped, peering over the top of the garment. "You awake?" he asked.

"Yeah," I said. "I'm awake."

"No," he said. "I was talking to the little dog over there."

"Oh," I said, perplexed, but determined to remain agreeable. There were some objects in the direction he pointed. Perhaps one of them looked like a dog to him.

Seeming satisfied in regards to the imagined dog, he finished putting on the sweater and sat down on the edge of his bed. Then he saw his socks beside the bed. So he put them on.

"Grandpa, you're getting into bed," I prompted. "Do you wear your socks to bed?"

"Sometimes," he said, vaguely.

I let it pass. Tucking him under the covers, I turned off the light and went back to bed.

Ten minutes later he sat back up and took the sweater off. Even later in the night he took off the socks as well.

Grandpa woke up often every night to go to the bathroom. Old age and prostate trouble will do that to a man. In the early days a good trip to the bathroom was when he managed to get out of the bedroom, use the toilet, and come promptly back to bed—all without turning on the light. Often a bathroom trip wasn't so good.

Turning on the bedroom light was a common necessity. This was very understandable, but having the light turned on was disruptive for me. Far worse than the light blinding me, having the light on meant Grandpa was likely to see something that would derail his train of thought. Instead of going directly about his business of getting into bed, or out to the bathroom, he would start doing something else. Maybe he would see a bit of junk on the floor that needed to go into the garbage. Maybe he would decide he needed to neaten his bed (at midnight!). Or maybe he would see the roll of toilet paper beside his bed which would then descend into several minutes spent carefully folding a few sheets of toilet paper. Or else he would decide to organize the top of his dresser. Just because. Anything could happen. The world is a fascinating place to the easily preoccupied, especially at 2:00 AM.

Those were common derailing activities which slowed the process of going back to bed. It was easy to see how his eyes rested on various objects and he thought something about them that put his mind on a different track besides going to bed. Usually his derailment didn't last more than a few minutes, but at 2:00 AM a few minutes with the light on felt close to eternity. He was thinking about straightening his bed. I was thinking, "Kill me now."

When I saw him become derailed I generally tried to prompt him with questions to keep him on track. If he insisted on his derailed thought I usually let him go on with it, otherwise the situation could turn into an argument. Disputes usually ended with Grandpa ashamed and humiliated, or angry. Wanting to avoid such results, I felt letting him set his own course (as much as possible, with prompting) respected his dignity best, and avoided needless strife.

But sometimes there was no keeping him on track.

§§§

I awoke again to the bedroom light. The clock said 1:00 AM. Squinting through the light blindness, I noticed Grandpa standing at the other end of the bedroom, dressed in one of his button down shirts. He had not been wearing that when he went to bed. After turning on the light he came over to his dresser and began going through the drawers. I wondered, in a befuddled sort of way, what was going on. I alternated between watching him and closing my eyes against the glare of the light. Eventually he found what he wanted on the floor—a pair of socks—and put them on. Then he told me to go back to sleep, turned out the light, and left the room.

Great.

He had left the bedroom door open, and lying in the darkness I could tell from the light shining in the room that more than the bathroom light was on. The kitchen light was on.

Something was up.

I lay where I was a little while longer, wishing he would come back into the room and get into bed. At such moments half articulated prayers and pleadings flitted through my mind. *Oh God, please...not a night like this. Let him come back and go to bed.*

That didn't happen. I finally dragged myself out of bed and went to investigate.

Grandpa was standing in the doorway to the kitchen trying to put his coat on. For a moment I thought he had gone completely unhinged and, imaging it was morning, he was starting his daily routine—in this case preparing to go out for the newspaper. Up to this point in his disease Grandpa had been very good at recognizing darkness as nighttime and daylight as daytime, but I reasoned that sometime that might change.

Then I saw the tub of peanut butter on the table and the spoon stuck in it, and I knew Grandpa was going down a different trail.

"You need help?" I asked.

"Yeah, I can't seem to get this thing to work," he said.

He had managed to twist the coat around so that he was wearing one sleeve properly and had turned the other sleeve inside out. With the sleeves in such disagreement it was impossible to wear the coat. I helped him take the coat off, righted it for him, and assisted him in putting it back on.

"You're cold," I said.

"Yeah. I ran and ran the water and it never got warm," Grandpa said.

I looked around and saw no running water and no mess, so I let that comment go.

"You go back to bed," Grandpa said.

I considered what to do. He obviously realized that it was still the middle of the night based on his repeated admonishment for me to go back to bed. I suspected he had got up some time ago to use the bathroom and had become concerned about the pipes when he felt the cold water from the sink. (I now understood he had an obsession about pipes freezing.) Being concerned, he then intended to check the kitchen sink for signs of freezing pipes as well. But after he had gone to the kitchen to check the faucet he became sidetracked by the peanut butter. The peanut butter made him decide to have a midnight snack, and while having his snack he had become cold. That made him decide to put on more clothes. It was like a version of "If you give a mouse a cookie" and it was at this point of returning to our room for more clothes that he had woken me.

In any case, he was up and he didn't seem to have any intention of going back to bed. I *felt* like chiding him that 1:00 AM was no time to have a snack. I *thought* about seeing if I could prompt him into going back to bed. But in the end I decided he seemed pretty determined to accomplish something, and he was in an agreeable mood that I didn't want to ruin with a midnight argument. Rather than just sit in the kitchen and watch him, I decided to try a subtler approach for getting him back to bed. Grandpa usually didn't like being alone, so I went back to the bedroom to see how long he would sit in the kitchen before the isolation made him decide to return to bed.

Of course this had the added benefit of allowing me to lie on my bed instead of sitting miserably in the kitchen wondering how much of the night I would have to waste in a hard chair in the brightly lit kitchen instead of my bed. Such vigils made the night seem very long.

So I lay in bed with the door open and tried to alternately doze and listen to the sounds drifting into the room for any hint of Grandpa getting into trouble. I went out every ten to fifteen minutes to check on him, especially if some sound seemed to particularly warrant investigation. I found him once getting himself a cup of milk, and another time simply wandering around the house, but never getting into any trouble or doing anything dangerous. Several times he told me to go back to bed, and I refrained from a tart comment that he should be heading the same place.

Finally the time reached about 2:00 AM and when I checked on Grandpa again it seemed he was beginning to settle down. He had collected various things and arranged them on the couch. He told me the newspaper wasn't working right. Sensing the occasion was finally at hand, I suggested that maybe we go back to bed. He agreed that maybe we should, but he didn't seem in a big hurry so I went back to lay down by myself. A few minutes later he appeared in the doorway, took off his hat, tossed it on his bed, and seemed to struggle to get his thoughts in order. Then he realized he had left the kitchen light on and left the room again. The kitchen light went off, but Grandpa didn't return.

I guessed what had happened but waited a few minutes before getting up (once again) and going to check. I found Grandpa lying on the couch in the dark. Most likely on turning out the light he had imagined that he had turned out the bedroom light and had gone to "bed." However, the last time I let him spend the night on the couch I found him later naked from the waist down, with a urine stain on the carpet. So I couldn't leave him out there this time.

"You ready to go to bed?" I said.

"Yeah, I ate some peanut butter," he said.

"Well, how about we go to bed," I prompted.

"Yeah, okay, I guess we should," he agreed. He got up off the couch, we went back to the bedroom, and I tucked him in. Then I went around the house and checked on everything to make sure nothing was amiss.

Then I went back to bed.

This is one example of how Grandpa would pass a night.

Grandpa had increasing difficulty relating properly to objects, and this started to show particularly in relation to his clothes. It happened in the day, but it also happened at night.

Years ago when he still had all his mental faculties, Grandpa carried around a wad of carefully folded toilet paper, or paper towels, for nose blowing. Like a boy scout, he was always prepared for the unexpected runny nose. He was neat and he was careful. But when I cared for him I often saw him using a garment to wipe his nose. It was a combination of regression to childish impulses, but also a true confusion of use—he sometimes literally mistook his clothes for a hanky.

Grandpa usually went to bed wearing an undershirt and undershorts. When early in my care he began worrying about wetting the bed he started wearing a diaper at night instead of undershorts. Sometimes he had a problem of forgetting to put the diaper back on during one of his many night time trips to the bathroom. This resulted in him either switching back to his undershorts, or going back to bed naked.

One night he returned to the bedroom after a bathroom trip wearing his undershorts (not the diaper) and carrying his undershirt balled up in his hands. Somehow in the process of going to the bathroom he had become confused into taking off the undershirt. I asked him if he wanted help putting it back on. He said, "No, I think I'll just go to bed."

Later in the night I woke to Grandpa coming back from the bathroom again. He didn't turn on the light. Instead, he felt his way over to his bed and sat on the edge. I could see him in the dim light filtering through the window. Since he didn't look much inclined to lie down immediately I sat up to see what he intended to do. I didn't have long to wait. Grandpa plucked at a leg of his undershorts, then promptly pulled the garment off. Balling it up decisively, he wiped his nose vigorously, then tossed it away in the darkness.

He was now sitting on the edge of his bed in the darkness, stark naked.

"Um...Grandpa," I said. "You think maybe you want to put something on?"

"Oh," he said, "I suppose I can put some socks on."

It was a giggle worthy moment, but I played it straight.

"No," I said, picking up the diaper he had discarded earlier in the night. "How about this?"

"Oh, that. Okay." He let me help him put the diaper on without the least sign of realizing what had just transpired. It was funny in an absurd sort of way, but also a reminder of his condition. The straight-laced Grandpa of yesteryear would have been horrified to see himself taking off his undershorts and blowing his nose on them. It would have appalled his sense of modesty to say the least.

At such times I might laugh because it was funny in a way, but at the same time in the back of my mind I was very glad Grandpa didn't realize what he did. Those moments of blissful ignorance were a small mercy for him.

§§§

SCARED

Helping Grandpa was labor intensive, time consuming, and required a large supply of patience. An evening with him, much less a day, was quite an adventure. It would have been easier to take charge of everything and micromanage him, but that would have removed all self-motivation from his life. But refraining from such strict control of his activity meant that often the simplest process turned into a major project.

Getting ready for bed was one such simple procedure that often morphed into an exercise of patience and perseverance. One evening clearly illustrates the situation.

It began when Grandpa went to the kitchen sink and began washing his dentures in preparation to soak them for the night. As usual he became side-tracked by the dishes in the sink. Since it was a harmless diversion, and he sometimes would eventually move on to cleaning his teeth, I kept half on eye on him and let him fiddle around with the dishes.

A little later I heard, "Awww...shit. Right down my leg." Muttering about the bathroom, and related things, made it very clear that *someone* thought they had just had an accident. I came over to see Grandpa rolling up and pulling up his pant leg as far as he could, like a man preparing to go deep water wading.

"Having trouble?" I queried.

"Yes," Grandpa said.

"Need to use the bathroom?" I asked.

"Yeah, didn't you hear me?" he said. "I already did it down my leg."
He started off toward the bathroom.

I checked the area by the sink. A quick inspection of the floor
showed no wetness. I immediately suspected that Grandpa didn't
actually have the accident that he imagined.

I checked the sink. The top portion of his dentures were lying in
the sink, the hose and sprayer sprawled in the sink with them. I
guessed what had happened: Grandpa, while confusedly using the
sprayer on his dentures, had managed to hit himself, but he was too
confused to understand the sprayer's wetness. As soon as he felt the
water on his pants his mind connected that with wetting himself,
which lead to dealing with this supposed crisis by using the bathroom.

Grandpa was heading toward the bathroom, but Arlan was already
using it. I followed Grandpa and explained that it was in use. He
seemed momentarily stumped as to how he should proceed, but
appeared to consider going into our bedroom. Concerned that he
might decide to relieve himself there, I suggested he use Grandma's
bathroom in the master bedroom suite.

He agreed and started toward Grandma's bathroom. I decided that,
considering his present state, I had better make sure he didn't do
something that would upset Grandma. We were still in the early
months of my care for Grandpa and he was still a little irritated and
shy about having someone watch his every move in the bathroom, so
as Grandpa entered the bathroom I hung back while watching to
make sure he didn't do something drastic, such as urinating in
Grandma's laundry hamper. He didn't do that, but next thing I heard
was a *sploosh, sploosh* and—quickly glancing in to the bathroom—I
saw Grandpa swishing his hands around in the toilet bowl water.
Satisfied, he took a sodden piece of toilet paper and began washing

the inside and rim of the toilet.

I nearly freaked out. If there is one thing we have all been taught from childhood it is that toilet water is *nasty*. But I caught myself, and said nothing. I reminded myself—firmly—that since Grandpa had already done it there was no undoing it, and it wouldn't help if I got all excited. Sticking his hands in toilet water was something I had already suspected Grandpa of doing previously (all that talk about the toilet water being *veeery* cold), and so I wasn't too surprised to catch him at it. Nonetheless, I had to suppress a wince and refrain from verbally snapping at him to tell him he shouldn't do it.

I wished I had been faster and caught him before he started, but at this point I simply watched. He couldn't get his hands any dirtier, and correcting him now would only humiliate him. In his right mind he *knew* you were not supposed to splash around in the toilet. Apparently he thought he was cleaning the toilet. I watched, and thought about how glad I was that the toilet water didn't looked used, and wished he would hurry up and stop.

Grandpa might have felt an inkling that something wasn't quite right with what he was doing because he suddenly stopped and threw the toilet paper into the toilet and turned to the sink to wash his hands. I tried to help him along by drawing his attention to the soap. We clumsily washed his hands, and eventually he lost interest and seemed to hunt around for a towel. I pointed out a towel and he half-heartedly wiped off his hands. I could tell he was getting increasingly confused, now very far afield from his reason for entering the bathroom.

"You want to go pee?" I prompted.

"Yeah," he said. "I've been wanting to go all this time."

So he finally urinated—in the toilet, properly. I stepped away for a bit to allow him to finish up with a semblance of privacy. I came back a minute later and he had already moved on—toilet paper in his hand, scrubbing at the floor around the toilet where there was absolutely nothing that needed cleaning. He ended up giving the entire exterior of the toilet and the floor around the toilet a good cleaning before he was finally satisfied. Only after he finished all of that did we finally leave Grandma's bathroom. By this time Arlan had left the other bathroom and Grandpa stopped in there to make sure things were all set, and check for anything that needed cleaning.

Once he was finished with the bathrooms he went into the living room and sat down to watch TV. His top dentures were still in the kitchen sink, and his bottom dentures were still in his mouth. I retrieved the container from beside the sink and put his top dentures in. Then I went and asked him for the rest of his teeth, and set them all on the counter to soak for the night.

§§§

Until Grandpa forgot the bathroom and his need for it, using the toilet absorbed much of his daily existence—and, as a result, mine as well. The tales surrounding that one little room could fill a book themselves. The experiences were at times funny, sad, poignant, frustrating, and depressing—all in measure, all mixed together. It was life. It was more than that. It was a microcosm of Alzheimer's, a window into the larger battle Grandpa fought against the disease, and for his dignity.

In the beginning, it appalled Grandpa to think of someone else coming into the bathroom with him. Did you think he was incompetent? (Not that he said those words, but he felt the sting.) He didn't want anyone in there watching him doing his business.

Reality moved inexorably against his wishes. Still, this is where he took his stand and fought tooth and nail to keep his dignity, and his bathroom independence. I decided to let him take the lead in this battle. It was his fight, and so it would be on his terms. I would help, I would be there at his side when he needed me, but I would let his problems prompt him to ask for help.

I wanted to allow him the opportunity and space to come to his own terms with Alzheimer's, and I figured if he recognized for himself that he needed bathroom help he would be more agreeable to assistance in this very touchy matter. It was a delicate and difficult balance. On the one hand, in my view, a puddle of urine on the floor was not a big deal in the long run. But, at the same time, I wanted to save him from the shame of that mess. I was never sure how to balance everything, and often Grandpa and I were both wretched where bathroom matters were concerned.

It was a messy learning process for both of us.

He started out spending a looong time alone in the bathroom. Sometimes I thought he used the toilet twice (at least, he flushed the toilet twice) and sometimes he came out with a bunch of "used" toilet paper that he was looking to dispose of (sometimes in an incoherent fashion). He had a compulsion to wipe the rim of the toilet, even when it didn't need to be wiped, and he used far more toilet paper than necessary. Then he might wrap that toilet paper in more toilet paper. It could get quite out of hand. He was afraid that he was screwing up, and he wanted to fix it all by himself.

Grandpa heading for the laundry room or bedroom instead of the bathroom was a common problem. Being unable to turn on the light was another early issue. Pretty soon I was often going into the bathroom with him to prompt him and keep him on track, just as we did when he got ready for bed. Following him into the bathroom required exceptional tact because Grandpa recognized it as another big blow against his self-sufficiency, and also a violation of his modesty. He was *very* modest. We tried to pretend this change wasn't happening, but we couldn't pretend for long.

§§§

Grandpa was always worse in the evenings. Some evenings he was better than others, but it was always worse than the day. Some evenings he was quite bad. Sometimes his confusion could add up, one confused mistake piling on top of another, making his muddled thoughts all the more confused until the situation spiraled completely out of control.

He tried hard to use the bathroom independently, but no matter the time of day, his ability to use the bathroom continued to decline. Once when his brother Doug was visiting Grandpa called him into the bathroom to show him how to urinate in the toilet. Doug kindly obliged. Another time Grandpa called Grandma into the bathroom because the toilet "wouldn't flush." With Grandma watching he put down the toilet seat and said, "See, it didn't flush."

Then there was the occasion when he had filled the sink up with water and called Grandma in. "Ma, I want to pump all the water out of the sink into there," he said, pointing at the wastebasket.

"You don't do that, Pa," she said.

"Well, how am I going to get it wet?" he said.

"You don't put water there," Grandma said. "We don't put wet things in the wastebasket."

"We don't?" Grandpa said, and then reached down to feel around in the snot tissues to ascertain that everything was dry. Then he straightened and said, "Then how do I take a crap?"

So Grandma had to show him how to put down the toilet seat, and instructed him to drop his pants, sit down, and when he was done he should wipe, and when he wiped he should *throw the paper into the toilet*. Grandma had a hard time with Grandpa's bathroom failures.

It was amazing how convoluted his thought process had become for using the bathroom. Who would have thought a person with Alzheimer's could have dreamed up trying to pump water from the sink to the garbage can so that he could take a crap in the toilet? It took a truly inventive mind. Grandpa's mind wasn't working properly, but he was trying hard to work the bathroom by himself. He was trying so hard.

Grandpa's earlier problem of sometimes urinating in the garbage grew into a daily problem. As a result, moving and emptying garbage cans was a fairly common pastime for him. I think sometimes he did it simply because it felt like a productive and right thing to do. The rest of the time it was because he realized after the fact that he had urinated in the garbage can and so he tried to fix his mistake. If he felt guilty about messing something up, changing the garbage bag was his vague idea of how to fix it. Sometimes he got it *mostly* right and did something sort-of right with the bathroom garbage can. The rest of the time he became side tracked and did something with the wrong garbage can because he remembered that he intended to do something with a garbage can but couldn't remember which one he intended to change. It could become sad game of "Who's on first."

Not quite six months into my time of care we reached the point where Grandpa was no longer cognizant of how to fix his bathroom problems (real or imagined) and began to actively call on others for help. It wasn't a need for total assistance, but it was progressing down that path. His concession to his needs made it easier for me to help him without causing conflict.

Previously, he had always wanted Grandma for all his troubles and I had to present myself and tell him I would help with whatever he needed. It took him months, but he finally accepted me as the expected person to help him. He still always wanted to know where Grandma was, and what she was doing, but now when he needed help he looked for me to assist him. He still might often call out "Ma!" as his default reaction, but it was me he expected.

It became quite common for him to call me into the bathroom. In his confused mind many of his troubles with the bathroom were related to malfunctioning objects, so he called on me to "fix" the bathroom, or at least assure him that everything was working properly. Sometimes he would call me in and engage in a garbled dialog about the stuff in the bathroom being "In alignment and in order and all set." An ongoing concern of his was the bathroom radiator, which was opposite the toilet. Sitting on the toilet left him staring at the radiator, and often he would call me in, wag his finger at the radiator, and ask me to "fix it." He obsessed over it. Somehow, it didn't look *right*. Other times he would simply ask me to look at the toilet and tell him if everything looked all right, or to make sure it wasn't plugged (even when there was nothing but water in the toilet). Another time he asked me to come in and look at the toilet because it wouldn't flush. So I came in (saw the toilet had nothing in it that needed to be flushed) and told him "You flush it by using this lever."

"I know," he said. "But it doesn't work." I pushed the lever and the toilet flushed. "The bugger," Grandpa sputtered. "It wouldn't—last time it didn't—" I have no idea if he had really tried to flush the toilet, or had just *imagined* that he had, but sinks and toilets were nefarious things now. For Grandpa they "broke" and no longer worked—only to start working again, as if by magic, when someone else used them. He needed to make everything work, and yet he couldn't, no matter how hard he tried.

As weeks progressed into months we saw increasing glimpses of where Grandpa was going with his bathroom troubles. His worst moments were still just that—occasional moments. But his departure from reality became increasingly severe. Grandpa urinating in the bathroom wastebasket instead of the toilet became such a frequent daily occurrence I limited the number of bag changes to only the worst messes. It was the beginning of an increasingly worse spiral.

§§§

I was working on supper when Grandpa came into the kitchen carrying a pair of his socks he had found in the hall. He asked if they were clean or dirty and should he throw them in the hamper. I told him they were probably worn before, but he could wear them again if he wanted, or put them in the hamper if he preferred.

Grandpa made indications that he wasn't going to wear them, and left the kitchen. Anyone who has cared for little children knows the "radar sense" you develop—some innate ability to know when things aren't going *quite* right, even if the problem is not in your direct line of sight. With my inner radar warning sounding, I stepped into the hall and sensed that Grandpa was in the bathroom. I knew he couldn't have walked down to the bedroom and then back to the bathroom in that amount of time.

Then I heard the toilet flush.

Hamper. Toilet.

A quick sprint to the bathroom brought me the sight of Grandpa standing over the toilet, watching his socks go swirly-swirly round in the yellow water, preparing for the downward plunge to a very nasty end in the guts of the toilet, or somewhere further along in the plumbing track. The socks had not completely sunk and with a quick snatch I grabbed them by some still dry parts.

Grandpa looked surprised at my intervention.

"Good guess, but that's not where they go," I said lightly.

"What," Grandpa said, "some things go here, and some things go there?"

"Yep," I said. "The socks don't go there." I hung them over the side of the garbage can to drip some of the liquid away.

The incident wasn't a surprise. I had been expecting it for weeks. His confusion about objects was such that sooner or later (and sooner more likely) the toilet would become the receptacle for all sorts of items; clothing, dishes—anything that could be "put" someplace was fair game to be put in the toilet. Or the garbage can.

This deteriorating situation frightened Grandpa. He wanted to win the battle and be able to use the bathroom as an independent man. He saw he was losing, and he was afraid of what that might mean.

One day I spent half an hour discussing with Grandpa how the bathroom worked and trying to coach him in using it. He would say, "I've got to go to the bathroom," and then he would go into the bathroom only to stop, uncertain and overwhelmed. Then he would mumble and point at the sink, the garbage can, and the toilet. He talked about getting them to work, or work together. He wanted to make sure things were in order, and rambled on about flushing, or things not flushing. He talked about which bathroom it would be better for him to use, decided he should use a different one, and walked out to the kitchen only to then return to the one he just left. He left his glasses on the edge of the sink in the upstairs bathroom and then went downstairs and flushed (without using) the downstairs toilet and came back up again. None of these things accomplished the urination or defecation which his brain was trying so hard to sort out.

He managed to work himself into a fine state of agitation trying to get the bathroom to come to sorts, and in the end he couldn't hold his urine any longer. "Oh! There goes two pints down my leg!" he said, and the sudden emergency unstuck his mind and he tottered for the toilet, finally remembering. He got some urine in the toilet, made something of a mess on the bathroom floor, and got his clothes a bit wet. After a half hour of anguish his need to use the toilet was finally over.

This was mentally and physically exhausting for him.

Grandma had gone off to her room to be alone, so after I got Grandpa into clean clothes I told him to come back and keep me company in our bedroom. The struggle to understand the bathroom had made him so confused and agitated he needed time to calm down. So while I lay on my bed reading he sat on his bed and kept himself occupied neatening up his socks and other little things lying about on his bed.

Later that day he had another accident in the bathroom. After I dressed him in clean clothes and cleaned up the mess I helped him to the kitchen for a cup of coffee and a little snack to eat.

Then the truth of Grandpa's worries finally came bubbling up.

"Well, I'm scared," he said, sitting down.

I sat down beside him to listen. Grandpa rarely expressed himself, and when he felt moved to do so I knew it was important.

"You're scared," I repeated.

"I'm scared that if things continue on like this I'll be too much to take care of and I'll be sent to a nursing home. You know how that turns out."

There it was. The awful idea.

Other times he had said he was "afraid" or "afraid of what might come down the pike" or some similar statement, but nothing so precise as this.

"Grandpa," I said firmly, "you don't need to worry about that so long as I am here."

It was the best promise I could give him. I couldn't say he wouldn't fall to pieces, I couldn't say he wouldn't lose every ability he had. All I could promise was that I wouldn't let him go.

§§§

VISITING

One of my weaknesses in caring for people is that I have a hard time just *being* there. In tending to Grandpa I had a hard time recognizing the simple value of *presence*. I wanted to be a problem solver, not company. If anything needed doing, fetching, fixing, or otherwise accomplished, I was ready and willing. Being helpful is good, as far as it goes, but taking care of someone encompasses more than *doing* things.

Active, purposeful presence is sometimes a greater balm than all the doing or fixing in the world. Often for Grandpa being present was what I needed to give. Grandpa wanted me to be there, sometimes to sit and do *nothing* except keep him company and share the moment with him so that he did not feel so alone. That simple act was attending to his person, and his need.

I had a hard time with that truth. I was always lining things up in my head to do. I was willing stop and talk or listen if Grandpa said, "Hey, I'd like to talk to you," but it rarely occurred to me to sit around with Grandpa, doing nothing, and just *be* there. He hinted at it often enough, and sometimes outright asked. I was often more reluctant to just sit than to fetch him a cup of coffee.

Grandpa appreciated being with people. In fact, he preferred simply *being* to doing something. About the only way he could get a thought out was to let it pop out when it bubbled up in its own good time. He couldn't engage in the normal communication of everyday life, so he spent most of the day feeling isolated. Most of the time there wasn't someone to just sit beside him, waiting to answer any question and interpret any event he didn't quite understand. Rather than paying attention to this need, I preoccupied myself. Whenever Grandpa wasn't in need of physical help I wanted to run off and get something done for *me*.

One day he seemed in a more social mood than usual. It was afternoon when he said, "Why don't you come out front with me." Usually I was the one who suggested going out and often as not Grandpa would decline. But today he suggested we go, so we went out front and sat in the full afternoon sun. Seated on the front stoop, we watched the world and the cars go by. We sat there for 15-20 minutes making small conversation. Then we went inside.

It was in the brief times like this that he could almost seem normal. He talked about how he would never want to ride on a motorcycle and contend with the cars, and how his depth perception was bad so he couldn't tell how low things were. I asked him if the tall pine tree in the front yard was older than him and he said no, Grandma's son Paul had planted it (he meant my great-grandma).

It was a meaningless little moment filled with meaningless bits of conversation. Except, it wasn't meaningless. It was the stuff of relationships, the stuff of caring. In the end, I cherished those moments more than nearly any other. It was the moments when I took the time to sit and watch TV with Grandpa and explain the commercials to him. It was when he fell asleep afterward, his head resting on my chest, breathing softly. We didn't say anything much or important those times, but more was communicated than what was said in words.

Sometimes I found myself forgetting that in spite of Grandpa's illness he was still a person who could enjoy the little things of life, same as anyone else. I was reminded of this another afternoon when Grandma asked me to take her to the bank for some business and the car wash to clean her very new car. We took Grandpa with us. His entire involvement consisted in sitting in the car and watching the outside world. It caught me by surprise when we pulled back into the garage after the trip and Grandpa said, "Well, very good. I really enjoyed that."

Since Grandpa was not inclined to go traveling, I had imagined that everything beyond his own house was a world he preferred to avoid. There was a good bit of truth to that, but it wasn't all the truth. The world was still a beautiful and interesting place, and if he could simply sit safe in the car and look at the world—that was one of the few enjoyments he had left.

§§§

Family was another one of Grandpa's few pleasures in life.

He tried to behave around company. The worse his disease became the less he remembered what behaving meant. In the early days, he strove to be dignified, polite, and quiet when we had visitors. He did well, too. When family came to visit people wouldn't have believed Grandpa was nonsensical at night based on his conduct when they were around. His behavior, if not perfect, was only slightly odd.

I felt almost a little bitter. The stories about how difficult Grandpa had become were circulating, but then people visited and he was so mild. I didn't want a scene, but at the same time it felt as if Grandpa was fooling them into thinking that caring for him wasn't a big deal. If only they saw how things became when they left, I thought.

But the sheen of normalcy couldn't last, and his odd behavior began to show. He started asking guests bizarre questions, or calling out in his agitation for people when he had no need. The time came when we had visitors and he did his usual things of driving his cane about on the carpet, moving chairs around for no reason, and falling down at odd times. All of this was part of "normal" life but up until this point it had been something he could control (mostly) when company was around. Six months after I moved in all of Grandpa's quirks hung out a lot more, giving the impression of a mental institution to visitors.

A part of me was glad that other people were beginning to see what Grandpa was like. But, paradoxically, I also found it irritating. When people looked sideways at him in his crazy moments and whispered among themselves something flared up inside me. *Yes, he is coming to pieces. Didn't you know that? Why are you acting so shocked? You should see how it is every day. And don't gape.*

I guess I didn't like the subtle disapproval and dismay, or shock with the suggested whiff of "If only he weren't this bad." I felt defensive. Didn't they understand how hard he was trying? As the months and years passed people grew better at accepting Grandpa's condition, though the finer points of how you had to help him, or communicate, remained difficult for some visitors.

The further the disease progressed, the sooner Grandpa grew agitated with company around, and the worse it became. Later, for big holiday family gatherings, he was only good for a few hours and then he needed to withdraw to his bedroom where it was quiet. He liked company, but his mind could only take so much before he became inarticulate and anxious and began shouting for people—named or unnamed—and asking guests to do impossible things.

That was towards the end, but even in the beginning of my caregiving Grandpa was never much of a traveler. Still, in spite of being a homebody before (and before was always "before Alzheimer's"), he would visit his brothers, sisters, and children with, if not great frequency, at least steady consistency. By the time I had arrived on the scene that consistency had vanished and he was rapidly approaching the condition where he wouldn't travel anywhere to visit. Traveling was stressful for him, and in some inexpressible way frightening, also. Being away from home increased his sense of foreboding.

Traveling with Grandpa was stressful for me, too. Events that wouldn't have been much of an issue at home—such as Grandpa forgetting his pants in the bathroom, or randomly starting to undress himself—could be huge issues in a public setting. The world does not understand Alzheimer's.

In the first year of my care, November waned late and Thanksgiving came, with a big family gathering in Pennsylvania. This was a rare event where all of Grandpa's children, their children, and even great grandchildren assembled for the holiday celebration. I took Grandma and Grandpa down for the party, but I knew the days of Grandpa journeying to such celebrations were numbered, and I took them with a heavy heart.

I remembered how at the previous Thanksgiving Grandpa had already begun exhibiting trouble recognizing grandchildren. It continued this year. "Who is that?" he would say to me. Or he would look at someone and say, "What is the name of Nate's daughter?"

Given how his disease had progressed in other areas, such as self-care, I was surprised how little his difficulty in recognizing people had progressed beyond the previous year. But perhaps he simply kept most of his problems to himself, overwhelmed or embarrassed at his inability to recognize so many people.

The noise and bustle and unfamiliar environment took a lot from Grandpa, but in a deep and abiding way he loved to see his family. This showed in his fairly good mood at the news of going out for Thanksgiving, in spite of all the reasons he had to feel reluctant. In fact, he also appeared still happy when we came back.

A big problem when Grandpa went out was that when he arrived somewhere he often wanted to go home almost immediately. This impulse pretty well ruined any reason for going in the first place. So another indication of how much he wanted to be at the Thanksgiving gathering was his willingness to stay *two hours* (which with travel time added was an amazing amount of time for him at that point). Even so, Grandpa had scarcely finished his dessert before he was asking to leave. "Okay, let's go," he said. "Let's get out of here."

The two hour visit was less than at the last family gathering. His endurance was shortening more and more.

People wanted family photos so Grandpa was forced to sit and wait while relatives pointed and jostled to get everyone organized. He found it impossible to look at the camera. His gaze constantly wandered off to something that caught his attention elsewhere. Grandma kept trying to make him look forward at the camera, but in the photos we have he is either looking away from the camera, or else staring rather vacantly forward like some poor lost soul. The one good picture of Grandpa has him looking sideways, his face caught in profile as he smiles at something beyond the picture.

§§§

It was late in that first autumn, the time when autumn edges into winter, when Grandpa decided he wanted to visit his brother Gene. Gene was one of Grandpa's older brothers, and his favorite, whom he loved dearly. He had previously made this trip in regular fashion, but now it was a herculean undertaking spurred on by his concern about how Gene was doing. There was no particular reason to be worried—best we knew Gene was in better health than Grandpa—but Grandpa constantly fretted about people being sick or freezing in the winter. In his mind the weather loomed as an ever-present danger.

Doug agreed to come along for the visit to Gene. Back in the day the three of them often got together, so this was a chance for a moment like old times. Thursday afternoon after I returned from the weekly grocery shopping I took them both.

The trip was about a half-hour drive. Grandpa had no complaints during the ride. He and Doug watched the Pennsylvania countryside slide past and shared memories about places and people from long ago. It seemed so normal. Then we arrived at Gene's trailer. Grandpa came inside, his expression a bit preoccupied, and said maybe two dozen words, consisting of little more than, "Yes, I'll have coffee. How are you doin?" and, "That's good."

I was never there for the good old times, but I got the distinct feeling that the situation was awkward and not at all like old times. Grandpa appeared only half present, and for a man who wanted to see his brother he apparently had absolutely nothing to talk about, nothing to ask, and nothing to say in response to any inquiry. Twenty stilted minutes ticked by. Grandpa made it halfway through his cup of coffee. Then he wanted to go home.

"It's time to get going," he said.

"Now?" Gene said. "You just got here."

"Can't stay," Grandpa said.

I had warned Doug in advance that it would turn out this way, and we had tried to warn Gene as well, but he seemed perplexed. Why travel all the way to say two dozen words and drink half a cup of coffee? Because, I would have said if I could have explained, Grandpa wanted to see Gene, but he didn't have any words to say, and being away from home put him on edge. The gray weather bothered him, the sky, the fading daylight. Once he had *seen* Gene that was enough and it was time to go home. It didn't make sense, and yet it made perfect sense if you understood.

I tried to explain to Gene that this was simply the way Grandpa was now, and I think in some way he understood. But I don't think he really understood Alzheimer's, or how it was changing his brother. Standing on the porch and watching us get in the car Gene said, "I guess we should really come down there."

I nodded. That was the future.

Gene only stopped by to visit once, over a year later. Grandpa was much changed then. While the guests sat around the living room, Grandpa sat on the couch and picked crumbs, lint, or imaginary things off the floor at his feet. Those little bits of nothing were more interesting than his visitors.

"So, how have you been, Ike?" Gene had asked, trying to make conversation and ignore Grandpa's peculiar preoccupation with the floor.

"Oh, pretty good," Grandpa had said, not looking up. "How about yourself?"

"Pappa, sit up and pay attention to your visitors," Grandma said, embarrassed.

Gene tried to say it was all right, but his discomfort was apparent. He didn't know what to do.

It wasn't that Grandpa was unhappy to have visitors—though perhaps it looked that way. He was glad Gene had come, but he simply had nothing to say. Alzheimer's had faded his social awareness to the point he was comfortable saying nothing. In his mind the visitors could sit quietly where they were, and he would contentedly pick up whatever tiny bits of rubbish he imagined he saw around his feet. For him, all was well. But in the strain of the silence everyone else felt what had been, and what was no more.

Grandpa hadn't forgotten entirely about people and the larger world—he simply lived in his own little moment. Either you could accept that, and join him there, or else there seemed to exist an unbreachable wall between you and him.

Maybe particularly because of that, Grandpa struggled with loneliness. There were days I could find him sitting on the arm of the couch, staring out the window at the world beyond. His world was shrinking ever smaller and smaller, and in his own way he felt the fact that it had shrunk to the four walls of his house. While a part of him had become frightened at the idea of going beyond those walls, another part of him felt trapped in his little world. The outside big world was frightening, but sometimes it held memories of better times. He wanted to see *that* outside world, the one which still had echoing memories of his past and better days.

§§§

WORDS NOT SPOKEN

I never heard you talk about your father's death," Kevin said to Grandpa. "I always wondered why. I wanted to hear about it from you."

"I couldn't say it," Grandpa admitted.

The confession came unexpectedly from Grandpa. The entire extended family was gathered at the house for an early Christmas celebration as 2006 drew near its end. After the meal people dispersed this way and that, the younger cousins congregating to play games while everyone else conversed in small groups. A few of us were sitting together when my uncle Kevin sat beside Grandpa on the couch and attempted a serious conversation in spite of Grandpa's failing verbal communication.

I was surprised by the directness of the question. I thought everyone knew the topic of Grandpa's father's suicide was off limits. But maybe that was why Kevin asked. Grandpa's days of communicating were drawing to an end—if you had a difficult question for which you wanted answers, the time for answers was running out. Perhaps that looming reality prompted Kevin to ask the question which was hard to ask, and which gained the raw confession from Grandpa.

"It was a shame," Grandpa said. "A terrible shame. Talking to other guys, they would say, 'My father does such-and-such. What does your father do?' It would be on the tip of my tongue, stuck there. I couldn't say it. I couldn't."

What I knew about that past, I had learned from other people, not Grandpa. My great-grandfather killed himself by drinking red lye out in the barn. Grandpa, then a boy of about ten years, had found his father dying. It was the second time he found his father after a suicide attempt. The first had been a failed hanging. Drinking red lye is a slow and painful way to die, but it was successful, in the end.

Why did the man do it? Rumors were all I heard, second or third hand. There were whispers about depression, an old head injury, or despair about trying to feed a large family. Nobody really knew. There was little care for people with mental illness in those days, and not much more understanding. Opprobrium touched all those around suicide.

Though the suicide haunted him, Grandpa said little about any of his childhood. "Those days are gone," was all he would say when his brother Doug starting talking about the old days.

§§§

When I was growing up Grandma and Grandpa lived in the country. Their residence was situated on the Pennsylvania-New York border, and to reach the house you had to drive along a road titled—fittingly enough—"State Line Road." Grandma and Grandpa's old house sat where a dead end road trailed off, their land butting up against a large tract of village owned forest.

As a young child, I felt a certain air of mystery surrounded their property. Behind the house ran a tiny creek and on the other side was a stand of trees that seemed the beginning of a dark and forbidden forest. To me, the neatly stacked heaps of dead wood and bramble cleaned up by Grandpa marked the edge of some ominous unknown. In the other direction, across the road, were the two small barns. If you went past them the world opened up to a distant horizon—a curiosity of forests and fields. Where the dead end road stopped beyond the house it became a forest trail that quickly disappeared under overhanging tree branches. In my child's mind that trail led off to where people became lost, never to return. Slightly safer was the pond out behind the house. That was far enough away to hold a sense of adventure, and yet not too far so that after I had looked at the water and frogs I could make a quick return to more familiar surroundings.

Timid and fretful, I saw hidden—or not so hidden—danger on every side. I failed to take advantage of all the interesting places I could have adventured if my sense of exploration had outweighed my sense of paranoia. But if my fears of the unknown kept me from experiencing many of the country pleasures, there was still one I could enjoy: tractor rides.

Grandpa had at least two old tractors which he was constantly fighting to keep repaired and running. The smallest was probably a prehistoric incarnation of a lawn tractor, created before anyone thought of inventing a mowing deck. What useful purpose it had served, or could still serve, I didn't know. To my mind it existed solely to give tractor rides.

Grandpa wasn't socially skilled, and entertaining grandchildren was no exception. His repertoire was limited to reading stories, and giving tractor rides. Tractor rides were a rare treat—partly because it usually didn't strike his fancy, and partly because a functioning tractor was often an uncertain and frustrating proposition. I remember hanging around the barn and inquiring if perhaps the tractor would be fixed soon, and would we be going on a tractor ride today. The answer was "Maybe" in the sort of way that spoke of patience strained by questioning little children, and uncooperative machinery.

But those tractor rides did come, and all the better when they came unexpectedly. The sound of the tractor engine—or the announcement that Grandpa was giving rides—would send me running outside. Grandpa had constructed his own sled to drag behind the tractor, and that tractor and sled would pull up in front of the house. At the command of, "Hop on," we would all clamber in. Then it was off across the yard, around and back, and around again. It was excitement—a taste of the country life, and grand adventure. Then, all too soon, it was over and the tractor returned to the barn until next time.

We have a picture of Grandpa giving a tractor ride. A gaggle of cousins are crowded on the sled, grinning like fools. Grandpa rides in front on the small tractor, staring intently ahead, hands held at the ready, perhaps carefully nursing the fitful machine along.

They are good memories.

If my childhood was a naïve and innocent time, filled with foolish worries and happy memories, Grandpa's childhood was the opposite. His childhood had a father dead by suicide, and brothers who had to drop out of school to help feed a large family. He never wanted to go back to those memories, but the strange turns of history and time worked their pull.

Glenwood Road was the street his story began on, and it was the street where his story ended. That street was weighted with memories. Grandma had lived there in her youth, too. Grandma and Grandpa had met on that street. They had courted on that street, walking up and down beneath the shade of the old trees. The first house Grandpa built for their beginning family was on that street—built on a tiny parcel of land bought from his widowed mother-in-law. The little house still stands there, and I have passed it many times, a small and worn thing.

Grandma had fond memories of Glenwood Road, and when the twisting path of inheritance brought them into possession of a new house on that street, she leaped at the chance to move back. The country house on State Line Road was left behind, and the house Grandpa ended up living in was just down the road from where he lived as a child. Grandma loved it. She could look up Glenwood Road and see the window to her childhood bedroom. Grandpa hated it. He could look down Glenwood Road and see his childhood home, and the barn where his father had killed himself. "They are bad memories," he said. "Things I don't want to remember."

It's strange how you can't escape the past. Doug would come down and talk about the past while the three of us sat around the kitchen table—two old men and one young, a thousand untold stories between them. "Dad's death left a hole in Mom's life," Doug said. "She missed him so much. I think it hurt her the worst the way people talked."

Grandpa said nothing. He looked down at the table, so no one could see his face. Sometimes, it is the silent people who hurt the most.

Maybe creating things helped Grandpa cope with life. Maybe it was just part of who he was. I'm sure growing up during the Great Depression taught him to be frugal, to make things for himself. The inclination to make things is a trait I share with him. I look at some leftover lumber scraps and think, "I wonder what I could make from that." I face a problem and ponder how I might come up with an ingenious solution fashioned out of what I have on hand—something that is cheap and effective. It is a challenge, a skill, and an art. For me, it is also almost like a game.

Many things Grandpa made in his life sprang from necessity. That first cinder block house he built was a necessity. It was a tiny house, and it wasn't beautiful, but he made it with the nickels and dimes he had. The walls of that house were no higher than they had to be, because cinder blocks cost money. Over fifty years later, he still had the wheelbarrow he used to mix the mortar for that house. I know, because I used it. The wheel is a simple metal rim, one of the handles has been replaced, and it has more rust now than it did those many years ago. Grandpa never got a new one, because what he had still worked.

Though Grandpa made, and fixed, many things out of necessity or frugality, it was what he made for amusement that earned him more recognition. A story told to me—with no small amount of marvel— was how once, as a boy, my uncle Kevin wanted a motorbike. In answer to that wish, Grandpa scrounged up the old engine to a rototiller and used that engine as a foundation to build a functional *wooden* motorbike. Yes, the entire frame was made from wood. It was the epitome of ingenuity. It was crazy, too. Grandma told me it had no brakes, and admitted riding it into the garage door. (What were you doing riding it, Grandma?)

Whenever an idle moment came upon Grandpa he would make something. It was as if his hands could not remain still. I remember as a child visiting one day and seeing Grandpa sitting at the kitchen table, snipping apart soda cans to make miniature metal airplanes. He made a collection of them, and they hung suspended from the ceiling as if caught in flight. While visiting our house for a birthday party Grandpa found some wooden oddity outside and began whittling it into a whistle. When he was done it worked, if you knew how to use it.

Grandpa fashioned many little wooden figures and carvings which then ended up perched on shelves and in nooks around the house. But he did more than carve. There also were the paintings and drawings that I never knew he created until I was much older, because he was ashamed of them and hid them away. Only later would I begin to appreciate how much I didn't see, and never would see.

Grandpa loved music, and had an ear for it. Without the money to afford lessons, anything he wanted to learn he taught himself. He taught himself how to play the piano, the guitar, and the mandolin. He could fix pianos, too. He could tune a piano by ear, and even attempted a piano tuning business. I have some of his business cards. There was an entire box of them sitting in storage, apparently untouched. "Accurate" and "Reasonable" the cards said. Accurate and reasonable he was, but a business man he was not. Unwilling to promote himself—as the languishing box of untouched cards testified —the business went nowhere.

Grandpa could do many things, and had many skills, and made all sorts of things. But to me the Indian he made stands out the most in speaking about who he was and what he could do. Grandpa always had a fascination with frontier American life, in particular with Native Americans. He would read about them, about how they did things, and how they made things. He made a pair of moccasins out of a deer hide. He fletched arrows. Then he made the Indian.

To call it amazing was an understatement. As a first attempt it was unbelievable. How, exactly, he constructed the life sized realistic figure, I don't know. He used some type of plaster for the skin, which he then painted after it was molded and dried. The effect was startlingly life-like. One day as a little boy I walked into the garage, arriving for a visit, and there the Indian waited. He stood tall and proud, his face creased with stern lines, his steady eyes staring into the distance. I looked at him, noticing every bit of care given to the details. The realism was enough to creep me out, just a little.

As a first attempt the Indian was certainly not flawless, but with raven black hair, loin cloth, bow, and pouch, he was undeniably a unique work of art. To simply walk into the room was to know it was art, made by a real artist. If Grandpa had refined his skill he could have made statues worth significant money and made a name for himself as an artist in his old age. Instead, he made the one Indian, and never made another one again. He didn't want to sell it, but when Grandma saw an opportunity she made sure it sold.

The Indian was Grandpa's most amazing work of art and it astounded my child's mind as something beyond the ability of any mere mortal, and certainly a Grandpa (so a child's mind thinks). But his first love was canoes. Grandma told me the story of how Grandpa was trying to make a canoe when they were first courting. At times she felt a little second place to the canoe, when Grandpa couldn't understand why she didn't like standing around watching him work on it. That canoe was never finished. The responsibilities of life washed it away. Still Grandpa dreamed of canoes. After he was gone I discovered some of his old papers tucked away in an oil stained bag. There I found photocopied canoe diagrams taken from books. From his notes it seems he was particularly fascinated by an ancient canoe called the *Sairy Gamp*, designed by J. Henry Rushton and designated in 1883 by *Forest and Stream* as "the lightest canoe ever made by man for practical purposes." (Ten and a half pounds in weight for a nine foot wooden canoe!)

Grandpa was more a scholar than he gave himself credit, more of one than many would expect from a man who never finished high school and never attended college. In the old packet I found extensive notes scribed in his careful hand writing, including lengthy quotes from books on canoes and canoe construction, the terms and methods precisely recorded, the title and publisher carefully noted. There were diagrams, sketches, and mathematical equations scrawled out as he tried to recreate what he saw as Rushton's greatest work.

Grandpa wanted to make the ultimate canoe. He never managed that dream, but he did assemble a canoe. It is fitting that as his first project was the canoe of long ago, never finished, his last project was also a canoe. He had worked intermittently on his project to make a canoe from scratch, but maybe he realized his time was running out and he would have to settle for something less. The story I heard was that he took an old broken canoe and reconstructed it, cutting it apart and refashioning the length, then refinishing the exterior.

It wasn't his dream, but it was a canoe, painted bright red. As a child I stood in their old garage on State Line Road and stared at that red canoe and thought, "You can actually make a canoe, all by yourself? You don't need some special machinery to make it? And it won't sink?"

It didn't sink. It seemed nothing was impossible for Grandpa. He even let me paddle the canoe out on the pond.

After the canoe, Grandpa never completed another major creative project. His days as an artist were gone. Hands which once carved an Indian's face or tuned a piano began to fumble, to struggle, as the day approached when they could no longer do the simplest things. Now those hands are stilled forever, but for me the Indian and the canoe will always remain as symbols of what he was, and what he could have been. Long after he lost many things to Alzheimer's he still remembered that canoe, put into storage in the barn. Many things he no longer understood, but when Grandma spoke about the possibility of selling the canoe, he perked up.

"What? You're not going to sell that thing," he said, angrily. "You're not going to do nothing with it!"

It was hard to know if his anger was at the thought of losing what was dear to him, or at the idea of selling what he considered a failure. Grandpa always judged his own accomplishments harshly.

In the end, we gave it to Kevin. I was against selling it too, but I knew it couldn't stay in the barn forever and I thought it should go to someone who cared. Someone who could understand.

§§§

The past can haunt, but sometimes it brings a gentle reminder of love. It was the Christmas season after Grandpa had died that Grandma was digging through her old collection of Christmas cards, thinking that since she had collected so many unused cards over the years she ought to do something with them. Then, there in the midst of her cards, she found a small plain white envelope addressed in the familiar tight handwriting of Grandpa, to my uncle Kevin.

The card was old, more than 16 years old. It had never been sent. There wasn't even a stamp. Inside the envelope was a small simple card. On the front was a pastoral painting of a red barn in winter. Inside Grandpa had written:

Dear Kevin -

Cards never seem to have the precise words to express what a person really thinks or feels on a Holiday season such as Christmas Time. So, [below were the printed words of the card:]

Wishing you a beautiful world

Through all the seasons of the year

Happy Holidays

[Then Grandpa concluded in his own writing:]

With much love and unbounded hope for the future

Mom and Pop

I was astounded to see the card. Not because I didn't know Grandpa felt such sentiments toward his children—I knew he did—but I was surprised that he actually ever *wrote* such a thing in a Christmas card. Grandpa didn't share those feelings—he kept them hidden away in his heart where it only came out in little glimpses if you were paying attention. And perhaps that was why the card had never been sent. Perhaps in the end Grandpa was embarrassed by what he had expressed and had put the card away so nobody saw it, until that day. Which was too bad, because I know Kevin wanted to hear those words.

Kevin did, in the end. Grandma gave him the card that Christmas. It might be a little disconcerting to get a card from a dead man, but still fitting, I think. You can't escape the past. Our deeds speak about us, even from beyond the grave.

Grandpa had a hard time saying many things. Sometimes we don't say what we really ought to say. I don't know if Kevin ever heard the things he wanted from his father at the time he wanted. But I think he understood that it was hard to say some things. I think he accepted it, and treasured what he got.

§§§

- 2007 -

A TIME OF SORROW AND LOVE

I broke my collar bone shortly before my third birthday. My older brother and I were playing Humpty Dumpty on the porch rail. (A parentally unsanctioned event, but we weren't observed.) In the game we would straddle the rail and then rock back and forth while singing the Humpty Dumpty rhyme. At the end we hopped back onto the porch to simulate falling.

I was a little too good at playing Humpty Dumpty. When it came to my turn I rocked back and forth with such abandon that I toppled head first off the rail and landed on my shoulder in the rocky drip-line beyond the porch. I still remember the impact. I remember not being able to see straight, I was crying so hard as I tried to walk back into the house.

It was a young age for a broken bone, but not remarkable. This was no disaster, no life threatening illness. It is the greatest excitement I can come up with for my young life, and it pales to insignificance when I compare my life against Grandpa's youth. It makes me think. I broke my collar bone when I was two—Grandpa's physical problems began before he was born. His death almost happened before his birth.

Grandpa's brother Doug was about five years older than Grandpa. He told me his recollections of the events surrounding Grandpa's birth, still vivid eighty years later.

"It was coming on to the New Year holiday," Doug said. "Mom was really pregnant, but she was cleaning the house like crazy."

"I remember, she was standing on a step-ladder at the top of the stairs," he said. "The ladder slipped and she fell down the stairs. She landed on the metal mop bucket full of water at the bottom of the stairs, right on the rim."

"I saw her lying at the foot of the stairs. There was blood." When Doug spoke his face had the faraway look of someone seeing a memory all over again, once more the little boy watching his momma lying on the floor.

"People were called," Doug continued. "Everyone was running about. Then they got her to the hospital," he finished.

Evelyn Purdy went into labor and struggled through a difficult breach birth. Somehow, both mother and baby survived, and so on December 31, 1927 Ivan Purdy was born to John and Evelyn. A baby who could have died before birth became their fourth son, and one day would be my grandpa.

But all was not right.

"His head was crooked when he came home," Doug said.

Grandpa had Torticollis (in that day commonly called wry neck). It was a shortening of the muscle and tendons on one side of the neck causing the neck and head to turn unnaturally to one side. The condition is the result of either trauma or genetic malformation. Given the events surrounding Grandpa's birth, the former is likely—if not from the fall then from doctors using forceps in an attempt to remove him from the breach birth.

In his childhood Grandpa was the little boy with the crooked head. Then, shortly before the age of ten, he underwent surgery to correct the problem. Afterward there was a neck brace, and physical therapy.

Vehicles were scarce during the Great Depression. To attend his physical therapy appointments he had to ride in to work with his father and then walk to the hospital. After his therapy was finished, he walked back to the vehicle and sat in the truck for the rest of the day until his father was let out from work. Grandma told me it was a cruel way to treat a little boy. It wasn't pleasant, I'm sure, but I don't know what could have been done differently given the circumstances. Times were different back then. Grandpa was lucky to get physical therapy. He was fortunate to have a chance to be whole, straight, and unbroken. He was blessed to be alive.

Grandpa carried the scars from that surgery with him for the rest of his life. The white lines ran down both sides of his neck, alternating a puckering ridge or shallow groove in his flesh. They looked ugly and cruel. Strange how the things that fix us can appear so bad.

The therapy was hard, but he was diligent. The doctors taught him to walk with an erect posture—a lesson that stuck with him so well that in his youth he had the upright bearing of a tin soldier. Old age and back pain eventually stooped Grandpa's posture, but his neck remained straight. If you did not see the scars you would not have known he had once been the boy with the crooked neck.

Doug said the year Grandpa's neck was fixed in surgery was the same year he accidentally stuck his hand in the corn chopper and lost the last joint off his pointer and index fingers. (It might also have been exactly the same year their father killed himself, and in light of Grandpa's life long sense of guilt I have wondered if Grandpa somehow connected his own health problems with his father's death and as a result blamed himself for the suicide.) In a different conversation Doug said he thought the boys were the cause of their mother's gray hair—partly in jest, but partly not. With stories of chopped fingers and such it wasn't hard to understand how a mother would feel stress. Grandpa carried those shortened fingers the rest of his life. One ended in a smooth rounded stump, the other held a small nub of nail that I had thought as a little boy was the end of a bone sticking out. Even in his last years Grandpa still remembered the pain from that day he lost part of his fingers. We all carry our own past, and its pain, but most of us don't have such physical scars.

I think about my youth and it seems trivial in comparison to Grandpa's experience. What do I know about pain and suffering? What do I know about perseverance, and making the best of a bad situation? Grandpa faced physical suffering, pain, and ridicule. He was the little boy who went to school with the crooked neck and faced that mockery. He was the boy who went to school with the mauled fingers. He was the marked one who never fit in.

He was the boy whose father committed suicide.

That was worse than the physical pain. That was shame and hurt deep inside where no doctor could straighten or fix.

His father's suicide left an emotional scar in Grandpa's life—a pain, anger, bitterness, and shame no less real than the physical scars his body carried. But even that was not the end of the hardship he would face in growing up. Not even a year after that suicide, World War II began and all of Grandpa's older brothers went off to war. There was no father, and now there were no brothers. Soon as Grandpa was old enough, he dropped out of high school and joined the military. He did not see combat, but was shipped overseas in time to participate in the occupation of Japan.

The summer of 1948 came and Grandpa was discharged from the army and returned home to a neighborhood slightly changed. Robert and Ruth Maslin had moved in and built a house up the street. There they lived with their children—and one of those children was a pretty teenage daughter named Janice.

Janice caught the young soldier's eye, and it wasn't long before they were taking walks hand in hand up the tree-lined street. Grandma blushed when a niece who had been a young girl at the time told me that little story. "I didn't know anyone saw us," she said.

It was a time of love, but sorrow too. Grandpa's mother Evelyn was dying from cancer. In the spring of 1949 she passed, leaving ten children orphaned. Scarcely twenty years old, Grandpa had to face his future parent-less. There would be no mother or father to watch him walk down the marriage aisle, or see him raise his children.

Then tragedy followed tragedy. That same spring Robert Maslin suffered a massive heart attack and died. Ivan had lost his mother, and Janice her father.

Grandpa never spoke to me about those days. He never shared his hopes, dreams, or hurts of his youth. The resentment he felt at his father for killing himself was never spoken, the sorrow at losing his mother so young never shared. I never expected to get any insight into his thoughts as a young man on the cusp of life, with sorrow and love so intermingled. Then, after Grandpa was gone, Grandma found an old love letter from him in her files, tucked away. She was promptly embarrassed by it, and hid the letter—but not before I slipped it away and scanned myself a copy.

Grandma was strange about emotions. She liked to fantasize about her grandchildren marrying, but she tried her best to not cry when Grandpa died. When she found his love letter she was visibly pleased— until she became mortified and said it was embarrassing. Well, it was embarrassing, in a way. Crying is embarrassing. Love is embarrassing. Both show us weak, vulnerable, and perhaps even foolish. I think she had a hard time with that.

Though Grandpa never spoke about that time, I think the love letter says something about his frame of mind.

> *Janice Darling,*
>
> *A day as nice as this shouldn't have been wasted in school or work. We should have been together, cause I'm sure we'd both have enjoyed it more. Don't you?*
>
> *Hope you're feeling good Jan. I do—always do when I've spent some time near you. I love <u>you</u> darling—for what you do to me and for me. You're just everything that's wonderful and good, all rolled up in one.*

On he went for several pages. Yes, so foolish by one measure, and yet by another so heartfelt. I read it, and I saw a young man clinging to love and hope, and a dream of a new future free from the hurt and death that has so filled his life up until that point. It was a letter almost wild in hope and love and optimism. I could see a young man who so desperately wanted his future to be something different from his past.

And so they were married late in the autumn of 1949, in the midst of a rare early winter snowstorm, a young man of twenty-one and a woman scarcely more than a girl at seventeen. They were young in love, so fresh and naive, full of hopes and dreams for the future, and yet older in sorrows than I am.

When I stop and think about Grandpa's life—really think about it —I feel small. My troubles and struggles shrink to insignificance. The lives of those who have gone before you can make you a little more humble, and a little more quiet. I look back on that time and marvel at what Grandpa lived through. He faced sorrow and hurt. He was a broken man, with his fears and doubts, his burden of shame and his fits of rage. But with all of those faults he held onto love. It seems a strange mixture—but I guess life is like that.

Time is sorrow and love woven together.

§§§

THE UNFIXABLE

When I was a boy my family moved to the country. One of our first pets were two Peking ducklings. They grew into adult ducks, male and female, and were inseparable. They loved to eat dog food. One morning a few years later I went out to feed them and found the male duck with his head ripped off, killed by a wild animal in the night. I can still see him in my mind's eye, a frost of fresh snow covering his mangled body. Shocked, I went back inside and burst into tears.

Over the years many animals joined our hobby farm. Having a soft heart, I became the boy who tried to be the nurse, tending the various animal ailments that came along. My care was mostly limited to helping sickly chicks and ducklings hatch out of their shells—or when a particular crippled duckling leaped into the pond and began drowning I leaped in after it to make a rescue.

I was about ten when we adopted two kittens. More precisely, the neighbor cat decided to have kittens somewhere on our property and with all those cute kittens prancing around *somehow* we ended up adopting two of them. One we named Phoebe because it was supposed to be a female. Later, it became clear Phoebe was male, but the name stuck. We had him for several years until one morning he was struck by a car. I didn't see Phoebe get hit, but I saw him walking funny, in a horrible, lurching, falling sort of way. He made it into the unheated back hall entrance before collapsing.

There were no external signs of injury, but it soon became very clear that Phoebe was paralyzed. How he had made it up from the road I don't know—maybe some preternatural cat determination to make it home before his body gave out entirely. There he lay, quiet and unmoving, but not dead. Dad said he was as good as dead, there was nothing that could be done, and it was only a matter of time.

I couldn't bear to do nothing. I made Phoebe as comfortable as I could. I slid him closer to the interior end of the hall where it was warmer, and laid him on a rag. As Phoebe lingered I thought about how he was probably hungry and thirsty. It was awful to imagine.

Phoebe was unable to even lift his head to eat or drink, so I took a bulb syringe and tried to squirt water in his mouth. Then I took pieces of dry cat food and stuck them in his mouth with my fingers. The cat swallowed what water he could, and attempted to chew the food as I stuck it in his mouth. But he was lying on his side so most everything fell out of his mouth and he accidentally bit my finger while trying to chew the food I stuck in his mouth. It's stupid to try to stick food in a paralyzed cat's mouth with your fingers, and—in case you're curious—it hurts a surprising amount to have those sharp canine teeth sink into your flesh. When those teeth went through the pad of my finger and the blood welled up, I wanted to pull my finger from the cat's mouth more than anything, but I couldn't remove it until Phoebe opened his jaw. He didn't mean to bite me, and I didn't blame him. He was just a dying cat, trying to accept the care I wanted to give.

In a day or two Phoebe died. Dad gave an epitaph of sorts when he came to remove the body. He said something like, "Well, he's gone. He loved us so much that he tried to make it home before he died, but we couldn't do anything for him." It was all I could do to keep from bawling. Not only was Phoebe dead, but I felt utterly unworthy of such devotion and wretched that in response to such loyalty I had been unable to do anything to fix the injury.

The bite on my finger become infected. Dad lanced the infection and soaked my finger in antiseptic while muttering about all the germs in animal mouths. I think he was appalled and perhaps a bit disgusted that I had tried to feed a paralyzed cat by sticking food in its mouth with my fingers. In retrospect even I could see it had been rather dumb.

I may have inherited my love for animals from Grandpa. His fondness for animals was tempered by a personality given to quick irritation—and I definitely inherited that. He couldn't stand disobedient or troublesome animals. They could send him into a fit of rage.

In his first year of marriage he attempted to work a farm, but quickly gave it up. The pay was terrible, but I think he also decided fighting with cows was not to his fancy. He never attempted the career of a farmer again, but animals remained a part of his life. Though at times they drove him to anger, he always tried to do right by them.

When my Dad was an infant he was diagnosed with an intolerance to cow milk. To deal with this problem, Grandpa acquired a milking goat. Each year the mother goat gave birth to baby goats and produced milk. One year a goat kid broke its leg. Grandpa took the animal to the vet, where he was informed it would cost more to set the leg than the animal was worth. So he went home and set the goat's leg himself, and made his own plaster cast. The leg healed up perfectly. That was the kind of care I wanted to give to the animals I had.

§§§

"Here, write a sentence." The doctor's assistant handed Grandpa a pencil and piece of paper.

"What should I write?" Grandpa asked.

"Anything. Whatever comes to your mind," she said.

"Well, all right." Grandpa thought a bit, looking awkward and self-conscious, then carefully wrote on the paper and handed it back to the lady.

She read the sentence. It said, "The goats are restless tonight."

"You like animals?" she said. I think she found it the most peculiar sentence she had ever read in response to her request.

Grandpa explained how he liked animals, and his daughter had goats and sometimes at night the animals became agitated. He grew flustered and trailed off.

The assistant was satisfied. The only purpose of the test was to check Grandpa's writing and thinking ability. The written sentence was only one small part in a entire battery of tests to see how advanced his Alzheimer's had become. It showed that his "time sense" was completely shot (year, time, age, etc.) but that his sense of place was still intact. I found it interesting how much *better* Grandpa had scored now, a few months into my care for him, than he had about six months ago. Back then when the neurologist had first scored him for his Alzheimer's the doctor had labeled Grandpa with the mental capacity of a two-year-old. This present test had taken place under the auspices of Grandpa's normal family doctor who put him at ease. While the test clearly showed cognitive impairment there were no dire declarations of imminent mental oblivion this time.

Afterward, the assistant told Grandma she wouldn't test Grandpa again. She explained that he would only get worse, and there was nothing they could do for him. Privately, I agreed it was for the best. The current round of testing had only embarrassed Grandpa and made him acutely aware that he struggled to answer questions which he knew ought to have been simple. The process did nothing for him. While I had an intellectual curiosity to chart his decline, there was no point in making him suffer repeated humiliation just so I could track his slide.

The next visit to the doctor three or four months later in March 2007 was just a regular physical. Grandpa had gained five pounds from the last time I took him in, and since he was underweight that was a good thing (and made me feel pleased that at least I was feeding him well). His blood pressure was back down to only seven points above what the doctor wanted, which wasn't worth doing anything about, she said. And that was that. He was hale and hearty, except for the fact that his mind was falling apart.

That was the same thing they said the last time I brought him in. Grandpa refused to take any sort of pill (for Alzheimer's or anything else), so there was really nothing doctors could do for him. Recognizing this, I understood it was pointless to take him to the doctors. The whole event was a source of stress, agitation, and embarrassment for Grandpa and it accomplished nothing. Why take him to the doctor so someone could check his weight and blood pressure and say both were okay?

Even Grandma agreed with me. We decided we wouldn't take Grandpa to the doctor again unless he had an actual need that a professional could address. That was his last appointment for a long time.

§§§

March of 2007 saw a milestone. Grandpa became unable to sign his name. It was a small thing, something that could pass without notice. But it was telling, and I took notice.

That morning didn't start out great for Grandpa to begin with. I don't know if he was simply exhausted from all the visitors we had been getting over the past several days, or if he was feeling a little under the weather, or if he was just feeling depressed. He said he wasn't hungry for breakfast and after drinking a few cups of coffee he quickly retreated to the couch and lay there dozing and looking forlorn and sad. I don't know if he remembered the bathroom accident in the middle of the previous night, but I wondered if he was thinking about it and feeling very down. When Grandma finally showed her face for the day he asked her if she might have some words of affection for him which only confirmed my suspicion he was feeling emotionally bleak, whatever the reason.

About mid-morning I finally managed to convince him to eat something—a piece of cake with another cup of coffee. Then at noon I persuaded him to eat some garlic bread I had made the night before (which he had really liked then). Finally at 1:30 PM he ate a normal lunch of soup.

The day didn't get better. He seemed off kilter all day, using the wrong words in conversation more than usual, and not making any sense. Then late afternoon came and I was taking Grandma to the bank. She needed Grandpa to sign a check before she left so she could cash it. But he couldn't sign his name.

We both tried and tried to coax him.

"Sign here, Grandpa," I said.

"Right on the line, Ivan," Grandma prompted

Grandpa stared blankly at the check put in front of him. "You want me to do what?" he said.

"Sign your name. Put Ivan Purdy."

"How do I do that?" Uncertainly, he took the pen in hand.

"Like you always do," Grandma said. "Here, practice on a piece of paper." A blank scrap of paper was shoved in front of him.

"Um. Okay." Grandpa took pen in hand, then paused. An uncertain meaningless squiggle. A pause again. "I guess I really don't get what you want," he admitted

He didn't understand our words, what we wanted, or how to do it. He didn't know what the request "Sign your name" meant, much less how he was supposed to perform the act. The idea was truly incomprehensible to him.

Afternoons were always worse for Grandpa compared to mornings, so I am sure that on a good morning around that time he could have still signed his name. But this failure was a threshold event. Signing his name was not a complicated task. If he couldn't remember how to sign his name on a bad afternoon, it wouldn't be long before he couldn't do it on a good morning. Grandma had said she didn't want to invoke power of attorney for herself until Grandpa was no longer able to sign his name. Well, now it was that time.

Grandpa's Alzheimer's never had some clear cut point where after a particular day he was starkly different. Everything progressed in shades of gray. But the endless progression made it *feel* as if some definite break with the past, with an attending drastic change of the future, was looming. It felt like one day everything would change and instead of things growing slowly worse some vital cog would come loose and life would become completely altered. A certain sense of waiting pervaded daily life. Perhaps this feeling sprung in part from an inability to imagine how some things could possibly continue their slow, progressive, decline. How could he slowly forget how to walk? How could he slowly forget how to feed himself? It seemed as if those were the types of things a person either could do, or couldn't. There was the tendency to subconsciously expect that one day Grandpa would wake up and not remember how to do anything.

With all that Grandpa had lost at this point, what stands out to me is how much more he still had to lose. On a very bad day in March 2007 it felt like there wasn't much left for Grandpa to lose. After all, how much is left to lose when you can't remember how to sign your name?

The answer is, a lot.

For all of the troubles Grandpa daily endured it was striking how I could still largely interact with him like a normal person. He was often a very confused old man, but he was still self-aware, and largely cognizant that he was sick and failing. The better half of his mind was trying to deal with it. The better half of his mind reached out to me and together we tried to deal with it.

It was painful to watch him struggle to speak, and see him *knowing* that he could not speak clearly. It was painful to have Grandpa call me into the bathroom every day and ask me to show him how to not urinate all over himself and all over the bathroom. It was painful to watch Grandpa mutter and curse at himself as he tried to make his feet work properly when they would no longer walk him across the room.

It was all very painful, but in a sense the pain was a reminder of how much he still had. So long as we still had this pain it meant Grandpa wasn't sitting on the couch staring blankly at the wall. The pain we daily faced was a reminder of how much he still retained.

Yes, they were reminders of what he still had, but they were also reminders that he was broken, and I couldn't fix him no matter how hard I might try.

§§§

A SONG FOR GRANDPA

Sometimes I wondered what Doug thought deep down as he watched Grandpa slowly lose his abilities. Doug was well into his eighties and still exceptionally sound of mind, so he had little danger of developing Alzheimer's disease himself. But there must be particular sadness in watching your younger brother lose everything he had—mentally and physically. In a man's sort of way, I think Doug had a lot of compassion for Grandpa. He came to visit every week, and was willing to do anything for Grandpa that he asked, even showing him how to urinate in the toilet. Doug wasn't scared of Grandpa's sickness, or the weird things he did. When Doug came over he would sit right next to Grandpa, which was the sort of thing Grandpa liked. Grandpa wanted to have people near—where he could feel their presence.

If Doug could be faulted for anything, it was trying too hard. I think sometimes Grandpa found him exhausting. Doug pestered Grandpa to go out and walk. He tried very hard to engage Grandpa in conversation. Doug did everything in his ability to cheer Grandpa up, and make it seem like nothing was different. I am sure he didn't want to lose his brother to the disease, and perhaps that made him try too hard.

It was a sad thing for Doug to watch unfold. Still, whatever his personal thoughts, Doug always had a jolly word, a joke, or a bit of a song. Mostly, Doug tried to reminisce about days gone by. Some days were better for Grandpa, and he joined in. Other days he didn't want to remember, or talk.

I was fascinated by the conversation, even if it was mostly one-sided. The visits from Doug gave me a glimpse into the past. He talked about his childhood with a freedom that Grandpa never showed and told all sorts of stories on himself and various siblings—including Grandpa. A lot of stories seemed to have something to do with one of the kids getting hurt in a particularly fantastical or rather gruesome way.

Then sometimes stories would veer into the later years when all the Purdy boys were men with families of their own. In those stories I learned that Gene, Doug, and Grandpa were a walking trio. When Grandpa was young and healthy he went for walks with his brothers and sometimes they would sing. One song in particular they sang, a song about Charlie's shoes.

From Doug I learned that *Charlie's Shoes* had been adopted as their walking song, the song they sang while walking back country roads. I suspect it was a bit of a joke at the time, but now it was also a memory of better times and happier days. But the more Doug pressed for Grandpa to sing it again the more Grandpa insisted that he could not, or would not.

It may have ended at that, except one day Doug showed up for his weekly visit with a music CD clutched in his hand and a twinkle in his eye. While out with one of his daughters he had stopped at a music store and found a collection of Billy Walker songs. On that CD was *Charlie's Shoes*.

"Put it on. Play it," Doug said to me, pacing around the living room with his usual energy. Grandpa sat on the couch, preoccupied with picking at the carpet between his feet.

I put the CD in the player and in a moment a cheery tune began to play, along with words I had never heard before. *"I'd like to be in Charlie's shoes, that's what I always said..."*

Grandpa's head came up. "Hey," he said, his eyes brightening, a smile spreading across his face. "Do you hear that? That's—"

"It's *Charlie's Shoes*," Doug said gleefully, and laughed.

For a moment it was like old times.

That was Doug. He was old, he had survived pancreatic cancer, and had already lost his wife a short time ago. He had every reason to be down, or caught up in his own life. But he took the time to visit every week. More than that, he went the extra mile to find an old song and buy it, just so he could see the surprised and happy expression on his brother's face.

§§§

I had a song for Grandpa, too. It wasn't a song from Grandpa's past, but it was an old, old, song that I introduced him too. It wasn't a happy song. The lyrics go way back to Ireland.

> *I wish I was in Carrighfergus*
> *Only for nights in Ballygrant*
> *I would swim over the deepest ocean,*
> *The deepest ocean to be by your side.*
> *But the sea is wide and I can't swim over*
> *And neither have I wings to fly*
> *If I could find me a handsome boatsman*
> *To carry me over to my love and die*
>
> *My childhood days bring back sad reflections*
> *Of happy times I spent so long ago,*
> *My boyhood friends and my own relations*
> *Have all passed on now like melting snow.*
> *But I'll spend my days in endless roaming,*
> *Soft is the grass, my bed is free.*
> *Ah, to be back now in Carrighfergus,*
> *On that long road down to the sea.*

Chorus:

But the sea is wide and I can't swim over
And neither have I wings to fly
If I could find me a handsome boatsman
To carry me over to my love and die

But in Kilkenny, it is reported,
On marble stones there, as black as ink.
With gold and silver I did transport her
But I'll say no more now 'til I get a drink.
For I'm drunk today, but then I'm seldom sober
A handsome rover from town to town
Ah, but I am sick now, my days are over
Come all you young men and lay me down.

The song is called *Carrighfergus* (or *Carrickfergus*) and I thought of it as Grandpa's song, for two reasons. First, I introduced him to a version of the song (slightly different than the version reproduced above) from the album *Elemental* by Loreena McKennit, and he loved to listen to it. Being of Irish descent, he liked nearly all things Irish. There were times I put him to bed and left the song playing on repeat as he drifted off to sleep.

But I also thought of it as Grandpa's song because of my own figurative meaning I applied to the words. In the song the singer laments for his lost love, and his own dissolution. In the Bible, in particular in the book of Proverbs, wisdom and understanding is personified as a woman, and that image is key to understanding the song *my* way. I don't know if it shows proper respect for artistic sensibility to reinterpret an old Irish song into a poetic lament about succumbing to Alzheimer's, but in my mind I saw it, and it fit perfectly. What else would you say, seeing your life and your mind slip away? The being drunk, of course, is only figurative for the state of confusion that the person with Alzheimer's finds themselves in.

I didn't think of the song this way before I started caring for

Grandpa. But after I made the connection I couldn't shake it and to me the lyrics became terribly, terribly, sad in a way they never were before. I put him to bed, and he lay there curled up as the music played and to me it seemed the song was his story and my heart ached. For someone slowly dying from Alzheimer's, the gulf between them and their former wisdom and intelligence is vast. The sea is wide, and they can't get over.

Day by day, that sea grew wider and wider.

§§§

SPECTACLE

I feel like I'm a spectacle that everyone is staring at," Grandpa said. His lunch had become a failure. In spite of his best efforts, and everyone's attempts to help, it had indeed ended as a spectacle.

I had some inkling before lunch that we were in for a bad spell. Maybe it was the fact that he couldn't find his clothes to get dressed when he got up that morning. Maybe it was the vague sense of being lost that had permeated the first half of his day. With an effort, and gentle prompting, he managed to struggle through eating most of his lunch, but when it came time to finish up the meal with his little tub of yogurt he hit a bad spot.

He started eating his yogurt well enough but then decided his bottom dentures needed cleaning. He pulled his dentures out and blithely splashed the remainder of his coffee over them, and then looked confused as he stared at his coffee covered teeth and the mess on the table. I hadn't been able to catch the situation before it occurred, but seeing what he had intended to do, I said, "Grandpa, would you like to clean your teeth?"

"Yes, that's what I was aiming to do," he said.

"Here," I said, "give them to me. I'll do it for you."

I went to the sink, washed off his teeth, and then brought them back. He had to turn them around several times before he figured out how they went in his mouth, but he finally got them in place. By this time he was completely derailed from the process of eating his yogurt. He pawed around the table, fiddling with everything but his yogurt. Grandma and I tried to nudge him in the right direction until he finally made his pronouncement about feeling like a spectacle.

"Okay," Grandma said. "I'll leave you be."

She walked out of the room to go do something else and I stepped out far enough so that Grandpa couldn't see me, but I could watch him and help if necessary. Grandpa continued to grope around in bumbling confusion. He latched onto his coffee cup which he struggled with for a bit, straining to bend the ceramic mug into a different shape. When that was unsuccessful he set the mug down and finally lighted upon the tub of yogurt sitting in front of him. He promptly turned the yogurt container upside-down and tried to stuff it into the coffee mug. When that didn't accomplish what he wanted he pulled the container back out and turned it upside down on the table. There was something strangely compelling about watching him try to accomplish *something* with such bizarre and frustrated results. I rooted for him, but seeing the situation rapidly heading toward an end which included yogurt all over the place, I intervened again.

"Grandpa," I said, "do you want to eat the yogurt?"

"I want...I...Make things...to do..." he sputtered and stammered, completely inarticulate in his state of confusion. At that point I wasn't sure if he could even remember what he had been *trying* to do, much less explain it. One failed action snowballed into another until Grandpa couldn't remember what he had been trying to accomplish, only the urgent sense that he had been trying to do *something*.

"Here," I said, removing the coffee mug and setting the yogurt tub upright in front of him. "All you need to do is this." I stuck the spoon into the yogurt.

Grandpa stared at the spoon in the yogurt and then laughed. "How did you do that?" he said. "I was trying and trying and it wouldn't go in. How did you make it go in?"

"Well, I...stuck it in," I said, not exactly sure how to answer the question.

"How is it so easy for you?" Grandpa asked. "I couldn't get it to do that."

"Well, actually, Grandpa, you were trying to do things with the coffee mug. That doesn't work so well," I said as gently, and lightly, as possible.

"I don't understand how you did it," Grandpa said with another little laugh. "I guess there are a lot of things I'll never understand."

Then he ate his yogurt. Simple as that.

Rarely, but becoming ever more common in the months of the first year, were these episodes of utter befuddlement when eating became an impossible task. A week or two previous I had given him a muffin to eat. He chopped the muffin up with a fork and then looked at it and said, "Okay, now what do I do with this? What am I supposed to do with this thing?"

"Well," I said. "You spear it with a fork and eat it. Or else you can pick it up with your hands and stuff it in your mouth."

"Oh." Grandpa looked at the chopped muffin. "That's all? Nothing more?"

"Nope," I said.

So he ate his muffin. But these times of confusion grew increasingly common. Eating was becoming a battle.

After lunch, Grandpa laid down on the couch. I was pleased to see that it looked like we were in an afternoon lull. Now I could go to my room and pursue some of my own activities without needing to worry about what was happening in my absence. So I thought. Alas, no more than a few minutes after I departed there came the tell-tale clatter of dishes from the kitchen. I hoped all would settle down, but after it continued for a few minutes I went to investigate and found Grandpa fiddling with the dishes in the sink. Apparently his rest had ended when it occurred to him that the lunch dishes needed cleaning. But Alzheimer's had twisted everything up in his mind so in spite of his good intentions he could no longer neaten or clean properly. Sometimes he couldn't even recognize what was truly put in order.

Grandpa wanted to neaten up the kitchen and while I was uncomfortable leaving him unsupervised I wouldn't order him to stop like Grandma often did. But I also didn't want to give up my quiet time so I could supervise his activities. Such was my dilemma, and so I waffled. Generally his cleaning up was fairly harmless—consisting mostly in turning on and off the faucet, trying to get it to work "right" and cleaning dishes (and his teeth) in the oddest ways. Often all this ended with him cleaning dishes with his dentures brush and cleaning his dentures with the dish scrubber. Harmless stuff, if perhaps maddening to some observers.

My concern was always the chance that he might in an unobserved moment veer onto a different and more dangerous course like turning on the stove, or playing with sharp knives. After pondering the situation for a moment, I settled with leaving him to what appeared to be his harmless occupation and checking on him every once in awhile.

I returned several more times and found nothing dangerous occurring. At one point I manged to determine that he wanted to clear the dishes off the table, and so I quickly cleaned them up for him before leaving again. When I next returned after I had finished my reading for the day, I entered the kitchen to find Grandpa stripped down to his undershorts standing at the table with a washcloth and a cup of water. I intuited that he had started out thinking about washing the table and had ended up thinking about washing himself and got the two mixed up. He often gave himself a sponge bath at the bathroom sink and sometimes he conflated rooms together. In this case the kitchen table had become the sink.

Grandpa swirled a rather large amount of water about on the table with the wash cloth and then began scrubbing at his armpits saying in a shuddering sort of way to himself, "Ohhh, cold, cold. It's cold."

"Um, Grandpa," I said. "Don't you think you want to do that in the bathroom?"

"Oh, I'm almost done," he said blandly. Then he took the cup and splashed some more water on the table (in his imaginary sink, maybe) and swirled it around some more with his washcloth. Perhaps at this point his brain clicked back in gear and he remembered where he actually was because suddenly without further comment he tottered off to the bathroom with his cup and washcloth and continued his bathing there for another ten minutes or so. When he came back out with his hair neatly combed, I helped him get back in his clothes.

The day didn't get better. Grandpa grew agitated throughout the afternoon. Part and parcel of the "bad days" (as I thought of them) was an increased level of agitation. It was almost as if the unease and confusion settled into his bones and he tried to fight it off by setting everything in the house—imagined or otherwise—to rights. The chairs needed to be set to right, and the couch cushions. And the magazines. And anything else he laid eyes on or could find in wandering around the house.

Those times were some of the most stressful for Grandma. Grandpa was physically and verbally agitated, and insistent, not to mention nearly if not completely incomprehensible. She wanted him to settle down and shut up so she could rest and relax. Grandpa would have liked to relax, too, but the activity was a compulsion. A person might as well have asked him to stop breathing.

The mix between the two of them became volatile. I tried to help Grandma by being the one to deal with Grandpa in his agitation. I tried to help Grandpa by listening to him and helping him in his struggle, and doing what I could for him. I answered him as best I could so that as much as possible he felt somebody was handling all those worrying things out there which needed fixing.

Throughout the afternoon I kept leaving my computer to deal with Grandpa. It was wearisome, but I kept at it. The day was waning on toward 5:00 PM and I had just recently finished preparing Grandpa a cup of coffee when Grandma finally got up from her easy chair and went into the kitchen.

"Papa, what are you doing?" she said, staring at Grandpa. By this time he had finished his coffee and was down on his hands and knees studiously running the bottom of the now empty coffee cup over the front of the kitchen cabinets.

"Grandma," I said quickly, "he is having a very bad day. So long as he isn't doing anything dangerous, just let him be."

"I'm removing the burrs," Grandpa said calmly, and continued to move the bottom of his cup over the woodwork of the cabinets, managing a very convincing imitation of the studious wood-worker perfecting his craft.

§§§

Personal hygiene was another battleground. Grandpa had struggled with shaving for a long time, and before I came to care for him he was switched from a razor blade to a cordless electric shaver. The electric shaver was both for his own safety when shaving, and for the convenience of anyone who might have to help him. Grandpa usually shaved every other day or so, and had good days and bad days. Sometimes it seemed like how well he managed with his shaving was a litmus for how the rest of the day would proceed.

The whole process was a struggle. It wasn't until I watched him that I realized how much coordination and attention the procedure required; from turning on the shaver and using it on his face to cleaning the device when he was done. My goal was to help him as much as he needed, but not much more than that. For the sake of his dignity I bit my tongue and restrained myself while he fumbled with trying to turn the shaver on, and struggled to shave himself. He was intimately aware that turning on the shaver was a pathetically simple thing that he should be able to do. Blatantly doing it for him felt like something of a put-down—even if it would have saved him a lot of frustration.

Grandpa didn't want to be a spectacle, but it became increasingly impossible to avoid. I tried to cushion the blow by acting as if all the failures were not a big deal. When we were alone that helped, but often enough I was not the only witness.

Eventually the cruel realities of life collided head-on with Grandpa's struggle for dignity. Sometimes for all of his efforts he could not get the blasted shaver to turn off after he was done. Then he was forced to let me help. Finally the day arrived when he couldn't even shave himself without help. We didn't suddenly reach a magical moment when he ceased being able to shave at all, ever again. But there was the first time he couldn't finish the job, no matter how hard he tried.

At first, he would sometimes shave the wrong thing. That began before I came. The first confusion was shaving the man in the mirror. That was a funny mistake to witness. I tried very hard to not laugh as he studiously ran the shaver over the mirror, fruitlessly trying to clean the fellow up. That particular confusion was not very surprising for someone struggling with Alzheimer's. After all, the face did look *exactly* like his own. It was eerily fascinating to witness his mind confuse the image in the mirror with his own body and so tell his hand to shave that other face—a very practical demonstration of losing the sense of self. Whenever that happened I gently coaxed him to shave himself, not the guy in the mirror. Once I had him shaving the right face his mind seemed to get sorted out and he had no more trouble.

Then it progressed (as it always did) from that point. On his best days he could still shave himself, haltingly, and with prompting, but on his worst days he now tried to shave objects which had no relation to shaving at all, like the place mat on the table. Verbally correcting him would not fix the situation.

One morning in February of 2007 he said he wanted to shave so I fetched him the cordless shaver and the little table mirror he used. I immediately knew this wasn't going to be a good day because when I set the shaving equipment down in front of him at the kitchen table and then moved the sugar bowl out of the way he reached out his hands and said, "Wait...I need to...reach all the stuff." He looked across the table in a vague forlorn sort of way, as if he saw many things he needed for his shaving.

I directed his attention back to the mirror and shaver and he followed my prompting to get started, but he proceeded with the peculiar method of someone who was following instructions that he didn't fully comprehend, and whose mind was someplace else entirely. Proving my observation correct, he picked up the shaver, turned it on, and then took his empty coffee mug and proceeded to diligently shave it.

"Grandpa, that isn't going to work very well," I said.

"I know," Grandpa said in a matter-of-fact tone that showed he didn't understand in the slightest what he was doing, or what I had said.

"You will have a hard time finishing your shaving that way," I prompted.

"I'm getting there," he assured me, working the shaver head around the mug.

"It's a mug. A cup, Grandpa. You don't want to shave that," I said.

I think he vaguely grasped that I had said a negative, the dreaded "Don't" but he still didn't grasp what I was getting at. He rather confusedly put down the mug which I quickly removed from his reach.

"Hey," Grandpa said, "where are you—I need—"

"You don't want to shave that, Grandpa," I said, as gently as possible. "You want to shave your face."

At that point he realized he was screwing up, or at least finally knew I thought he was screwing up, even though he still couldn't figure out all the whys or wherefores. He stopped and held out the shaver and said woodenly, "You want to shave me?"

"No," I said. Shaving him was easy, but I didn't want him to be a failure. I didn't want him to abandon the fight. "You can do it," I encouraged him. "You just need to get started." I started the shaver on his cheek and then guided him in using it. For the moment it looked like he was back on track.

I got up from the table to take care of something else in the kitchen, but by the time I reached the counter and turned around to check on Grandpa he had finished half of his cheek and had moved on to shaving the table. "Grandpa, that's not going to work," I said.

"Why?" he asked, continuing to meticulously move the shaver around in a circle on the table top.

Then Grandma looked up from her breakfast (having been blissfully preoccupied) and took notice of what was going on. She promptly started laughing.

There was nothing that cut through Grandpa's confusion faster than laughter. If he knew nothing else, he knew when he was being laughed at. You could carry on a deadpan conversation with him about the most absurd things, and extract him from the most embarrassing situations without fuss if you responded as if there was nothing particularly unusual taking place. But laugh *at* him the least little bit and that cut sure and swift right to Grandpa's heart. He might not know what, why, or how, but he knew laughter. He knew condescension.

Even I had moments when I couldn't keep the laughter at bay but I knew enough to quickly excuse myself and laugh quietly elsewhere until the impulse had faded. Then I could return to dealing seriously with Grandpa and his troubles. But Grandma didn't (or couldn't) exercise the same self-control. In this case she began to alternately laugh and give him instructions about how and what he was supposed to shave.

Grandpa, of course, couldn't understand. "What do you mean I'm not supposed to shave this?" he said. "How—What—But—" As Grandma continued to laugh and give directions he finally just *gave up*, with complete finality. So I came over and took the shaver, sat down, and shaved his face for him. It stopped Grandma's laughing, and saved Grandpa from the struggle and humiliation.

But still, we had lost.

§§§

Shaving was not the only place these increasing problems became visible. More people began to see. One day Doug was over for lunch and we were eating the leftover pizza-rolls I had prepared for supper the night before. A few difficult mouth-fulls into the meal Grandpa realized he had taken out his teeth sometime in the morning and it was very hard to eat lunch without them. Once he realized his problem, and made clear his need, I went looking for the dentures. They were in the sink. I rinsed them off, brought them to the table, and gave them to Grandpa to put in his mouth.

But he couldn't remember how to insert his teeth in his mouth.

"You put them in upside down?" he asked, turning his top portion the wrong way around.

Everyone stared.

I tried to prompt him but once again it was one of those situations where all the words in the world would have done no good because he didn't understand what the words *meant*—at least in relation to the objects he was dealing with. So I tried to start over, taking back the upper section and giving him the bottom portion of his teeth. The bottom portion he inserted in his mouth okay, but when I gave him the top portion again he still couldn't remember how they went in.

By this point the whole situation wasn't helped by Doug earnestly trying to offer words of encouragement and Grandma laughing uncontrollably and trying to give instructions at the same time. Grandpa, quite mortified that he had become the center of attention, started pushing the teeth about on his plate as if trying to get them to scoop up food in the futile hope that this would somehow resolve his problem. Probably he just wanted to disappear.

I saw this was another failure moment, and realized ending it as quickly as possible would be the greatest mercy. I picked up the teeth, righted them, and inserted them in Grandpa's mouth for him.

Situation resolved, but too late.

Grandma felt bad for laughing at Grandpa's expense, and Doug *tried* to make him feel like it was all just fine, but with no success. Requiring someone else to stick your dentures in your mouth for you is a pretty low feeling, and Grandpa knew it. And he felt all the worse because his incompetence was put on display before company. It was not a good moment.

After lunch when he tried to say something and lost the words he asked, "What is wrong with me? What is my problem? What causes it?"

"Your Alzheimer's is what causes it," I said. "You have Alzheimer's, Grandpa."

Grandpa looked at Doug. "Did you know that?" he said.

"Yes," Doug said. "I knew that."

§§§

.

Dread the Night

One night Grandma went to bed at 10:00 PM and for some reason Grandpa stayed up, determinedly resisting all my suggestions about heading in the same direction. I don't know if his unwillingness to go to bed was tied to the fact that he had been eating large quantities of chocolate cake all evening, or some other reason. With no one else up (and me making myself scarce in the bedroom reading), I hoped he would become bored and decide to retire for the night.

After Grandma went to bed I went out to check on Grandpa and he asked me to put a movie on. More precisely, he was trying to get the remote to work and, being unsuccessful, was asking for another remote that worked. When honesty forced me to confess that the remote did work he then asked me to put something on for him. So I put on the old Turner Classic Movies channel and left him watching some black and white adaptation of a Sinclair Lewis novel.

I went back to my reading and stopped every once in a while to check on him. I knew he was starting to reach his end when I came out once and he told me I could sit down with him. I told him no, I was going back to the bedroom. (Hint, hint.) Maybe ten minutes later he opened the bedroom door. He was carrying his T-shirt and wearing nothing on his upper body.

"Mind if I bother you?" he asked.

"No, come on in," I said, sensing victory.

"Then prepare to be bothered," he said.

"You want that T-shirt on?" I inquired. "You ready to go to bed?"

"Yes, I want this on and this off, and I'm ready to go to bed," he said.

So I helped him put on his T-shirt, and prompted him on the rest of the steps for going to bed. Then he wanted to say goodnight to Grandma. She had already gone to bed, but I decided it had been a short enough time that she probably wasn't settled down. After guiding him through the process of saying goodnight to Grandma I got him back to his bedroom and into bed. Then I put on the Bible on CD for him to listen to.

We went to bed late, but he was trying to live on his terms. I understood that.

I would like to say I understood, and everything was easy for me. If not that, I wish I could say that the hard days were few, and I managed fine. But it wasn't easy, and I didn't manage just fine. It was hard, sometimes so hard that I felt like I was driven to utter exhaustion. The truth is, sometimes it felt like I barely survived through the day. Then the night came, and it could be even worse.

Many things contributed to make caring for Grandpa difficult—some small, some big. Physically the hardest part for me was the sleep deprivation I had to deal with on a daily basis. The watches of the night were long, and then morning dawned with no respite.

Since I slept in the same room as Grandpa I had first hand experience with his night time escapades. The situation started out fairly manageable. He tended to turn in early (usually by nine), but whether it was early or late he didn't really settle down until 11:00 PM. So I effectively didn't get to sleep before 11:00 and usually he was up by 7:00 AM and in-between I had to get up several times during the night for 10 minutes or so when he went to the bathroom. It always took me much longer to get back to sleep, so what on paper might look like eight hours of sleep was more like six. It wasn't as restful a sleep as I would have liked, nor quite as much as I really needed, but it was not so bad as to make me non-functional.

As Grandpa grew increasingly confused, the nights became worse. The bad nights and lack of sleep were at their worst probably during my second year (2007-2008) of caring for Grandpa. That marked the time when he was still mostly mobile and yet also very confused. After that point it became progressively easier as Grandpa was more exhausted at night and so slept better, and also he simply became less physically able to get up. But at the worst times there were nights that felt hellish to the point of insanity, and the sleep deprivation like some form of torture.

People asked why I didn't arrange some other sleeping situation so that I had my own room. The answer is that I felt Grandpa needed someone around to watch over him at night. If I was there I could make sure he got back to bed as promptly as possible, and had the best night possible. Leaving him to his own devices would exacerbate the worst of his failures. And, practically speaking, if I hadn't slept in the same room I would have lain awake worrying about what was going on with him. So lack of sleep was a sacrifice I made, and physically it was the hardest sacrifice.

In the early days Grandpa recognized the impact of his night time activity, and he felt very guilty, embarrassed, and worthless all at once. He might not remember exactly how many times we got up in the night, but come breakfast time he did remember that it was a lot. "Go back to sleep," he told me when he got up in the morning. And, "You don't need to get up with me."

He was always talking about how I didn't get enough sleep, and I was going to end up killing myself. His concern was endearing, but not practical. Of course I would have loved to go back to sleep, but since he couldn't make himself coffee or breakfast I couldn't exactly unleash him unsupervised on the rest of the house. So I ended up crawling out of bed a few minutes after him no matter how bad the night before had been.

§§§

A Saturday in early March of 2007 found me attempting to lay linoleum over the carpet in our bedroom. You don't install linoleum over carpet—the idea is ridiculous. But it was the best solution I had to keep the carpet clean. Repeated urination on the bedroom floor by Grandpa—and the following requirement that I carefully remove all of the urine from the carpet at whatever odd hour in the middle of the night—had made it very clear that we needed a better solution. Finding some spare linoleum in the barn became the best solution I had.

To start my problems with the linoleum, I knew from eyeballing the leftover roll that it probably wouldn't cover the entire room. It wasn't until I rolled it out in the garage that I knew exactly how little I had. By means of some careful cutting and re-piecing I managed to construct an L shaped section of linoleum which covered the space between Grandpa's bed and mine, under the commode and to the bedroom door.

With my design figured out, I then sliced up the linoleum and taped it back together in the proper shape. Laying the linoleum loose on top of the carpet and taping the sections together looked incredibly stupid, but I reminded myself that it was serviceable for the intended function—keeping accidents off the carpet and easy to clean up. Nonetheless, the stupidity galled me a bit. There is nothing like attaching linoleum to carpet with double-sided tape to make me feel like a Do-It-Yourself idiot.

By Saturday evening the room was usable, but since the linoleum was only lying on top of the carpet it had a bit of a ripple which made it hard for the door to open and close. Sunday morning I fixed this by taking the door down and slicing a quarter inch off the bottom with a circular saw. The room was now ready (ready as it could be) for whatever storms might come.

Perfect timing. I rose 2:00 AM Monday morning to use the bathroom and as I walked down the hall I thought, *gosh, I don't remember waking up for Grandpa going to the bathroom once tonight. Either I've slept completely through his trips or else he hasn't gone all night. If he hasn't gone all night then either he has wet himself, or he's going to have to go really bad sometime tonight.*

As I was finishing up in the bathroom I heard a sound from the bedroom that suggested Grandpa was getting out of bed. *Yep,* I thought, *he's going to need to use the bathroom.* As I returned to the darkened bedroom I saw the shape of Grandpa standing in the middle of the room between our beds.

"You need to use the bathroom?" I asked. And, in that very moment, I realized—as much by splashing sounds as sight—that not only did he need to use the bathroom but he had dropped the front of his diaper and was urinating on the floor, *right now.* To make matters worse, I noticed that he was aiming in the general direction of the dark blob which was the clothes I had taken off before bed.

Things happened very fast. I thought something like, *Yaaaahhh! Don't aim there, not my clothes!* And simultaneously thought, *What difference does it make? You'll only have to wash them.* But somehow I still preferred to mop up the floor with paper towels than have to deal with my clothes soaked in urine.

I uttered a strangled, "Don't do that there."

To which Grandpa gave a reply something along the lines of "What do you expect me to do? I can't hold it in."

In the process of responding to me Grandpa shifted slightly so my clothes were no longer in the direct line of fire which gave me some small sense of relief. The spigot was open now and I could tell by the sound that he was unloading full bore on the linoleum. I flicked on the light and said calmly, "If you could get it in there," (pointing to the commode) "it would be nice." Then I stepped around him and removed my clothes from danger.

Grandpa dutifully waddled toward the commode but only

managed to get maybe a quarter to half a cup actually in the device, the rest making a second large and spreading puddle on the linoleum underneath the commode. While he finished voiding his bladder I made a quick trip to the kitchen and grabbed the roll of paper towels. I returned to the bedroom and tore off several longs strips and tossed them over the larger puddles to keep them from spreading any further. Meanwhile, Grandpa dropped his (until then still clean) diaper in the puddle he was standing in and proceeded to attempt to strip. There wasn't any point in undressing since his clothes were dry, but Grandpa's feet were wet, so he imagined everything had to go. His mind worked that way. Being barefoot myself I didn't particularly care to join him in the puddle. I tore off two sheets of paper towel and laid them on the untouched floor beside his bed and after helping him out of the diaper which was around his ankles I encouraged him to go over to the bed and dry his feet.

His feet now dry, I quickly fetched him a fresh diaper. With him dressed, I tucked him back into bed. One thing I was very thankful for was that by this point in my caring for Grandpa he let me handle his messes without attempting to deal with them himself—and attempting himself was always a greater disaster if he did try.

Once tucked in bed he promptly fell back to sleep. With Grandpa taken care of the situation was stabilized and cleanup became routine —but only because I had the linoleum covering the floor. This meant the better part of a roll of paper towels was sufficient to mop up the mess. The final step was spraying disinfectant over the linoleum. Then I went back to bed.

I was so very glad that I had made the time to finally put the linoleum down. I had known that a bedroom disaster was only a matter of time in coming, I just didn't know how close I had cut it. Now, with the linoleum in place, so long as Grandpa didn't decide to use my bed as a urinating spot we were all set.

A week later I woke to Grandpa sitting on me.

This time I somehow was exhausted enough, or he was quiet

enough, that I slept through the unfolding disaster and only woke to face the results. I first started waking when Grandpa sat on my bed in preparation to lie down. Dragged into a half-awake state by the sensation of someone almost sitting on me, it felt like too much work at that moment to explain to Grandpa that he was on the wrong bed. So I lay there waiting for him to realize he had made a mistake. He seemed to realize something was wrong with the bed—a funny lump or something—because he kept trying to re-situate himself. Finally, seeing that he wasn't going to quickly realize his mistake and get up, I made some groggy comment about how he would have more room in his own bed.

Grandpa made some remark (probably about his mistake), laughed, and got up and moved to his bed. Normally I always tried to tuck Grandpa in when he went to bed because if I didn't I had to listen to him wrestle with his blankets and mutter for ten minutes as he tried to cover himself. However, that night I was exhausted and still only half awake, so I listened to him mutter and struggle. I reached over with one hand and turned on my bed light, hoping that would be enough help, but the light shone in his eyes and he asked me to turn it off.

In the darkness once more, I heard him say, "Ahhh, it's all wet."

Wet? I thought. *That's not right. Okay...time to check on him,* I decided.

Groggily, I sat up and swung my feet over the side of the bed and set them on the linoleum—right in a cold puddle of urine. *That* woke me up.

Eeeyaaah, I thought, and reached over to turn on the light, wishing I had something handy to wipe off my wet foot. A good look at the room in the fresh light of my bed lamp showed it had become a disaster area. The sheet was half off Grandpa's bed, and his blanket was half on the floor and various items were scattered about on the floor. A quick check confirmed that his blanket was only wet where it had fallen on the urine covered floor—Grandpa had peed all over the floor, not all over his bed. One small mercy.

Grandpa's winter hat lay on the floor, and his glasses wallowed in another puddle of urine over by the commode. After picking my way around the room for a survey, I determined that all the urine had been contained on the linoleum, forming a rather large irregular lake. He had never made it out into the hall to track his trail of wetness to the bathroom, or cause any further messes there.

It was quite the mess. The continual night time messes were running me to the ragged edge and I must have been very exhausted to have missed the entire show without waking.

Situation assessed, it was time to move into cleanup mode.

I wadded up the slightly wet blanket with the other wet clothing items and chucked them into the corner. I took one of my spare blankets and gave it to Grandpa. Next I put him back to bed, then wiped up the floor, and finally cleaned his glasses. Situation restored to normal.

After that night I decided it was time to keep a roll of paper towels permanently in the bedroom. I didn't want to have to walk all the way to the kitchen when I needed something desperately for cleanup—like wiping the bottom of my wet foot, or stopping a tide of urine.

§§§

I came to dread the nights. It wasn't that I dreaded the tides of urine I might have to face—during the day that hardly caused me to break my stride. What weighed me down was the requirement of being constantly ready for whatever might come. My rest was frequently interrupted. There was no rest.

I knew Grandpa didn't mean to do it. I knew he wasn't trying to be malicious. I knew it all made him as miserable as it made me. I tried very hard to be kind, patient, and understanding. But often at night I was not at my best. Then irritation and impatience seeped through that Grandpa felt.

One Tuesday night Grandpa woke at about 1:30 AM to go to the bathroom but when he returned to bed he didn't promptly fall back to sleep as he normally did. I lay in my bed and listened to him sigh and stir and move about on his bed, shifting restlessly. I dreaded the next act. I had a feeling I knew what was coming, and sure enough a little later I heard the sound of a dresser drawer opening.

I flicked on my bedside light. "You want something, Grandpa?" I asked.

"Yeah, I guess so," he said. "Something to put on."

"What?" I looked at him. He was still properly dressed for going to bed.

"You know," he said. "Something to split your palm and cover your modesty."

It was nonsensical and a little funny, but I thought I knew the gist of what he was trying to get at. "Are you cold?" I asked.

"No, I'm not cold," he said.

"Well," I said, "the only thing you don't have on is a pair of pants, and you don't need to wear pants to bed. I don't understand what you want to put on."

"Never mind," he said, somewhat impatiently. "You'll have to ask your mother about that. I mean, your wife."

I didn't have a wife, but he certainly made it sound like the issue was slightly indecent—whatever the concern.

I turned the bedside light off. I wasn't feeling really agreeable. On a night when I felt particularly long-suffering I would turn my bedside light on and keep him company, watching as he did various re-arrangements of his dresser. That gave him a sense of help and support even while I occasionally prompted him in the direction of bed. This night I didn't feel like doing that, so I put a T-shirt over my eyes and decided I would just lay there until he finally tired of looking for the imaginary something.

I think he sensed my answer was a little bit more abrupt and final than usual because as he continued to fiddle around with stuff in the dark he said, "Well, I guess Arlie doesn't want to have anything to do with this." (At that time since Arlan had lived with them much longer Grandpa used the name of Arlie for any boy unless he was thinking very hard to remember my name).

His statement made me feel a bit guilty so I told him, "Grandpa, if you can tell me what you want I'll be glad to help you." But I still didn't sit up in bed and turn on the light and keep him company in his hunt to fix the unknown problem. Bereft of a proper resolution, I got to listen to Grandpa return to bed and his restless turning and sighing. After doing that a while he sat up and scratched his head very loudly. Then he began to fiddle around and fumble with things on top of the dresser, eventually succeeding in knocking my clock onto the floor. (I turned my bed lamp on to pick that up, then turned the light back off.) Finally Grandpa got out of bed and turned the main bedroom light on. He checked the room out, then turned the light off and left. I heard him go to the bathroom, then the hall. He returned to the bedroom, turned on the main bedroom light again, walked over to his bed, then went back to turn the light off. Then he went back and climbed into bed.

He repeated the entire agitated procedure maybe three or four times. Generally it consisted of scratching the itches that need itching, trying to set the bedroom to rights, finding glasses, going to the bathroom, trying to determine if anything needed to be set right or fixed in the bathroom, then going (probably) to check the time on the stove clock in the kitchen and then coming back to the bedroom and trying to get everything right for bed again.

Did it feel like torture? Yes, it felt like torture. There was no point to it, and it felt like there would be no end.

These types of situations took on a nightmarish hue for me. When there was a midnight mess that needed cleaning up I was in control of the situation. While it might not be fun I could at least clean it up in my time and go back to bed. But if Grandpa became agitated in the middle of the night I could only wait until he exhausted himself. I could not stop him.

When Grandpa became agitated five minutes ran into ten, and ten into fifteen and fifteen into half an hour. I would wonder how much of the night this would take, and then imagined being up all night watching Grandpa trying to set things right. I wasn't in control and I couldn't "fix" the situation. I couldn't even ignore it.

In these situations I tried to prod Grandpa in the direction of bed, but success was doubtful at best. In the early days when he became side-tracked from going back to bed the fiddling preoccupation usually ran a much shorter course before he was satisfied. A year into his care the restlessness had become pathological, and the best I could do was sit and wait for events to run their course. If he latched onto something and I resolved that problem he simply moved on to another object that needed "fixing."

On and on it went.

So it was that night. He had no defined goal, no end he was trying to reach except peace in his mind, and no logical suggestion I could offer to help him along. It was an infinite loop of activity until he became either mentally or physically exhausted.

I lay in bed and waited, keeping track of his activities by sound, until somewhere around the fourth circuit he finally stopped in the middle of the bedroom and said, "Well, do you think you could help me get all these things set to rights?"

"Sure," I said, taking the cue and sitting up. "I'd do anything if you'll lay down and go to sleep."

I removed the bathroom towel that had made it onto his bed (neatly folded) and the box of tissues that had also migrated there. Thus clearing the bed, I straightened out various other sundry disorder, approximately neatened his covers and folded them back. Then he willingly got into bed and I covered him up. It was now about 2:30 AM. This was, unfortunately, a typical night.

§§§

READ TO ME

When I was little one of the few things Grandpa would do with his grandchildren was read them a story. If we were visiting, the question would always come, "Will you read me a story?" Usually he said yes, and we would gather round while he read a short picture book, a cigarette smoldering between his fingers.

Shortly after 2007 began, I started reading to Grandpa when I put him to bed at night. The impetus came when I noticed that during the day he would sometimes pick up a magazine in the living room and try to read it. I figured that instead of leaving Grandpa to read the same half dozen magazines again and again I could provide him with a little more variety. I knew that because of his Alzheimer's and his failing eyesight I had to be selective in what I offered him, or else the idea of him reading it would be doomed to failure from the start.

The next time my sister came visiting I asked her to bring *Caddie Woodlawn*, which is a novel of probably about sixth grade reading level. It is a good story that anyone can enjoy. When I offered the book to Grandpa he seemed mildly interested and later I saw him make an attempt to read it. But I could tell he wouldn't be able to finish the story. Reading the book appeared laborious for him. He had to really apply himself and even then after a few pages he would mark his spot and stop. In spite of that difficulty he did seem interested enough to make an attempt—he just was no longer capable of following through.

Back in the day Grandpa did read books. I realized that I was picking up various subtle signs that maybe reading was something that had *unwillingly* fallen out of his life and something that, just maybe, he wished to continue.

I hesitated before suggesting that I read to him. I always tried to be very careful when I brought up ideas and suggestions with Grandpa. It was hard to judge how he would react and I didn't want to say anything that would wound his dignity. By the time I asked I was pretty certain he would appreciate hearing a story, but I feared he might feel I was treating him like a child to suggest that *I* read to him. I remembered the years of his reading to me. If he remembered, too, the obvious role reversal might have hurt too much.

Finally, one evening I gathered the courage and made the gentle suggestion that I read to him. Surprisingly, Grandpa readily agreed. I figured I would see how it went. Perhaps, I thought, he was only humoring me and after a night or two he would grow tired. Sometimes he was ambivalent about something and would agree to it for a short while before wearying of it.

But Grandpa didn't weary of the reading. In fact, I quickly discovered that he very much enjoyed it. For as long as he was awake he preferred that I kept reading. And so I kept reading, every night. Sometimes Grandpa would fall asleep shortly after I had begun, sometimes he would remain awake through a few chapters and so then I stopped before he fell asleep. I usually read for between a half hour and an hour as I lay on my bed opposite him.

Once I started reading to him at night it was almost as if he looked forward to going to bed, as if the story time was something enjoyable waiting for him at the end of his day. As a kid there were few things I enjoyed more than listening to a good story, so why would it be different for him now? I know the strong pull of hearing a story.

But there was something deeper than just hearing a story. If all

Grandpa wanted was a voice droning on I had always previously started the Bible on CD playing so that as he drifted off to sleep he heard someone reading the Bible aloud. That man could read well. And yet, over that, Grandpa preferred to hear me read. It wasn't just the sound of words he wanted—What he longed for, and savored, was the deeper thing that goes on when a story is read. When someone sits down to read to you they are giving a part of themselves—a part of their time—to you. It is a gift.

Anyone who has had their mother read stories to them realizes that what they enjoy from it is more than just the *story* that Mom is reading. It is that *Mom* is reading the story. It is Mom being there with you. When you listen to a recording it might be interesting, but it isn't the same thing. The recorded reading is dead words, not the sharing of one person with another. The man reading the Bible on the CD was very good—but he was, in the end, only a disembodied voice. What we all hunger for is the presence of somebody near and—for just a little while—to not feel so alone.

Still, I had this niggling question: How much did he understand? Answer: When he was paying attention, he understood much. Once he was following the story well enough to correct my mispronunciation of a word. (Him with Alzheimer's!) But he often fell asleep halfway through the chapter. I knew that part of the effects of his disease was that his mind tended to wander, so I suspected he often followed what I was reading for a time and then his mind drifted off in his own thoughts even while he continued to listen.

In the end how much he understood didn't really matter. What mattered was that at the end of a chapter I would stop and if he wasn't asleep he would open his eyes and when I asked him if he wanted me to keep reading he would say, "Yes." The bedtime reading was a time when he could escape from all the confusion and fears of the day, a time when he could rest and someone would talk to him and tell him a story that required no effort and demanded nothing of him.

It was perhaps the one time in the day one might say he was

peaceful.

In reading to Grandpa I stuck to the same general sixth grade level of fiction. After working through *Caddie Woodlawn*, I moved on to *Moccasin Trail*, and then *Maniac Magee*. Grandpa continued to enjoy both the stories and the reading in equal measure. Often he fell asleep before I finished reading, so I wondered how he could possibly keep engaged in the story. Somehow he did, at least enough for himself.

When reading *Moccasin Trail* aloud I was concerned that the writing might be too difficult for Grandpa to follow. The chapters were longer than *Caddie Woodlawn*, the interaction more complex, and the conflicts between characters more subtle. But in spite of my concerns he seemed to enjoy the story very much. At one point he asked, "How much do we have left? Is it almost over?"

"No," I said, "we're only about halfway through. Are you getting tired of this story?"

"No," he said. "I was afraid it was almost over."

There is no finer compliment that can be given.

I don't want to give the story away for anyone who hasn't read it, but at the end of *Moccasin Trail* there is a final gripping conflict when a particular character is in danger. One of the last chapters ends with one character distraught, screaming at another character and the other character running off to attempt a daring rescue. Grandpa was gripped. I finished the chapter and looked up, and he wasn't lying on his bed drifting off into dream land. He was sitting up, watching me intently. When I closed the book and said that was the end of the chapter for tonight he said, "Awwww..."

Yes, he enjoyed that story.

Next we started *Maniac Magee*. I was a little uncertain on this choice because it was a story about a kid in modern times, and I wasn't sure Grandpa could relate to any story set beyond the Great Depression. However, I chose the story because I suspected that any story dealing with the every day struggles of people was one Grandpa could relate to in some way. Besides, half of his enjoyment was in hearing the reading, whatever the particular story. In any case, he enjoyed *Maniac Magee* as much as the previous book.

Later, I found out exactly how much the story reading meant to him.

Arlan and I had begun splitting the weekend for going home to visit family. He went home to see the family on Saturday, and I went home on Sunday. Between us, there was always someone with Grandpa. I came back one Sunday evening to learn it had been a bad day for Grandpa. When I returned from my visit home Arlan was cleaning up a mess in the bathroom and told me he had to get Grandpa two pairs of new pants during the course of the day. The rest of the evening Grandpa was very agitated and confused. It was a bad day for him all around, but I think part of his evening trouble came from his exhaustion. When I finally got him into bed I left the room briefly to get a drink and a quick bite of dessert before I started reading to him. I stuffed a bit of food in my mouth, took a quick drink, and three minutes later I was back in the room. Grandpa was already sound asleep.

Talk about falling asleep as soon as your head hits the pillow. It was only 9:00 PM.

Nice, I thought. Grandpa was down early for once and I was so tired I needed to go to bed early myself. This was a chance to catch up on my sleep. So I finished up what I was doing on my computer and got into bed by about 9:30. I slid under the covers, turned out the lights, and settled down to go to sleep...and Grandpa woke up. It was about 10:00PM. He had to go to the bathroom. So I got back out of bed and assisted him. He finished his business in the bathroom and I helped him back to bed.

Then Grandpa sat on the edge of his bed and said, "Well, I guess it's probably too late to read me any more story." He had fallen asleep before his story reading, yet in the midst of all the confusion and forgetfulness of his mind and all that Alzheimer's had done to him, somehow he managed to remember he had missed his dearly loved story time.

"Yeah, it's too late," I agreed, thinking of my intention to go to bed early, and how it was already heading toward quarter after ten. "It'll have to wait until tomorrow." But then I started feeling guilty. He had pretty much come right out and asked me to please read to him, and we were both awake already, and I probably wouldn't have to read all that much before he fell asleep again. Besides, what difference did it make, anyhow? Weren't some things more important that a full night of sleep?

So I read him some *Maniac Magee*.

Another night I was preoccupied (not to mention tired), and I wasn't keeping up with Grandpa as much as I should have, and he was already lying down in bed when I came to check on him. He was dozing lightly so I touched his leg and asked him if he wanted me to read him the story.

"Sure," he said. "I'd love it if you'd read...I mean, if it isn't too much trouble and if you don't mind..." It almost broke my heart that he was so eager, and so worried about being a trouble.

So that night we read about McNab the giant bully and his confrontation with Maniac Magee over baseball. Toward the end of the conflict McNab leaves the field, supposedly to take a wizz in the forest down by the creek. "He took a long time," the story said, "but the kids supposed that someone as big as McNab needed to take a long wizz. They figured he might make the creek rise." I glanced up and saw Grandpa grin. He was following the story at least that well.

The next book I read was *Heidi*. Grandpa definitely enjoyed listening to *Heidi*, and it was a bit of an odd turn of family history, I suppose. When my Aunt was little Grandpa had read the story to her. After we finished *Heidi* Grandma suggested that I read my own book, *The Stuttering Bard of York,* to Grandpa. I had considered it, but at the same time I questioned whether Grandpa could really appreciate the story. The subject wasn't among Grandpa's interests and I thought that maybe the writing level was a bit too advanced. The real reason to read my book to him was if he knew I wrote it and simply was interested in knowing what I had written.

I decided I would give it a try. Doug was reading my book, and when he came over he would talk about the story with Grandma and that left Grandpa out of the loop. If the book was read to Grandpa I thought maybe he could follow any conversation on the subject, or at least feel included.

Since my story was humorous, I wondered if he would get any of the jokes. He did laugh at one or two (the most obvious, unsubtle, and simple jokes, but still...). More importantly, he didn't seem bored out of his mind.

The first time Grandpa laughed it was early in the novel when the hero Ben came to town for help and the mayor said to him, "You must bring your eyewitness account to the king so he will be moved by tender emotions and come to our aid. You must fetch the army of the king, Ben. Just like your parents told you. And never fear. Let not a concern touch your empty and innocent mind."

Grandpa got that one.

I'm glad I spent those months reading to Grandpa. The bedtime reading took away from my personal evening time, but those occasions were some of the most special moments I had with him. I wish I could say I read stories to Grandpa up until the very end. But I didn't. The days grew more exhausting, the evenings seemed ever shorter, and the time—well, it took time. A hymn or two was quicker, so it turned into that. And then we were both so tired, it was easier to just finish with a kiss. It was such a short time in the broad perspective of life, but somehow it was too much to continue. I regret not making more of an effort to keep it up, but at least I have these memories.

§§§

SEEING THE DECLINE

We were both lying in our beds in the dark when Grandpa spoke up. "What was the Battle of Hastings about?" he asked. "I'm thinking, and I can't remember."

Caught unprepared, I answered him as best I could, scrounging around in my memory of history. Battle in England, king killed, turning point in history—I couldn't give more, but he seemed satisfied. Eventually he was silent, and drifted off to sleep. I lay in my bed and wondered why he was trying to remember the Battle of Hastings as he went to sleep. It wasn't exactly what I thought a person with Alzheimer's would ponder.

Grandpa often sat silently on the couch. Sometimes he seemed to doze, other times he simply sat. I suspect at those times his mind wandered from one thought to another, drifting along in that way we all do when daydreaming, only to come back to the present and realize an hour or more has passed. As a healthy child or adult we usually daydream about past events, future plans, or imaginary adventures. But what thoughts wander through the mind of someone with Alzheimer's?

Probably Grandpa's mind sometimes wandered through memories of the past, concerns of the present, or thoughts about the future—

just like anyone else. Other times I think his thoughts simply wandered, perhaps unconsciously seeking out things forgotten. He sometimes asked questions out-of-the-blue. As a youth he never finished high school—quitting to join the military—but he read a lot and taught himself more than many people ever learn in high school, or even college. As a result, many of his questions were about things many people never knew, much less had a chance to forget—such as the importance of the Battle of Hastings.

A common source of questions for Grandpa regarded the meaning of words. Typically, they were unusual words he had once known, but then with time and the progression of his disease he only retained the memory of the word without its meaning. The questions popped out at the oddest times.

"What is a hedonist?" he asked one night while lying on the couch.

"What does occlusion mean?" he asked after supper one day.

One of the funniest word occasions was mostly because of context, but I also found his explanation very telling. It was around lunch time one day either late in 2006 or early 2007. Melinda, Grandpa, and I were sitting around the kitchen table. Suddenly, Grandpa spoke up.

"I sit there and I think and I think," he said. "I think until I think I've finally got it all thought out. Then I think *earwig* and I don't know what that means."

His condition so succinctly stated.

I explained to him that an earwig was the name for a type of bug, and tried to explain what the bug looked like. Grandpa didn't seem to have any recognition of the bug I described, though I know he had seen them many times during his life, and called them earwigs himself. After a few of my futile attempts at explaining, he seemed to lose interest.

His mind had probably already wandered off again.

Earwigs, hedonists, occlusion, and the Battle of Hastings were just a few of the things that shuffled through his wandering, thinking, mind. As his disease progressed such coherent pondering became less, but much later—in March 2008—there was another similar incident.

It was 10:30 PM and past time to get Grandpa to bed. I went into the living room where he sat slouched on the couch, studiously reading (or, more likely, pseudo-reading) the fine print in some magazine.

After an initial verbal exchange where I managed to get him to agree to having a bedtime snack of shredded wheat, he went on from that to a long discourse about people doing this and that, and things occurring like such and such all of which sounded very important and productive and made no sense at all. Once he ran out of steam I said, "So, would you like me to get you that shredded wheat?"

"Actually," he said. "I really need to go pee."

We started down the hall, arm in arm, heading toward the bathroom. Halfway there Grandpa stopped, scratched his head, and said, "You know, I've learned more about cells this year than I've ever known before."

No, we didn't have any science magazines lying around the living room for him to read—if he were even capable. There was no way for him to have read extensively on cells that year, so you can try to figure out that comment if you like. It was given in the most sober sense of reflection, so whatever was behind Grandpa's thought, he wasn't joking.

Perhaps he was remembering a year many, many, years ago.

But then, perhaps he wasn't really thinking about cells at all, just as his long convoluted conversation about things and people doing things was really an attempt to say he needed to go pee.

§§§

One day in the spring of 2007, I was sitting in the kitchen working on supper and Grandpa stood in the entrance-way, looking at me. Grandma came by and Grandpa said to her, "I can't tell them apart."

"What?" Grandma said.

"I can't tell the boys apart. I don't know which one that is," he said, looking at me.

"Oh," Grandma said. "Well...just call him 'Hey You.' That should work."

The attempted jest was the best Grandma could do in the situation, but I don't think Grandpa found it very funny. He had stood there, watching me intently, trying to make himself remember.

Given the progression of his decline, I was a little surprised by the times when he showed such clear self-awareness of his increasing problems. Another day when Grandpa was trying to communicate with me and struggled with his usual difficulties—he used the wrong words, nonsensical words, or sputtered and stuttered, unable to get *any* words out. Finally he stopped and said very clearly, "I don't know how anyone can understand what I say."

Grandpa continued to slip, but he struggled against Alzheimer's mightily. Beyond the typical messes and mistakes in using the bathroom, he began to have more trouble *finding* the bathroom. He increasingly required me to physically take his arm and lead him there. Sometimes, it was unintentionally comical.

One evening as we prepared for a trip to the bathroom Grandpa said, "Okay, I'm going to walk straight and when we get to the right place you say 'Gee' or 'Haw' and then I'll turn."

He was quite serious. He had no clue where the bathroom was located (little more than five feet from where we stood), and he figured it was best to just follow directions. When we walked down the hall he would have kept walking right past the doorway if I hadn't taken him by the shoulders and turned him into the bathroom.

Then there were the times he was completely oblivious to his own crazy antics. Such as when late one afternoon he started to get undressed in the living room.

"Do you want to take a shower?" I asked, observing his progress.

"Yes," he said.

So I went to the bathroom and I adjusted the shower water to the right temperature (had him test it several times to make sure it was right for him), then fetched him a washcloth and a towel. I made sure he got *completely* undressed—no taking a shower with half of his clothes on—then told him the shower was all ready, and to call if he needed anything more. He said okay, and I shut the door leaving him in the bathroom to tend to himself as he preferred.

I came back a few minutes later and could tell by the sound coming through the bathroom door that the shower stall door was still wide open. I supposed he had probably forgotten to close the stall door when he had climbed in the shower. I opened the bathroom door to swipe out his old diaper and replace it with a fresh one for him to put on. At least, I tried too. Grandpa was standing in front of the bathroom door. Still stark naked, he had the sink faucet going full blast along with the shower, and was vigorously lathering up his hair at the sink. The man knew how to bathe with gusto. There was so much hot water pouring out of the various faucets that the room had become like a sauna. It was something of a scene to open the door to great billows of steam and find Grandpa standing naked in front of the sinking, lathering up his hair for all he was worth. I tried to gently prompt him to use the shower but to no effect, so I let him be. A little later I checked back in and at that point he had moved on from his hair and was cleaning the sink for all he was worth. Later, he came out of the bathroom his hair all washed and neatly combed and I helped him get dressed.

§§§

If some of his antics were harmless, others were less so. What worried me was where his decline created truly dangerous potential. A minor issue was sharp knives, but I found that "out of sight out of mind" worked well enough to keep them out of use. It no longer occurred to Grandpa to look for implements in drawers. But more troublesome was his developing habit of fiddling with the knobs for the burners on the gas stove. This held the triple danger of Grandpa possibly burning himself, starting a fire, or leaving the gas on but unlit and so blowing us all to kingdom come once enough gas had poured into the house. I eventually removed all of the knobs from the stove and only replaced them when I was actively cooking. While inconvenient, this brought me greater peace of mind.

I had easy solutions for the danger of knives, and the stove. Not dangerous like those issues, but far more frustrating was Grandpa's continued attempts to make the toilet work.

He started throwing all the contents of bathroom garbage cans into the toilet, bag and all, with regular frequency. He thought it might make the toilet work. First urinating in the garbage cans, and now this. It was the last straw for the garbage cans. They had became too much of an issue. Grandpa was constantly trying to get them to "work" with the toilet when he was in his "I don't know how the bathroom works" agitation. Something was supposed to go in the toilet—that he knew—he just couldn't remember what. Maybe if he dumped the garbage can in the toilet he wouldn't have to go pee anymore.

As I fished the garbage bag out of the toilet for one of the last times Grandpa asked, a bit peevishly, "Do you always have to do that?" as if I was undoing all his hard work. I answered, as lightly as I could, "Well, every time you throw it in."

The upstairs bathroom garbage can was the first I removed, but the downstairs bathroom can soon followed. One day I went down to check on him and found him tottering out of the bathroom with his pants around his knees, intent on grabbing a throw rug and adding it to the garbage bag and contents already plugging up the toilet. Apparently he figured that if the first addition hadn't made the toilet start performing maybe another addition would help. So that was it. No more garbage cans in bathrooms.

The throw rugs were the next banned item. Grandpa became increasingly preoccupied with them in a bad way. With the garbage cans no longer around, his fixation switched to the throw rugs and they become associated with his bathroom needs. One day Grandpa told Grandma he needed to go to the "sewer" and then promptly dropped his pants and took aim at the rug in front of the refrigerator. When Grandma protested that he wasn't supposed to do it there he turned to her and said, "Well then where am I supposed to do it?" A different day he *did* pee all over the throw rug in front of the kitchen sink.

The problem wasn't just the throw rugs, but they were a prime illustration of a larger issue: By this time whenever Grandpa was seized by the sudden and desperate need to use the bathroom his blind instinct was to first drop his pants and then find the proper receptacle (or *any* receptacle) for his business. It could be a garbage can, it could be a throw rug, or something else entirely—which included, at some point, the kitchen table, the bathroom sink, and the shower.

I noticed around this time that not only was Grandpa forgetting how to use the bathroom, he was also having increasing difficulty interpreting the signs that he needed to go. He would take off his pants—usually a good sign he needed to use the bathroom—and then say, "What am I supposed to be doing?" If I suggested he needed to use the bathroom he would deny it, saying, "No, not now." Then a few minutes later he will suddenly say, "I've got to go, bad!" and he wouldn't be able to make it to the bathroom. He was becoming unable to recognize the need to use the bathroom unless he had the *desperate* urge, which was too late. Because of this, I became something of a broken record, asking him whenever he did the least thing, "Do you need to go to the bathroom?" in the hopes that I could get his mind on the right track, and him to the toilet, before desperation struck.

In speech Grandpa also suffered significant losses compared to a year before. By the end of the summer of 2007 he was more often than not verbally incomprehensible for conversation. He could shout a one word summons well enough, but in carrying on dialog he was maybe 90% incomprehensible for *most* people. I say for most people because after a year of caring for Grandpa I had become very adept at reading between the lines and contextualizing his attempted communication to get the gist of what he wanted. While his words often (in and of themselves) made no sense, most of the time I could still piece everything together enough for communication of a sort. If most people couldn't understand him 90% of the time, I *could* understand him 90% of the time.

We could have a conversation like this:

Grandpa says, "I—I—I the hunnhh and I the thuuuu we go things. Ok?"

I look at him. "You mean you have to go to the bathroom?"

"Yes!" he says.

Someone else trying to understand would have been entirely lost, but I knew that if Grandpa wanted to "go" somewhere it likely was the bathroom. So while he was often incomprehensible to most people, Grandpa and I still communicated well enough to get things done.

Nothing drastically worsened over that summer, but the evident loss of ability in every regard by summer's end was stark compared to when I first started helping Grandpa the previous autumn of 2006. September came with the anniversary for my first full year of caregiving. The man who could take himself to the bathroom was almost completely gone.

Grandpa's bathroom competence was by now in some ways similar to a toddler on the edge of continence. Except, a toddler was heading in the positive direction of becoming fully continent while Grandpa would soon enough become completely incontinent. About this time I began to set him on the toilet whenever he wanted to go to the bathroom. We had tried this some months earlier without success, but it had finally taken hold as an improvement. Before Grandpa always wanted to urinate standing up—and that method was more and more often ending in some type of a mess, either on himself or the bathroom. Around the middle of the summer I somehow managed to convince him that sitting down was acceptable—except he couldn't figure out how to do it himself, so I had to help. When he needed to use the bathroom I guided him to the appropriate room, positioned him in front of the toilet, pulled down his pants, and lowered him onto the toilet much as you would a little child. This removed all decision making from Grandpa and, as a result, eliminated the opportunity for mistakes. Reaching this point required him to give up his battle with trying to figure out the toilet, and also to surrender the larger measure of his dignity. Gone was the man determined to use the bathroom by himself.

I knew I really needed to start wiping his bottom after his bowel movements. *That* was a dicey proposition to bring up, so I kept delaying. What should I say? "Hey, Grandpa, you're not wiping your butt good enough anymore so I have to do it for you." I imagined all sorts of reactions. Where do they teach you how to discuss the issue of butt wiping with your Grandpa? There was no good way to bring the subject up—at least, none that I could imagine. In the end, I decided the best course was to not make an issue of it—I just started doing it. A few times Grandpa complained, but I found if I was quick, prompt, and very business-like we managed to avoid any real fight.

Grandpa's continuing decline also brought the matter of his bathing to the fore. I contemplated with great reluctance the prospect of bathing him. The quality of his self-bathing had been suspect for some time, and I knew I needed to become directly involved. I needed to be there and make sure everything was washed. Soon enough I would have to *do* the washing. All of this would take much more of my time, but the touchy issue of his modesty was the real problem. I cringed thinking about Grandpa's response. I could easily imagine how he would lash out at me touching his most private areas.

I saw no happy solution for either of us.

§§§

WALKING TROUBLE

Lunch finished, Grandpa left the kitchen and headed for the couch, ready for some afternoon rest. His shuffling gait took him through the entryway, and he seemed on course. Then, two steps shy of the couch, trouble struck. Suddenly, his feet wouldn't move. His heel was half-raised, and his knee bent, but his toes would not leave the floor. He strained, foot trembling, legs jerking, but still his foot would not move. It was as if some unseen force nailed his big toe in place.

"Move! Move dammit!" he commanded his feet, to no avail.

"Need help?" I asked.

But he was determined to make it by himself. Thwarted by his own feet, he made a lunge for the couch, covering the last two steps in something of a controlled fall, grabbing the couch as he came in for a landing. Turning himself around, he sat, breathing hard.

"Geez, I don't know why that happens," he said.

"It's the Alzheimer's," I explained.

"Yeah, well, I don't understand it," he said. "I wish it wouldn't do that."

By the end of the summer in 2007 Grandpa's walking ability had taken a noticeable decline. It was sad to watch. The fundamental problem was his worsening Alzheimer's, but this was aggravated by congenital back and hip problems that gave him intermittent but severe pain and a loss of strength in his legs. It was more pleasant to attribute his problems to simple physical ailments, and so talk about how his back hurt and his legs were weak. But the reality was that in his strange stammering steps I saw the beginnings of Grandpa forgetting how to walk.

The Alzheimer's was doing him in. My cousin Melinda's maternal grandfather died as a result of Alzheimer's, and she mentioned one day that Grandpa was walking just like her other grandfather did before he forgot how to walk. It was confirmation of my own observation. I had noticed that Grandpa was more confused at the times when his walking ability was worst. Sometimes it seemed like he forgot *how* to move forward.

As a method of compensation, I often ended up "driving" him, especially in the later portion of the day when his mind was worst. This involved me standing behind him, putting my hands in his armpits, picking up some of his weight and propelling him forward. The maneuver was much like you would do to help a toddler just learning how to walk—except Grandpa was about as tall as I was and weighed in the range of 125 lbs and was forgetting, not learning how to walk. The maneuver broke just about every rule of good body mechanics and ergonomics, but I did it anyhow because it allowed Grandpa to maintain some fiction of independence in walking. It wouldn't last, but I was sorry to see him lose his ability to walk and so tried to enable his attempts for as long as possible.

Normally, I supported a portion of his weight which gave him added stability and a sense of security, as well as guidance as to where he should be going. But sometimes, when he was feeling especially poorly, I would support most of his weight. Once on a bad day he simply picked up his feet and I carried him over to the couch hoisting him by his armpits. I felt very fortunate that he wasn't too heavy for me to easily carry.

§§§

The autumn passed and November gave way to December of 2007. Grandpa's difficulty with walking continued to increase. Even before I had come to care for him he had developed a noticeable shuffling gait, a great change from the man I had seen running in my childhood. What was shuffling began to turn into a sometimes stuttering and stumbling step. The incidents where Grandpa suddenly seemed to have a foot nailed to the floor, unable to move, became increasingly common.

When he seized up near his destination he would make a lunge or dive to finish his journey, but if his feet failed him halfway across the room his only choices were to have someone help him, or get down on his hands and knees. So he began crawling around the house sometimes. Looking back, it seems so clear how that marked the significance in his decline. A year ago we had walked up the street. Now he was at times crawling about on the floor.

Grandpa noticed his walking problem, but he didn't understand the cause. He complained, "Why can't I lift my feet better?" The problem both perplexed and frustrated him.

Sometimes, a suggestion could unstick his mind and help for a moment. "Goose step," I told him once. "Lift those knees high!" By following my instructions and engaging in a ludicrous high stepping walk he managed to get his feet off the floor and moving. But when he went back to normal walking, his feet wouldn't move again.

As the winter wore on, his ability to walk continued to degrade as a result of his mental and physical problems. Because of increasing clumsiness, weakness, and the physical pain in his back, I started picking up Grandpa's feet and putting them in bed for him when he laid down for the night. I offered him medicine for pain relief in his back, but Grandpa maintained a steadfast aversion to taking *any* kind of pill whatsoever—even when he said his back hurt so much he was nearly out of his mind. I helped him as much as I could, but there wasn't much I could do to fix his increasing difficulty with walking.

His back pain didn't *cause* his trouble walking, but if he was in severe pain that did make the walking problem much worse. Drastically worse. Over a several week period he suffered some particularly bad spells of agitation combined with back pain. He became increasingly agitated more of the time, which meant he was getting up and going around the house doing "things" which mostly consisted of pointless wandering and fiddling. The worse his agitation or confusion the greater his tendency to try to move things—such as the kitchen table—which really wasn't a good idea for an old man to move, and certainly not an old man with back trouble.

Try explaining that to him.

All of his activity commonly exacerbated his pain, and then exhaustion added on to that. If he had a bad day of agitation and activity, he often ended in the evening clutching at his back and nearly unable to stay upright, much less walk at all. I felt sorry for him, and suggested he sit on the couch and stop walking around and trying to move things. But he was his own worst enemy. He refused to sit still.

This was all part of the continual worsening that I knew would eventually end with Grandpa no longer able to walk at all. If he wasn't aware of the end result, he was at least cognizant of his worsening ability. He commented, "People tell me to pick up my legs to walk better, but if I could I would." He complained incessantly that he couldn't get his legs to work properly.

As Grandpa worsened, any walking without support became a lurching stumbling gait. He often fell or lunged in the direction of his destination, careening off corners and grabbing at various objects until, breathing hard, he made it to his goal. It was nerve wracking to watch, and I worried that he would accidentally end up pitching himself down the stairs while attempting some careening transverse of the hall. I fretted especially about night time walking. Not only was it possible he might escape the bedroom while I slept and then fall down somewhere, but it was also possible that one night he might go to the bathroom and not have the strength to get back to the bedroom.

Walking had become physically draining and mentally taxing for him—not to mention dangerous. At night I became attuned for signs and sounds of trouble. One night I came out of a dozing light sleep to hear the familiar *thump-thump* of Grandpa's shoulder, supporting himself as he worked his way along the wall, sliding toward the bedroom door. Then came the clawing rasp of his hand fumbling for the doorknob. It all sounded confused.

I scrambled out of bed and opened the door to find Grandpa sagging against the hall wall in the dark. "Boy am I glad to see you," he said, almost panting. "I didn't think I was going to make it."

"Need help?" I asked.

"I guess," he said

Taking his hand in one of mine, I put my other hand in his armpit and bodily hoisted him up. By supporting some of his weight I managed to guide him back into the bedroom and bed.

His weakness and failing ability to walk meant it was unlikely he would wander off—in his condition he wouldn't make it past the end of the lawn, if he even made it out the front door. But there were other problems. Potentially anywhere in the house he could have a failure in his ability to walk, and this began to happen. For him some times and places of failure were more distressing than others. And some were more mental than physical.

Twice he had a crisis in the garage (which was part of the basement). The first time occurred when he decided to change the kitchen garbage. It was after dark, he didn't need to change the garbage, but since a bit of gentle persuasion from me didn't dissuade him, I didn't argue the matter. In the end I let him carry the bag of garbage downstairs. I made a mental note to check on him if he didn't come back in a reasonable amount of time, then went back to what I was doing.

A short time later I heard loud shouts of distress from the basement. "Help! Heeelllp! *Heelllp!*"

I ran downstairs and opened the door to find Grandpa in the darkened garage. He was unhurt, and besides standing in the dark appeared in no trouble. I figured out what had happened quick enough. The light switch to the garage was in the finished part of the basement and the door between the finished part and the garage was a fire door which automatically swung shut. Grandpa had walked out into the garage without remembering to turn on the basement light and the door had promptly swung shut behind him, plunging him into darkness. By the position of the garbage bag I deduced he had at first thought this was no big deal and intended to continue to the trash can in the dark. Halfway there he thought better of it and turned back. He probably intended to open the door and turn on the light—instead he had grabbed the handle to a filing cabinet drawer, opened it, and stuck his hand inside the drawer. At this point I think he realized he was utterly lost in the dark.

He was shook up when I arrived, but tried rather weakly to jest. "It sure took you a long time to get here," he said, sounding quite relieved. "I thought I was going to be stuck down here forever. I thought I was a goner." When I got him back upstairs he said to Grandma, "I thought I'd never see you again." He didn't precisely think any of those things, but behind the joke was the faint echo of the real terror he felt when he couldn't find the door to get out.

The second time he got stuck in the garage was on a day when he was in a fit of agitation which involved going inside and outside, upstairs and downstairs trying to do "things" which he wasn't quite sure what they were, and generally making himself utterly exhausted. He was completely unwilling to heed my suggestion to sit down and take a break.

As he went downstairs (yet again) I had an idea he was no longer fit for traveling. After a few minutes of him downstairs in the garage and not returning I went down to check on him. There I found him, stuck. His ability to walk—or, more precisely, his remembrance of how to do it—had expired at the front of the car. I found him bracing himself against the car, looking like someone who couldn't figure out how he was going to make it to the door. Exhaustion and confusion had combined to lock up his brain and he couldn't move himself forward.

I took his hand and tried to encourage him to move. At first he staggered and shuffled in place but with my coaxing his feet finally unlocked and we made it to the door. After that his brain relaxed and he made it back upstairs by himself. If I hadn't come for him I don't know how he would have made it. As it was, I had considered for a moment the possibility of being required to carry him up the stairs.

As Grandpa's ability to walk continued to dwindle I pondered the problems that came with that decline. What should (and could) I do to help? I couldn't make him walk better, but what about preparing for when he couldn't walk at all?

Even Grandma noticed his increasing trouble with walking. Attempting at alleviate the problem, we borrowed a walker from Doug who no longer needed it for his now deceased wife. Once, Grandpa gave it a try.

That evening he had particular trouble walking, so I guess he thought to limber himself up on the walker. It didn't work. He pushed the walker along in front of him, and for about thirty seconds it looked like it might work. Then after six steps his brain froze and his feet stopped moving. The fact that he had a walker didn't help. His feet were stuck, but he continued slowly sliding the walker forward until he was stretched out leaning on the walker far in front of him. This wasn't an improvement, as he now was in more danger of falling than ever before. I came and unstuck him by physically bending his knees for him and moving one foot and then the other. But then he walked another six paces or so, only for his brain to seize up again. If he struggled mightily with his own body he could (as if in a desperate gasp) get his own feet unstuck—but the walker added no more support or help, and it introduced more possibility of him injuring himself.

I asked Doug if we could borrow the wheelchair he owned, but no longer needed. At that point Grandpa didn't *desperately* need a wheelchair—but yes, he did need one. It was time to admit that. We were edging into the gray territory where sometimes a wheelchair would be useful, and on a rare occasion—such as Grandpa needing to leave the house—it would be a necessity. When he couldn't move himself around the house I could pick him up and move him. This allowed me to say we didn't *need* a wheelchair. But, really, that was more a statement of my ability to carry him than it was of the lack of his need. Sometimes, he needed a wheelchair.

It was also a good idea to have the wheelchair for the times when Grandpa couldn't get himself around while I was out of the house. If only Grandma, my sister, or some other person was around who couldn't physically carry Grandpa, they would need the wheelchair.

For several weeks after Doug brought the wheelchair it sat in the basement. I was reluctant to broach the issue with Grandpa. It was easier to leave things as they were. Then I decided I had better bring the wheelchair to where it was more accessible, and visible, and perhaps even use it myself to begin familiarizing him with the device.

Grandpa didn't resist the wheelchair, but neither did he prefer it at first. He preferred to get around by himself. There was no way he could figure out how to maneuver the wheelchair, so self locomotion meant either on foot, or by crawling. In spite of his preference for independence, the wheelchair was definitely the easiest and most comfortable way for him to travel. He was safe and secure in the wheelchair, and movement required no thought or effort on his part. In a large measure this passivity was the problem—from his perspective. Being dependent on someone else to travel in the wheelchair offended his dignity a bit (though he had lost much of that). More to the point, the wheelchair got in the way of his habitual self-reliance. It was impossible to wander around the house in a wheelchair, and Grandpa couldn't easily accept that.

I began to use the wheelchair regularly to take him to the supper table. He didn't *need* the wheelchair to get to the table in the early months that I used it, but I decided a regular occasion for the wheelchair was the best way to get him into the habit. Grandma liked it because Grandpa was sort-of restrained when the wheelchair was parked up against the table with the wheels locked. In that position he couldn't easily get up and wander around the table and mess with dinner. It was more a means of discouraging the activity than a true prevention because when he became frustrated with the table and how everything wasn't "working" he would stand up from the wheelchair and heave the table out of the way. For a skinny old man he still had a lot of strength.

After we had the wheelchair firmly introduced into the normal routine everything was in place for the time when Grandpa could no longer walk. But until Grandpa gave up walking, his failing ability to walk raised its ugly head over every day. On his good days he was still good enough at walking, but on the bad days it was bad, and getting terribly worse. He seemed to have the worst trouble when he was trying to go somewhere in particular and do something—his perennial trouble being making it the last few steps to the couch. It became bad enough that sometimes he couldn't even make it close enough to perform his lunging landing, and was forced to let me help him.

He was light enough that I could easily pick him up and carry him, but that was less than ideal. Like all old people he loathed having his feet off the ground. I found the best solution was to give him the clear sensation that he was being firmly supported. When his legs stopped obeying him he became afraid of falling, but when I was at his side supporting some of his weight that was sometimes enough to get his brain and legs working again.

He had fallen on occasion before, but he began to fall regularly. In such circumstances it was a great mercy that he was a very light man and we had thick wall-to-wall carpeting. Even so, his falls were alarming—especially when he crashed into something on the way down. It put me on edge. One time he knocked the keyboard tray off my desk in his descent, though he somehow emerged unscathed.

The causes for his falls were various, but all centered around the fact that his sense of balance and coordination had severely deteriorated. He could try to bend over to pick up a bit of garbage and go down. Or when trying to sit on the couch he would not make it. Then there were times he would simply lose all sense of balance when doing nothing in particular. Once I saw him standing perfectly still and suddenly almost pitch over backward like a felled tree.

He refused all suggestions of staying in his chair, so short of tying him down, there was little I could do to eliminate the problem. This forced me to make a hard choice. In a nursing home they would have medicated him, and restrained him if necessary, to prevent the hazard of falling. I knew Grandpa in his right mind would have preferred to suffer a broken bone than be restrained or medicated. There was no question what his wishes were—now, or previously when he was still competent. But his wishes were putting him in danger. A fall could leave him seriously injured, or potentially be the cause of his death. Should I over-rule his wishes for his own physical well-being?

It was a difficult choice. If something bad happened as a result of my decision I couldn't take it back. So would I restrain Grandpa for his own good, knowing full well it went against his wishes? I decided no. His right mind was deserting him, but I would still respect his long-standing wishes. I would not medicate him into complacency.

The decision made, events would now take their course. I told myself it was right that Grandpa should be allowed to live on his own terms. But every time he fell I cringed. Every time I wondered if I would end up regretting my decision for the rest of my life.

The walker was a complete failure, but by happenstance Grandpa came upon his own substitute. He gradually became infatuated with the kitchen chairs and began to take them with him around the house, like a wandering traveler with his luggage. The chairs were sturdy, and offered good support. Also, if he got tired he could sit on them.

He was content. It irritated Grandma to see him walking the kitchen chairs around the house, but I was glad that they kept him occupied, and a little safer.

On his very worst days it was painful to watch him fighting with his body, trying to make it remember how to walk—legs jerking, feet trembling. It was then I wished he would be content to sit in the wheelchair where I could push him wherever he wanted to go. I wished he would stop fighting the Alzheimer's and rest, so I wouldn't have to watch him struggle. But I knew that when he stopped struggling that would be the end of him. This was his battle, and he was fighting it. Still, in the matter of walking I hoped he would give it up before a serious accident happened.

Unfortunately, he did not.

§§§

MUDDLED UNDERSTANDING

Supper was winding down, but Grandpa—slower than everyone else even on his good days—was dawdling. His attention wandered from scraping the food around on his plate to surveying the table on the chance something might strike his fancy. Then he turned to picking at his clothes.

His gaze wandered to the empty spot on the floor beside him. "Hey, you there," he said in an agreeable voice. "I see you looking up at me, looking up with your big eyes. You want some, don't ya? Here, have a bite."

The spoon, with a bit of food perched precariously, was lowered toward the floor. "Come on, take it," Grandpa said.

We watched.

"What do you see, Papa?" Grandma asked.

"Huh," Grandpa said. He returned the spoon to his plate, seeming slightly puzzled. "I think that little dog around here is cute. Sometimes I see him, then he's gone."

It wasn't only a little dog that Grandpa sometimes thought he saw.

His mis-seeing was an interesting phenomenon. Sometimes he

clearly misinterpreted real objects, other times what he thought he saw was so far removed from reality that it was a complete hallucination. Or maybe it was a memory leaking into the present. When I was a boy Grandma and Grandpa had a little black dog named Didi and perhaps his constant seeing of a little dog in the house was triggered by the memories of when there was such a dog around. Whatever the explanation, Grandpa's bizarre acts were a reminder of his muddled grasp of reality.

Often he saw animals, and they were always farm animals—no strange exotic creatures like lions or crocodiles. He was remarkably agreeable about what he thought he saw, no matter how strange such a reality would have been.

Lunch one day found him staring across the kitchen out at the back porch. He stared, blinking with such fixed intensity that Grandma became a little unsettled and finally asked, "What is it you see, Papa?"

"Well, I don't know," he said. "It looks like—is that thing out there a cow?"

"Nope, no cow out there," I assured him.

"Huh. It looked like it to me," he said, and went back to his lunch.

Cows and dogs seemed to be regular recurrences. Another afternoon Grandpa and I were sitting on the couch, and I noticed he was looking across the room in a puzzled, searching, manner. Finally he said, "I don't know if I'm seeing what I think I am."

"What do you think you're seeing?" I asked.

"Well it looks to me like that is a cow standing there," he said, pointing at a kitchen chair he had dragged into the living room earlier.

"No cow there," I said. "That's a chair."

"Really?" He sounded surprised

"Yep," I said.

He shook his head. "I don't know why I think I see some of the things I do. It don't make any sense at all."

Oddly enough, the thought of having a cow standing in the living room didn't bother him.

The strange things Grandpa saw never seemed to alarm him. Some were amusing, cute, or odd to him. Some he didn't doubt existed. Others he wondered about. I never argued with him about the menagerie of people and creatures that occasionally showed up in his perspective. If he asked, I answered him honestly about what I saw. If he didn't, I let him enjoy his imagined company as best he could.

Some of the muddled imaginings brought us into a bit of conflict— but that was always about things that needed doing or fixing, not about imagined guests.

Early one evening in the winter of 2006-2007 the sun had gone down and it was dark. Grandpa walked into our bedroom and saw I had left the blinds up so he proceeded to try to put them down. My clue that he was trying to do this came when I heard the sound of my bed springs squeaking, indicating that Grandpa was climbing on my bed. I went into the bedroom and found Grandpa wrestling with the window latch.

"What are you trying to do?" I asked.

"Shut this window," he said.

"Here, let me help," I offered. I took the pull cord and dropped the blinds.

"How did you do that?" Grandpa asked.

"I unlocked it up there by pulling the string," I said, and I shook the pull cord to demonstrate.

"Oh. Now shut the other window," he requested.

"What?" I said.

"You shut that one," he pointed at the window. "Now shut the other window," he said, pointing at the back of my bed. My bed had a somewhat ornate white metal backing on it that ran along the wall.

"That's not a window," I explained.

"It's not?" Grandpa said.

"Nope," I said. "I shut the one window. I can't shut that because it isn't a window." In this case his muddle wasn't exactly an hallucination. The cross bars on the back of my bed struck him as a window, and thus it became one in his mind. Something was there, and in an abstract way it might look a bit like a window, but he wasn't making proper sense of it.

"Well, okay, if you say so," he said.

I started to leave the room, but at this point his mind must have dropped back into gear because as he followed after me he laughed and said, "Next thing you know I'll be having you tear up the sidewalk." I took the statement as his way of acknowledging he had just asked me to do something both pointless and impossible.

Alzheimer's didn't affect all parts of his mind equally, or consistently. As strange or impossible as it might seem, his mental condition truly fluctuated. I found the juxtaposition between what he remembered and what he didn't particularly amazing (and perhaps slightly bizarre). One thing he seemed to remember well was old movies that he had seen before. One night Grandma was watching *The Yearling* on TV and Grandpa decided he would go to bed. As I put him to bed he told me about how the first time when he had watched the movie he had thought it was pretty good but that over the years it had begun to strike him as childish. Here was somebody who struggled to remember how to use a toilet and yet he could still recall all the times he had seen a movie, and express his opinion about the movie, and how his opinion had changed.

The disjunct in cognitive ability felt almost unbelievable.

§§§

Doug showed up for another weekly visit and sat down on the couch next to Grandpa. "How are you doing, Ike?" he said cheerfully.

"Good," Grandpa said. "How about yourself?"

"Fine," Doug said.

"That's good," Grandpa said. Then his gaze slipped beyond Doug to the corner of the couch. "And how about you?" he said. "How are you doing?"

Doug looked puzzled and glanced at the couch.

"What's your name?" Grandpa said. He pointed at himself, speaking in his happy I'm-talking-to-a-little-kid voice. "My name is Grandpa. I'm Grandpa. What's your name?"

Doug looked even more uncertain, and at a loss for words.

"He doesn't want to talk to me," Grandpa explained to Doug, and sounded disappointed.

It was both endearing and a bit heart-breaking at the same time, seeing Grandpa cognizant of himself as a grandpa, trying to socialize with an imaginary grandchild, and being hurt that he was getting no response.

It had started with animals, but Grandpa began imagining little children around the house. In a way it was a small blessing. He loved little children, so in the midst of his loss and confusion his children visitors were a small flash of joy—even if they weren't there for anyone else. And so what? When family came to visit, there might be a few extra guests they couldn't see, but Grandpa was happy to see them.

This was hard for people to understand. Their natural reaction was to find it very uncomfortable, weird, and perhaps even threatening. There was a certain impulse to argue, to say, "No there *isn't* a little boy there"—as if that might somehow stop the detachment from reality. I tried to assure people who were a witness to Grandpa's imaginary friends that it was okay, and to not worry about it. When Grandpa and I were alone I tried to let the issue slide unremarked as much as possible. I knew his grasp of reality came and went fluidly and arguing with him didn't fix anything, and really it didn't matter. Either he figured out his mistake for himself or else he lost interest in the imagined person. If he happened to ask me for confirmation I always told him what I honestly saw, or didn't see.

This slippery nature of existence had its dangers, and by accident I allowed Grandpa to stumble into a less pleasant blending of reality. One day I sat down beside him, and he began to talk about how sad it was. He seemed genuinely upset and I was puzzled. Nothing unusual had happened that morning. What was wrong?

"It's horrible," he said. "You look at them, and you just want to cry. It's sad, sad, sad, and you can't do anything about it."

"About it?" I ventured, hesitantly.

"Yes," he said. "Their faces. They'll be like that the rest of their lives, and it shouldn't be."

I was utterly confused, and I could not for the life of me figure out what had put his thoughts in such a dark place where, apparently, children were being mistreated. But as he rambled on about what seemed a truly horrible situation, somehow I finally pieced together that he had seen an advertisement in some magazine for a cleft lip humanitarian agency. The ad graphically displayed third world children with cleft lips. For Grandpa, with his blurry reality, they had been more than pictures. The cleft lip children had been very real in an excruciatingly immediate sense. It had been for him as if the children were there, right with him in the living room, and his anguish on their behalf was palpable—and yet bereft of any understanding of what the humanitarian agency was doing for the children.

I felt guilty. Unable to do anything else, Grandpa spent endless hours amusing himself by flipping through magazines on the couch, carefully folding them, and sometimes tearing out the pages to fold up into neat little squares. It was a harmless quiet activity—until he came across the unexpected sad little cleft-lip child.

After that incident I went through all the magazines and tore out the pictures of the cleft lip children.

It was one thing for Grandpa to happily chat to the pictures of cute little babies and coo at them like they were really present. It was a pleasant way to pass time, talking with him about what the babies were like, or what their mommies thought. What I didn't need was him plunging into a pit of despair every time he stumbled across the advertisement for a cleft-lip humanitarian agency. Grandpa's reality needed a measure of guarding. He had enough of his own problems without adding the problems of the world to them.

The misinterpretation of visual information was not the only source of Grandpa's seeming hallucinatory behavior. Sometimes Grandpa's thoughts or literal memories leaked into the present so that he might be *thinking* about someone and that thought slipped through into the category of present reality. He might think the person he was remembering was actually present—not because he thought he saw them, but because he *thought about* them. Or, sometimes he remembered events from earlier in the day and thought they were still ongoing.

If someone didn't understand this and didn't know what Grandpa tended to think about, or didn't know what he had been doing earlier in the day, some of his comments could come out sounding like pure lunacy. But if you were able to unravel the personal context of his utterances there usually was at least a bit of scrambled sense behind them.

Sometimes the confusion was as simple as I might ask him if he wanted a cup of coffee which he was then served and drunk. Two hours later someone else might ask him if he wanted a cup of coffee and he would say, "Yeah, that other guy said he was going to get me one." There wasn't an imaginary person bringing him coffee—he had simply forgotten about the previous cup of coffee.

The more interesting occasions were when the muddle of past and present, reality and fantasy, merged in a more complex soup of experience. The intricacies of these conflated events led to unique conversations.

On Saturdays when Grandma was feeling well she liked to go out with my Aunt Daryl and shop. One Saturday evening Grandma tried to converse with Grandpa about what she had done that day.

Grandma concluded her description of what she had done by saying that Daryl would pick up a card for her because Grandma had run out of energy. Daryl's daughter Julie would have her baby any time now, and Grandma wanted to make sure she got a card.

"Oh," Grandpa said. "Was the baby crying this morning?"

"No," Grandma said.

"Oh," Grandpa said again. "I thought probably I imagined it, but the screaming sounded so realistic." Here was a peak into how Grandpa tried to deal with his own mind.

An observer might think at this point that he *had* imagined things, or was going completely nuts. But I had been with him all day, and I knew what had just happened in his mind. "That was the TV, Grandpa," I said. "There was a cowboy movie on this morning," I told Grandma. "And there was a baby crying in it."

Grandpa was silent a minute, thinking. "That was the one with the guy with a rifle," he said.

"Right," I said. He had apparently been following the movie well enough to pick up that the distinctive feature of the hero was that he only used a sniper cowboy rifle instead of a six-shooter. But in the vague muddle of his memory what had stayed with him was the baby crying, and now in talking with Grandma he hadn't been able to separate out what he had watched on TV from what she had done. It made sense—except if you didn't understand it made no sense at all.

Grandpa was silent a little longer. "Well," he said, looking at Grandma, "you going to shoot a path for me?"

Grandma looked at him, and then looked at me. "I'm turning that one over to you," she said.

"She wants you to explain it," Grandpa offered.

"Yeah, I know," I said. Grandpa was trying to talk to Grandma, Grandma wanted me to interpret Grandpa, and Grandpa was explaining to me that Grandma wanted me to interpret him for her. Such was life.

"Well, are you going to do it?" he said.

I was stumped. I knew he wasn't literally talking about wanting someone to shoot for him. I knew he was muddling up the cowboy movie of that afternoon with whatever he was trying to talk about now, but I didn't have a clue what he was trying to get out. So I gave the situation my best shot (pardon the pun).

"I can't shoot a rifle in town limits," I said. "And I'm not quite sure what you're using the metaphor for. You want to go somewhere? I'll take you if you want to go someplace."

"You want to drop in on someone?" Grandma said. "You want to see Helen and Hugh?" Then she looked at me and started laughing.

"No," Grandpa said. "Someone should tell them we don't need them to come around anymore."

"I don't think they'd appreciate that," Grandma said and started laughing some more.

I was getting a little annoyed with her. Grandpa had been trying to have a serious conversation, and she was making fun of him, and on top of that confusing him all the more. I suspected that Grandpa needed to use the bathroom, and had simply used the wrong words to ask for help. But with Grandma offering jokes about going to visit people Grandpa wouldn't be able to get his thoughts sorted out. I suspect he realized Grandma was making fun of him at this point, and his suggestion that someone tell Helen and Hugh they didn't need to come around anymore was his attempt to offer a deadpan joke in return. Regardless, the whole exchange got us no closer to understanding his issue.

The conversation moved on, Grandma talking about the weather and I said I hoped Arlan arrived home before the rain turned to freezing rain.

A little later Grandpa looked at Grandma again and said, "So are you going to shoot a path for me?"

"I passed that on to him," she said, pointing at me.

"I'll take you anywhere you want to go, Grandpa," I said. "You just need to tell me where you want to go."

"Well...you got the vehicle?" he said. "You're not afraid to go?"

"I'm not afraid," I said, still wondering where Grandpa was trying to go with the conversation. "Maybe you could come up with a place I'd be afraid to go."

"Well...I don't want to be a cripple," Grandpa said. "I wish I could go someplace where—"

"He wants you to shoot a path to where he won't be a cripple anymore," Grandma said.

"Oh, come on, Ma," Grandpa said, catching on that she was having fun at his expense.

"I was just using your metaphor, honey," she said defensively.

Somehow the conversation got on to living someplace else and I asked him if he wanted to move, knowing how he didn't like the current location. After talking about the subject in general terms for a bit he said that if it came up he would have to seek and think about it. Then he wanted to know if he was making my life miserable (and by implication that I wanted to move to get away from him).

"No, no," I assured him, and felt bad once again that he had to even consider the thought that he might be making me miserable. "You're not making my life miserable," I said. "I just want to make sure you're happy."

To this day I'm still not entirely sure what Grandpa wanted when he asked me to shoot him a path. Like so many other things Grandpa tried to say, its meaning was lost. He lost much of what he wanted to share.

§§§

Everybody knows Alzheimer's is about forgetting. That reality eclipses another truth. With all that is forgotten, many people don't realize what can still be remembered, and what still remains. With all that is lost, few understand that in Alzheimer's *one can still learn*. To be sure, the things remembered are dwarfed by the things forgotten, and the things learned do not measure up to what was once known. But the gains are still meaningful, and in the context of Alzheimer's ravages perhaps all the more meaningful.

It seems contradictory: Isn't forgetting the opposite of learning? We think they can't both have a part. And yet, they can and they do. On the one hand, for the caregiver it is about learning—learning how to take care of the person with Alzheimer's. On the other hand, for the person with Alzheimer's it is about *learning* how to live with forgetting. How difficult the journey of Alzheimer's becomes depends in a large part on how well both the caregiver, and the sick, learn to deal with the forgetting.

For the person with Alzheimer's the learning how to deal with forgetting begins long before any outsider is aware of it. There are subtle habits—perhaps even unconscious at first—developed to cope with the first problems of forgetting. Then it grows worse, and becomes obvious—the person with Alzheimer's stops old activities or changes his daily routine because things he used to do he can no longer remember how to do. It is easy for the observer to simply think the person "forgot" and no longer remembered that they used to do the particular activity. But in my experience of caring for Grandpa he forgot *how* to do something (like use the bathroom) long before the memory that it was *supposed* to be done was also lost. The person who is learning well how to deal with their Alzheimer's stops an activity because they realize they cannot do it. The person who is not learning how to deal with their Alzheimer's will keep trying and trying—and always end up in frustrated failure.

It is hard to learn how to deal with Alzheimer's. It is hard for the caregiver. But I found in my times of frustration that it was good to remember that learning how to deal with Alzheimer's was even harder for the one with the disease. I, at least, still had all of my mental facilities. Grandpa was in the un-enviable position of trying to use his increasingly broken mental abilities to figure out how to deal with those very same broken mental abilities. Getting through everyday life was mentally exhausting. It was physically exhausting too, and he looked it when I put him to bed. He laid there, limp, sometimes almost asleep as soon as his head hit the pillow. It was another day survived. Another day in the battle of learning how to forget.

Early on, Grandpa was more articulate in his attempts to learn how to deal with his forgetting. In one example, when he first began to have trouble making it to the bathroom during the night he let it be known that he needed a "can" beside his bed so that he could use it when he couldn't reach the bathroom. That was Grandpa thinking about the problem as best he could, and trying to come up with a solution. The problem with the solution was that in his muddle in the middle of the night making sense of the "can" was generally no more successful than reaching the bathroom.

He couldn't find the best solution to his problems all by himself, so I had to help him through the process. I found the ideal method was to coach him (both verbally and physically) toward the desired result, taking it slowly as he learned the new routine. It was a joint effort—I saw the direction things needed to go and I coached Grandpa, and he learned to accept my lead. If every time I realized something needed to change I tried to impose the new reality on Grandpa then friction (to put it mildly) would have often been the result. We had to learn together.

Grandpa didn't simply wake up one morning and forget how to live his life. It was a *process* of forgetting, but also a process of learning how to let go. Independence is a difficult thing to give up—and it should not be quickly taken from someone either. When facing Alzheimer's the caregiver can become so fixated on the fact that the Alzheimer's victim is "forgetting" that they fail to help the person through the steps of learning how to deal with that forgetting. I tried to avoid that trap. My goal was to be with Grandpa wherever he was at in the process, not force the end result on him before he was ready.

It is hard for a person to learn that they are forgetting everything.

For Grandpa, sometimes the learning wasn't precisely acceptance, just resignation. The process wasn't always smooth for Grandpa and me. There were times and situations where he struggled long and hard —like with using the bathroom. Other times he accepted his losses with better grace.

It is natural to imagine that all of the things in life which are hard to learn—such as math, science, or playing a musical instrument—are the beautiful and great things. But I think harder than all of those is learning—and accepting the reality of—forgetting. In its own way navigating the process and accepting the disease of forgetting requires as much grace and skill as a concert musician.

Grandpa took the battle on his terms, with his own frailties and strengths. While helping him in that great struggle, I tried to recognize and cherish the small accomplishments. I tried to acknowledge the victories for what they were. They may have been unimportant things, but for me the little victories were reminders that Grandpa still interacted with the world.

One small example was Grandpa learning to tuck his elbows in when I took his wheelchair through a doorway. When I first started taking him around the house in the wheelchair he would leave his arms jutting out over the side. If I was paying attention I would remember to tuck his arms in when we went through a doorway. But I forgot often enough that he occasionally banged his elbows on the door frame. After several such events I noticed that when we started wheeling down the hall toward the bedroom Grandpa would quickly tuck his elbows in. He had learned that if he left them out they would get banged. Of course he didn't always remember, but it was something he had learned even in his disease.

What Alzheimer's takes and what it leaves is a mystery. As important as it is to care for those ravaged by the losses of Alzheimer's, it is equally important to recognize the things gained, or held, in spite of those losses. Respect is an important part of caring for a person with Alzheimer's.

§§§

- 2008 -

FALLING

With winter came a lull of sorts. This is not to say it became easy street. Both Grandma and Grandpa's health continued to decline, but neither of them at that time were in the midst of a crisis. I felt like I had found a small bit of equilibrium in a world continually out of balance.

I worried that this lull was only the set up for the next crisis.

When January 2008 dawned the most immediate problem I faced was my own health. I had discovered about a year earlier that I had an inguinal hernia, something I realized at that time was probably a congenital defect I had unwittingly been dealing with all my life. The doctor told me it was mild, but agreed that if it was starting to bother me now it would be best to have it repaired.

I didn't want to have the surgery then. It was a relatively minor procedure, but I wouldn't be able to lift anything heavy for (at least!) a week after the procedure. Having the surgery would make it difficult to care for Grandpa until I had recovered. That made me reluctant to do anything about my problem so long as Grandpa was still in the picture. Weighing against that, the hernia *was* starting to bother me and I worried that if I didn't have it repaired it would suddenly become worse some day when I was in the midst of trying to move

Grandpa.

Neither possibility was pleasant to contemplate.

After wrestling with the choice of waiting or going forward with the surgery, I reluctantly opted to go forward. I decided it was better to have a known and scheduled period of disability than a sudden and unexpected disability at the most inopportune time. The date for the procedure was set, and I lined up family help to care for Grandpa for the first few days after my surgery.

I hoped—perhaps with excessive optimism—to be fully recovered before the next crisis in caring for Grandpa. While it may have been naïve to think that he would kindly hold off having any real problems until I was fully recovered, the surgery itself went exceptionally well. It was an outpatient procedure, and I was scheduled for the early morning. I was in the operating room for only about an hour, and was home not too long after 1:00 PM. I had very little post-operative pain and I took no pain medication immediately after coming out of surgery. The only pain medication I took *at all* was two Ibuprofen later in the afternoon for a headache that developed—probably a reaction to the anesthesia I was given for surgery.

I thought this a promising start. I don't know if the lack of pain was due to me being young, healthy, and fit, or because I only had a minor hernia that was congenital and thus not the result of a recent injury. Or maybe it was the result of the surgeon's skill. Likely it was some combination of all the above. Whatever the cause, I ended that day in an optimistic frame of mind.

With scarcely any post-operative pain, my recovery progressed rapidly. With every day it seemed more likely that I would be completely recovered before Grandpa had any problems requiring much help. I had the surgery on Monday, the 7th of January. My dad came down to take care of Grandpa for Monday, Tuesday, and Wednesday. By Wednesday I felt I could do all required normal caregiving functions for Grandpa so long as nothing disastrous happened. Dad went home Wednesday evening.

Thursday evening disaster struck. Of course. The minute I thought everything was good it took a turn for the worse in dramatic fashion. Thursday evening Grandpa spontaneously fell over backward. This time he didn't escape unscathed.

There was no outward cause for the fall. Grandpa was simply standing in the living room, doing nothing. He was staring off into space, lost in his thoughts. I happened to glance over from where I sat at my computer and noticed that he was beginning to sway like a drunk. About five seconds later Grandpa also realized he had become unsteady and started to turn to grab something. With that slight movement he toppled over backward as if someone had given him a hard push. He went down and struck the back of his ribs against a recliner.

By the time I reached him he was gasping, "Don't move me! Don't move me!" in a pained, tight, voice. I first confirmed that he had not hit his spine, and the pain was in his side. I felt a bit of relief then. If the pain was in his side, over his ribs, we weren't dealing with a possible broken vertebrae. I managed to coax him to roll over into a more comfortable position. Then, after allowing the pain to subside somewhat, I helped him up.

It was unclear how badly he had hurt himself. He was not articulate about his pain, and this forced me to decipher the situation on my own. He could clearly stand, and though obviously in pain it did not appear unbearable. I asked him if he wanted some pain medicine and he said no, so I figured his discomfort was not severe and all he had suffered was a bruise, a pulled muscle, or a temporary spasm. Such an injury was not fun, but given that he was an eighty-year-old man who had just toppled over backward, he had escaped better than I feared.

So I thought.

But his injury was not quite so minor as at first it seemed. After his fall Grandpa sat quietly on the couch for awhile, but I could tell by his quietness and stillness that he was in significant pain. I asked him again if he would take some aspirin and this time he readily agreed. Still, since he wasn't moaning or groaning I figured that two aspirin would take care of most of the discomfort he felt.

Later in the evening we completed his bedtime routine of snack, bathroom trip, and then to bed. Everything seemed okay until I helped him lie down and then he exclaimed, "Oh! That's where it hurts!"

We had a problem.

Grandpa *always* laid on his left side in bed, and that was the side he had injured. At this point I had the first glimmer that it might be a difficult night. Nonetheless, hoping for the best, I tried to get him comfortable, tucked him in, and sang him some hymns. He seemed quieted, but not asleep as he normally was by that point. I turned out the light and left, hoping that he would fall asleep and sleep well that night.

Such was not the case. When I arrived later to go to bed myself I found Grandpa up and the room in a state of disarray which showed he had not been resting quietly. He was hurting too much to sleep. Now I had the strong premonition that the night was going to be a *very* bad night.

I tried to get him to lie down again, but it quickly became apparent that his back was hurting him worse. He absolutely *couldn't* lie on his left side and he wouldn't lie on his right side because then he would be facing the wall and that wasn't acceptable. The solution was to move him over to my bed so he could lie on his right side and not face the wall. He felt less discomfort in that position, but it still wasn't comfortable enough for him to rest.

A normal healthy adult with a muscle injury usually discovers that there is one position in which the injured muscle hurts them least. A normal functioning adult will then stay in that position where nothing hurts and apply heat or ice as needed. If Grandpa had been such a person he probably could have passed the night in fitful sleep. But he was no longer a normal functioning person, and the more miserable he was the less coherently he functioned.

The night passed as an exercise in futility for me. I tried to get Grandpa comfortable while he continually worked contrary to his own best interests. I doubt I would have been any more successful if I had been in the peak of my health, but tending him was made all the more difficult by the fact that I had gone through surgery on Monday and this was only Thursday and I was not at all sure how much physical straining I dared do. In such a condition myself, rearranging Grandpa on the bed in search of a more comfortable position was a difficult affair.

In the end, it didn't matter. I would get him marginally comfortable and then he would have to go pee. I would get him comfortable again, hold him in my arms, and carefully rock and stroke him like a little child until he drifted asleep...and fifteen minutes later he would cough and give himself a pain and wake up. Instead of lying still until he fell back to sleep he would shift and that would hurt more, and then he would decide to sit up. It went downhill from there. Then there was no rest, or quiet.

He would not lie down, he would not sleep, and his sitting in bed muttering and moaning incomprehensibly meant I could do nothing for him. It was impossible, and I finally gave up and left him to do what he would. I lay and listened for the second half of the night as he moaned and groaned and muddled around with things in the bedroom. I realized that he would probably have felt most comfortable sitting up on the couch, but I wasn't sure he could make it on his own two feet that far, and at four days out of hernia surgery I was *sure* I wasn't supposed to carry him.

Eventually, as the night waned on toward dawn, Grandpa crawled out of the bedroom and on down the hall. I think he left in search of the bathroom, but forget his reason or destination. His journey simply ended halfway down the hall and he lay there on the floor. At that point, halfway between bedroom and couch, I thought I would try to move him the rest of the way to the couch. With much coaxing I got him back to his feet, but I only managed to persuade him to take a few steps before his mind and body gave out and he just stood where he was and wouldn't go any further. How I wished I could use my normal solution and pick him up!

Instead, I had to be inventive. I brought the wheelchair around and eased him down into it. I then moved him around to the couch and transferred him from wheelchair to couch, surely doing more lifting than I was supposed to in that final transfer. Once I had him situated on the couch I wrapped him up in a blanket and went back to bed. It was 5:30 AM.

I don't know if Grandpa slept, sat quietly, or did something else entirely. All I know is that I woke at 8:30 AM to him peeing in the hall outside the bathroom. So Friday began.

I had to go grocery shopping Friday. My sister came to watch Grandpa, though there wasn't much to do because he spent the entire day sleeping, making up for his sleepless night. While he ended the day more rested, his injury did not seem improved. In the first days following the accident I wasn't sure Grandpa would walk again, ever. He appeared to have lost all ability to hold himself upright, and he made a quick descent to the floor any time he tried to get up.

I worried, but in the end he did recover. Friday night I dragged my mattress out and threw it on the living room floor so I could sleep comfortably while Grandpa slept on the couch. The night passed more sanely than the previous. The next day he was much recovered and after that we were back in our normal beds. Grandpa was still not entirely comfortable, but he could sleep.

I suspect Grandpa suffered more than a muscle injury when he fell. I'm pretty sure he cracked his last rib. On that first most miserable night I was running over in my mind whether I should take him to the emergency room. For anyone else the answer would have been an immediate yes. But his mental condition had deteriorated to such a degree that taking him into a strange noisy place with so many strange people asking him to do so many incomprehensible things would have been like immersing him into his own private hell. A catastrophic reaction from him would have been unavoidable, and that gave me pause.

Under such circumstances I weighed the benefits of taking him to the hospital against the reaction it would provoke. Besides prescribing pain medication and advising limited activity there is little that can be done for a cracked rib, and I knew that. So I decided that unless Grandpa's symptoms became worse the gain from taking him in to the hospital for a prescription of strong pain medication was not worth what it would cost him physically, mentally, and emotionally.

A week later he was much recovered, though his side was still tender. The amount of improvement confirmed to me that I had made the right choice in deciding to not force him to go to the hospital for an examination. But I was still unhappy about having to make such a decision.

Unfortunately—but unavoidably—Grandpa's Alzheimer's induced problems with balance persisted. He almost fulfilled my worst fear, nearly killing himself in another fall.

He had a tendency to want to play on the stairs. Obviously this was very dangerous, and it made me incredibly nervous. I wanted to gate off the stairs, but Grandma was against that. Unless I was going to physically restrain him (already ruled out), there remained little I could do besides encourage him to occupy himself elsewhere.

One evening around supper time a few weeks after his previous fall he was fooling around on the stairs. I asked him if he needed to go to the bathroom. He said yes, and started up the stairs toward me. It was a split flight of stairs with a landing at the halfway point where the front door entered. He was about halfway up the second flight of stairs when I turned away to switch on the bathroom light. I heard a sound and turned back in time to see one of those things you never want to see.

Grandpa had been hit by a sudden bout of vertigo and promptly pitched over backward down the stairs. I caught sight of him just has he began the inexorable plunge, the path of his fall sending him head first toward the steel front door. I only had time to shout.

If he had hit the door he would have died, but God was merciful. Grandpa was still hanging on to the rail and when he reached the end of his arm he pivoted on his grip, his head just missing the door. He came to land somewhat gently on his back. While greatly shaken, he escaped with only a minor scrape to his hand.

Never again did we have so close a call. From that point forward Grandpa began to spend more and more time crawling instead of walking. With so many falls fresh in my mind, I could only see this change as a good thing. Eventually he gave up the stairs. Somehow we made it through the loss of Grandpa's ability to walk without him permanently breaking something, or ending his life. Navigating through this transition period from walking to not walking without some worse injury felt nothing short of miraculous.

§§§

PATIENCE

When I was a little boy, I always asked questions. I wanted to know why. I guess I still do. My parents were tolerant of my inane questions and encouraged the thoughtful ones. Grandpa had less patience. The endless questioning grated on his nerves. One day (after I don't know how many questions) he burst out in frustration, "That Rundy! It's always questions, questions, and more questions! Can't he just accept things the way they are?"

I didn't understand Grandpa's exasperation. I was young, and not self-aware enough to realize I was asking too many questions. But I was, and I did, often.

When I grew older I came to understand Grandpa's loss of patience. I still ask questions, even today, though not in the same endless stream. I don't think anyone should be ashamed of questions. But I do understand now how endless questions can become wearying beyond measure. Call it irony, or call it fitting, but whatever you call it when I cared for Grandpa I received the same endless questioning I had given. He gave back to me questions in equal measure, and more, than I had given him as a little boy.

After Grandpa's fall and injury in January of 2008 he experienced a stretch of time where his night activity was less troubled. It seemed his problems had stabilized, perhaps even improved a little. His number of midnight trips were less frequent, and accidents were rare. The spring of 2008 moved on and I started to think that maybe I no longer needed the linoleum which I had crudely placed on the bedroom floor.

Then in late April we began our descent again. It started with Grandpa being less prompt, efficient, and agreeable for the midnight bathroom trips. He would wake up and then moan and groan for ten or twenty minutes before conceding to the needed bathroom trip. Or we might go to the bathroom and then he wouldn't want to go back to bed. Or some variation.

The bathroom accidents and bedroom messes returned with a vengeance. Two nights in one week we ended up with a lake of urine on the bedroom floor, and once with the hall carpet soaked. On and on it went.

Contributing to this was Grandpa's increasing inability to make prompt trips—or even remembering to complete the journey—to the bathroom. For example, the mess in the hall was because he made it halfway to the bathroom and ran out of steam or forgot where he was going.

Midnight crabbiness also became worse. On Grandpa's part it was due at least in part to his increasingly confused state. If he couldn't comprehend what I was trying to do—or how it would help him do what he wanted to do—then as far as he could tell I was just persecuting him. He didn't understand why I was always dragging him down the hall, making him go through doorways, and making him sit down. Why was I bothering him and hurrying him along so much when he just wanted to go to the bathroom? From his view I manhandled him for no reason. For my part, an increasingly unhelpful patient, and increasingly lengthy and disastrous midnight trips, marked an equal increase in my lack of patience.

I felt caught between a rock and a hard place. If Grandpa couldn't understand what I said or what I was trying to help him do, why try?

If he couldn't remember that he needed to go to the bathroom a minute after he has got out of bed, why take him? I could easily change his wet diaper and save myself the fight over getting him to the bathroom. But (the other half of me said) maybe if I explained things a little more he would understand. Or if I was a little more patient and slow we could make it to the bathroom without nearly having a wrestling match. What could I do better? What should I do? These were the unanswered questions that came in the middle of the night when the minutes grew long, and there was no sleep in sight.

By default, my normal course of action was to offer Grandpa assistance if he seemed cognizant of a need to use the bathroom and was willing to accept help. If he got out of bed and was apparently unable to recognize his own need, or if he started to become contentious about my assistance, I let him be. If he got out of bed and started opening dresser drawers or moving stuff around the room I might then ask him half-heartedly, "Do you need to go pee?" or I might not. A year ago such a question would have likely gained a prompt "Yes, I need to go!" at which point I took him, he did his business, and we'd both get back to bed. Now that question could get a "No, not now," (even if it really was yes) or, "Uh...maybe. I don't know." Even a "Yes," didn't mean he would take the journey agreeably, or do anything once we reached the bathroom. Sometimes he agreed that he needed to go, then demanded, "What are you doing to me?" when I tried to take him to the bathroom.

Often enough I took him to the toilet only for him to sit there for two minutes, then get off without having done anything—not remembering he had anything to do. Ten minutes later he *really* had to go and couldn't hold it until we reached the bathroom. Too often he had already gone no matter when I took him and his diaper was wet and the entire trip was wasted effort. It was discouraging when halfway to the bathroom he would stop and demand, "Jeez, why are you dragging me along like that—let me go!" Or we would arrive at the bathroom and he would grab hold of the sink or door frame and refuse to enter, saying, "What the hell are you trying to do?"

I could carefully explain and gently remove his hands. I could try to block him from grabbing things and slip him into the bathroom before he had a chance to object. I became very good at getting him places in spite of his resistance, but it began to feel more like a grappling exercise than a trip to the bathroom.

Because of all these things, the act of taking Grandpa to the bathroom began to feel completely pointless. Then added on top of that feeling was Grandpa getting crabby at me because I was hustling him along, and my attendant desire to say something snappy back. It was rapidly approaching the point where getting him to the bathroom for urination *was* pointless, and he wasn't even thankful for the effort. In the end it felt like the best solution was to just lay in bed and do nothing.

The conclusion might seem obvious, but life isn't quite that simple. I was emotionally invested in the issue. On the one hand it felt like a concession to my lack of patience if I decided to not take him to the bathroom. On the other hand I was disillusioned by the pointlessness and continual effort required to avoid becoming angry over Grandpa's irritable refusal of my less than perfect help. So I lay in bed and wondered if I was doing what was best in a bad situation, or just doing what suited *me* best in a bad situation. I lay there and wondered if this really was the best, even for me.

Everything had worked so well *before* ("well" being a relative term) because Grandpa understood he needed to go, he wanted me to take him, and I could get him to the bathroom promptly. He would then empty his bladder, and we would both get back to bed in quick order and be able to fall back to sleep. Now his failure to use the bathroom meant that he got out of bed and became a derailed train careening about. When that happened neither he nor I got any sleep. Was there something I could do to keep him from becoming a midnight train wreck? Anything besides just lying in bed?

I didn't come up with any answer. I thought maybe some day I would find one. Or maybe this was just how it would be.

Regardless, there was the cost in lost sleep. Sometimes it was a half hour. Sometimes an hour. Sometimes more. One night Grandpa got out of bed at 11:00 PM probably because he needed to go to the bathroom. In the following *three and a half hours* he sat on his bed and talked incoherently, opened dresser drawers repeatedly, then sat on *my* bed and talked incoherently, bumbled and moved things about the bedroom, and finally ended up on his hands and knees in the corner by the door, completely lost—not knowing where he was, what he wanted, or where he was going. By that point he was so exhausted that he agreed to my suggestion of going back to bed. He was so exhausted and confused I had to physically drag him back to bed. It was not the first time in those three and a half hours that I had put him to bed, but it was only then, at the end, that he finally stayed there, and fell back to sleep.

At 7:00 AM we were up for the day.

It was easy to think, "Woe is me," but however hard it was on me, all of this was much harder on Grandpa. He wasn't doing these things for fun. Alzheimer's made him do it. The compulsion and confusion of the disease drove him. If it was a form of misery for me, it was double the misery for him. As much as I suffered, it ought to have given me compassion for Grandpa. Worse than a few hours lost sleep was losing sleep along with not knowing where you were, where you were going, or what you wanted—and then wetting yourself to top it all off. I had the lost sleep. Grandpa had lost that and everything else besides.

I was reminded of this one day. I had taken Grandpa to the bathroom sometime in the morning and sat him on the toilet to do his business. On my leaving he promptly stood, turned around, and urinated all over the toilet, himself—everything. A little later I was in the bathroom cleaning up the mess with a weary patience. Grandpa stood and watched, and said in absolute misery, "I should just find a bridge to throw myself off. I haven't done anything productive in a long time." The comment reminded me of how he felt in all that was happening, and I chided myself for thinking only about how weary I felt.

§§§

GENE

Doug leaned forward, a twinkle in his eye and said, "Remember the time you pushed Gene out the window?"

"Oh yeah, I remember." Grandpa gave a small laugh. "'Give me a push' he said, so I gave him a push and right out the window he went!"

The details of this story were murky to me, but Doug often returned—with much laughter and goading—to "Remember the time you pushed Gene out the window?" I was told that as children the three boys were playing upstairs in the unfinished construction of the new family house (where they were told they were *not* supposed to play), and Grandpa had pushed his older brother Gene out the window. The boy had fallen a full story to land unscathed on a pile of lumber. Gene was always getting hurt, and this was perhaps one of the few times he escaped injury.

The first few times I heard the story I presumed it was entirely, precisely, true. I imagined that for some reason Grandpa as a little boy had suffered a fit of ire at his older brother which had incited him to push him out the window. Grandpa certainly found the story slightly embarrassing, which seemed part of the reason Doug found it so funny to dig up that particular bit of old family dirt.

As Doug continued to return to the story, and more details slipped out, I began to wonder if my initial impression was correct. Gene was Grandpa's favorite brother, and had been since he was a little boy. I had heard from multiple sources that Gene had looked out for Grandpa when they were growing up, and that Gene was an easygoing guy who got along with everyone. It seemed odd that this easygoing boy who was his younger brother's idol would end up pushed out a window in malice by the idolizing little kid.

Grandpa commented about Gene asking for a push only after Doug had brought up the story on multiple occasions, but this lent a distinctly different impression to the story. Now the boys were horsing around, and Gene, swinging from some piece of construction, had asked for a push to swing harder. An overly vigorous push from Grandpa had sent Gene quite accidentally out the window. Or so it might have been. Doug's mischievous implications left me thinking that Grandpa may had been entirely innocent in his intentions but the result had appeared shady and Doug found humor in suggesting that Grandpa had intended to knock off his brother. Grandpa—having a sensitive conscience—squirmed just enough at the old story to amuse Doug.

This was the teasing of an older brother, even in their senior years.

Grandpa never went out to visit Gene again after I took him early in my time of caregiving. But Gene was never far from Grandpa's thoughts. At random odd times he would stop his activity and ask, "What is Gene doing? I hope he is okay. I hope he isn't freezing, or sick. Somebody should call him to see how he is doing." Once Grandpa became stuck on such a persistent jag of fretting about Gene that I offered to call Gene up so Grandpa could talk to him. The offer was seriously considered until Grandpa chickened out and decided he wasn't able to talk on the telephone.

The articulate worrying about Gene progressed to something different. Grandpa began calling for Gene throughout the day. Sometimes it was a quiet questioning, "Hey, Gene, you there?" Other times it was a shout, "HEY GENE!" demanding a response. Then he would pause as if waiting for an answer.

Reality was growing more fuzzy.

When Grandpa first started this calling I caught him once or twice shaking his head afterward and muttering to himself, "He's not here." Grandpa knew, but he was having a harder and harder time remembering that Gene wasn't present.

"You want Gene?" I asked after a repeated series of calls.

"No, not really, I guess," Grandpa said. "I just want to make sure everything is okay, and he is all right."

That was where it started, but it grew into something more. The sensible part of Grandpa's mind—when it was clear and working— worried about Gene and wanted to make sure he was okay. But I sensed a deeper urge stirring in Grandpa. Some more basic impulse compelled him to call for the Gene who had cared for him, and been there for him.

Since at the start of this Grandpa could remember—when he stopped to consider—that Gene was not present, I wondered how he rationalized the endless calling. Curious, I once asked him why he called for Gene. He said, "I don't know. I know he isn't here. I guess just because he is my favorite brother."

"You like him a lot, don't you," I said.

"Yes," Grandpa said. "I do. He is a real decent fellow. He's...special."

It was an odd moment of striking self-awareness. Grandpa could realize how foolish it was to call for Gene, and yet he couldn't stop. Time progressed and the impulse of calling for Gene grew stronger. The rational understanding that Gene wasn't present began to fade.

Who was Gene really?

Bed time came and I took Grandpa's arm as he tottered down the hall. "Time to go to bed," I said cheerfully.

"Yeah, okay," Grandpa agreed. "HEY GENE!" he bellowed, then finished in a normal tone, "It's time to go to bed. Come on."

Then came the days when in the afternoon Grandpa paused in his activity, confusion suddenly clouding his face. The shout came next, "Hey, Gene!" or "Come here, Gene!" "Help me, Gene!"

Some of the time the calling found its root in an emotional mood. Grandpa felt lost, lonely, uncertain, confused, or any number of other things, and his reaction was to call for someone to set it right, to explain, or whatever. Gene was the big brother who personified the one who could do all those things, and fix all things. He was company, comfort, and Grandpa's other half that was supposed to be there, always.

Gene became the most common word on Grandpa's lips, and with the increased frequency the reason for Grandpa's calling grew less distinct. Sometimes the call was for Gene to come and fix vague metaphysical confusion of why things *were*. Other times the call for Gene came because of a real need—such as required assistance in the bathroom. There wasn't just *one* reason he called for his older brother. Or, I should say, called the *name* of his brother. Gene had come to mean more than the old man living in his trailer down in Pennsylvania. Yes, Grandpa could call for the literal, physical, presence of his brother, but "Gene" was becoming the indistinct *other* of every need and want.

He needed Gene to rescue him from Alzheimer's.

I began to realize I was becoming merged with Gene. When Grandpa called for Gene it was me he really wanted. This didn't happen in a neat transition. Grandpa didn't wake up one morning having melded Gene and I into one person. It was a slow process wherein Grandpa's mind I took up the mantle of all that Gene had come to stand for.

Less and less he called for "Ma," (Grandma) and more and more he called for Gene. Or, really, for me. Rational thought was fuzzy, and Grandpa expected "Gene" to be present. In a way, Gene was present. What Gene had been to him at the beginning of his life I had become at the end.

Initially when Grandpa called for Gene I would answer, "He's not here. What do you want?" which would get varying responses along the lines of, "I want Gene," or "Where is he?"

Sometimes Grandpa would tell me what he wanted, or make something up on the spot when he hadn't really wanted anything at all. As Grandpa began to consistently call for Gene it grew tiring to constantly say, "He's not here," before inquiring what Grandpa wanted. It was then I realized that Grandpa was in the beginning stages of conflating me with Gene and there was no point in saying Gene wasn't present. Instead, I defaulted to simply answering his call of "Gene!" with, "What do you want?"

At first maybe half the time Grandpa would say, "You're not Gene." Then I would say, "No, but Gene isn't here, so I'm answering for him." Soon enough that passed and my answering for Gene satisfied him.

I answered for Gene, and I helped in his stead, but I didn't ever *wholly* became the one and only Gene. I became *a* Gene. I embodied what Gene had been for Grandpa. Even so, in the midst of Grandpa's confusion and forgetting he still maintained some muddled distinction. One day long after I had become accepted as "Gene" I answered Grandpa's call and he said, "No, I don't want you. I want the *other* Gene."

Yes, I was Gene, I was called by no name other than Gene, but at least sometimes Grandpa could still remember he had *another* Gene.

§§§

I drove the wheelchair up to the couch and stopped in front of Grandpa. He was engrossed in carefully folding pages he had torn out of a magazine.

"Ready for lunch?" I prompted.

"It's that time already?" He said and looked up, his expression half perplexed, half shocked, as if lunch has come up on him unexpectedly.

"Yep. Will you come eat?" I asked

"Yeah. Yeah, I guess so," he said. He carefully set aside the torn bits of paper, smoothing them in a neat pile.

I hoisted him to his feet, then turned and lower him into the wheel chair. "All right, Georgie Porgie," I declared with almost maniacal enthusiasm, "it's time for lunch!"

I wheeled him off toward the kitchen. Depending on the day I either threatened to crash the wheelchair into some object or sang loudly for the whole world to hear, "Georgie Porgie pudding pie, kissed the girls and made them cry! When the boys came out to play, Georgie Porgie ran away!" The end of the song would usually find us pulling up to the table. I would then tuck him in at the table and comment in some way on his wickedness for kissing the girls. Grandpa would shake his head and say, "I don't know about you."

I didn't know about me either.

He knew when I was being silly. Sometimes he would indulge me in the deliberate craziness and attempt to articulate some comment to further develop his supposed activity with these imaginary girls. It was fun. Stupid, but fun.

Lighthearted and fun it might have been, but those moments of levity and foolishness could not erase a larger problem: Grandpa was having increasing difficulty understanding the reality of the world around him.

For Grandpa, his ability to understand what he saw began failing before his ability to understand what he heard. I have written about how he would see imaginary people and things. I knew it was getting worse when he began to *not* see things that were right in front of him. Better said, he began to not *comprehend* the things he saw.

Objects lost all meaning.

His visual understanding of the world around him was not consistent. People who weren't around him on a daily basis had a hard time understanding that his visual cognition could fluctuate so drastically. Some days (or at certain times of the day) he was better. Other times he was worse. The trend was downward, and by the end of autumn 2008 one thing I noticed was his increasing difficulty visually comprehending every day objects, and even spatial existence itself.

People of sound mind easily understand what they are seeing. We interpret what our eyes see without even realizing we do it. For Grandpa it became something he struggled to grasp. Recognizing people and things was mental effort for him, much akin to attempting to solve a difficult problem. And when it became too much work, or he was not paying attention, he simply didn't interpret or make sense of his surroundings. He ended up just being "someplace" with "things" around him. Then he didn't know where he was, and he didn't know where anyone else was around him.

In that situation he felt alone no matter if there were other people in the room because he couldn't comprehend their presence. This was apparent when he asked Grandma where she was when she sat right in front of him, right before his eyes. But sometimes the inverse was also true. He sometimes talked to Grandma as if she was present when she wasn't in the room. One way or the other, he wasn't anchored spatially in the world. He asked people where they were, and asked them where he was, and asked them where things were—and understood none of the answers.

"I'm sitting in my chair," Grandma said in response to his query.

"Where is that?" he asked, looking right at her.

"Why don't you sit on the couch," she said.

"Okay, where is that?" he said, still standing beside the couch.

This was Grandpa at his worst. He was as good as blind then— worse actually, because a blind man still knows how to orient himself. Grandpa not only failed to understand what he was seeing, but he couldn't relate objects to each other within space. At a doorway he could turn left or right, but had no understanding which direction would take him where, or why he would want to go in either direction. He simply went on impulse, or faint memories—which meant when he came out of the bathroom he was just as likely to go to the bedroom as the living room. He had no idea of his destination, and no surety even in the direction. I couldn't point things out to him, or explain to him how things were done, because what he saw had no meaning. Objects had no meaning. We existed together in a dream world where anything was possible.

He was not at his worst all the time, but by the autumn of 2008 he was rarely at his best, and his best was far from what it had been a year previous. Most of the time he hovered somewhere in the middle— understanding some things, but existing in a limited state of awareness of his surroundings. It was an awareness I could see shrinking with every passing month.

There existed a strange tension between the sickness of his failing mind and the retained cognitive ability he still possessed. His mind could not keep him anchored within the present, so people and things suddenly appearing was accepted without question. Since—to his mind—people came and went without rhyme or reason, it was perfectly natural for him to suddenly start talking to an imagined person sitting on the couch. There was no thought that it might be strange to have someone appearing in his house whom he didn't remember coming, and may not even recognize. After all, he couldn't remember *anyone* coming into the house. He lived utterly in the present. The only thing that mattered was that the person (the imagined person) didn't respond to his conversing. Then he could become indignant or hurt.

For a long time Grandpa's hearing was his great support. Though his eyes deceived him, his ears would reassure him. If he called for someone and they answered he would be able to place them in relation to himself and would be comforted. But by autumn 2008 his ability to understand what he heard had begun to noticeably fail as well. Sometimes he would call and someone would respond and he would say, "Where are you?" sounding very much like a person lost in a great dark void. In reality the person responding might be in the living room with him, or just over his shoulder in the kitchen.

He was losing the ability to spatially place sound.

He was also losing the ability to distinguish sounds. We recognize people when we see them, and we recognize people when we hear them. Grandpa had for some time struggled to recognize who he saw—his own sons and daughters, and even increasingly Grandma. This problem began to spread to his hearing as well.

I must distinguish between *recognizing* and *knowing*. He never demonstrated any forgetfulness that he was married and had children, grandchildren, and even great grandchildren. His failure was that he couldn't recognize, or recall, *who* he was seeing. For example, he might say, "Who is that?" And I would say, "That's Daryl" (his daughter, one of my aunts) and he would say, "Oh, how are you doing, Daryl," and then he would prove that he knew who she was by asking (without any outside prompting) about her daughters, showing that he truly knew who Daryl was—he just didn't connect the knowledge of his daughter and granddaughters with the person in front of him. There was some comfort in seeing that he still knew he had a family, but it was a small comfort, and still incredibly sad to see his increasing difficulty recognizing people and remembering their names. The real marker of decline in this regard were the few times he was uncertain about Grandma's name, or unable to remember it. These began as very rare blips, but that they occurred at all with Grandma's name indicated the depths of the problems he faced. It showed how far the fuzzy edges in his life had progressed.

Since I had discovered how much simpler it made life for me if I answered Grandpa when he called for Gene, I started answering when he called "Ma!" as well. Soon, I was answering in the place of whoever was called—brother, wife, children, or imaginary people.

At first Grandpa would say, "You're not Ma" when I answered his repeated shouts for "Ma," but he began to protest less and less. I initially thought he was becoming accustomed to someone answering for Grandma, as he had with Gene. Then an incident revealed that at least some of the time he had trouble distinguishing who answered him.

One evening he said, "Hey Ma!"

"What?" I said.

"Why don't you come sit down beside me," he said.

"Okay," I said and got up from the computer and went over to sit beside him.

"Not you," he said, seeing me approach. "That woman said she would come sit with me."

"No, that was me who answered you," I said.

From that point on it became increasingly clear that he often couldn't distinguish (or perhaps simply couldn't remember) *who* answered him. The answer was what he wanted, and who gave it wasn't important. This discovery made life much easier for me because now when Grandpa called incessantly for anyone (not just Gene) I knew I could answer and quiet him. If he said, "Ma, how are you doing?" I could say, "Just fine," and he would be satisfied. Or if he said, "Ma, where are you?" and I would say, "Over here," and he would be appeased.

It was not as if he never recognized who was speaking. Sometimes he could distinguish voices, just as sometimes he could still recognize what he saw. But I think he had to pay careful attention to distinguish who was speaking, and sometimes that wasn't important. Sometimes when he called "Ma," all he really wanted was someone who cared about him to answer.

His abilities continued to deteriorate. Reality came unglued more and more. One day he was hollering, "Ma? Ma? Ma?" so I came over and said, "What do you want?"

He stared at me for a long minute. "Well?" he finally prompted. "She asked you what you wanted."

That was a new one for surreal exchanges where I somehow ended up being responsible for carrying on both ends of the conversation as two (or perhaps three?) different people.

Again, later, he was calling for Gene but seemed to have no

particular want in mind. When I came and inquired, he muttered and mumbled various unintelligible things while pointing at the chairs and objects around him. I assured him that everything was all right.

"Well, yeah, okay..." he said, and turned back to his fussing. Ten seconds later, "Hey, Gene!"

"Yeah, what do you want," I said. "I'm still standing right behind you. I came last time you called."

"Oh, geez!" He startled sharply. In the space of two breaths he had already forgotten I was there. "Yeah, I guess you did," he said. "Well, how am I going to distinguish between when you and I speak?" he asked.

Grandpa wasn't stupid, and Alzheimer's wasn't making him stupid. It was making it difficult for him to interact with the world because he was increasingly unable to recognize the meaning and function of objects, sounds, people, and even distinguishing between what was real and fantasy. But these were problems of perception, not intelligence. In his worst states of confusion he was still keenly aware of being considered stupid. He could detect the slightest whiff of contempt in a phrase, the least hint of disgust in a tone. I learned to be very careful how I expressed myself around him. An errant sigh, or a slightly curt response could wound him deeply. The sense of my words mattered much less than the *attitude* they expressed. I could be incredibly silly in the actual words I said, but if the tone was loving, that was all he really cared about.

I learned to not be picky over the logic of words and just let the love come through. Grandpa called for "Ma" and "Gene" because he wanted someone there who loved him, and when I responded he knew I was there and I loved him, even if I called him Georgie Porgie. Maybe he knew I loved him especially because I called him that.

So life went on. Things grew crazier, but somehow the crazy talk and nonsensical living was starting to seem normal. After a year and more of caring for Grandpa, the strange no longer felt strange anymore. I called it living like Alice in Wonderland, typified by the following evening:

I was rushing around the kitchen trying to make supper. Grandpa was busy doing his thing. In the evening this usually meant either messing around in the kitchen while I worked, or else sitting on the couch and calling for someone to tell him if everything was set to rights, and complaining that the pillows weren't working. This evening he was sitting on the couch, but around the halfway point in supper production he had to go to the bathroom so I stopped what I was doing and got him to the toilet. I then returned to the kitchen where I kept half an ear on his continued muttered complaints about the (to him) incomprehensible and malfunctioning nature of the world.

Finally a plaintive squawk became loud enough that I decided it was time to check on him. A quick dash away from the food on the stove to the bathroom and I asked, "What's the matter?"

"I can't get this to work right," he said, holding up the carefully folded hand towel.

Seeing that he was done using the bathroom I said, "That's okay, I'll take care of it for you." I hung the towel on the rack. "There you go. You're all done," I assured him, and then rushed back to the food on the stove.

He didn't follow, and as I worked the food on the stove I heard continued befuddle mumbling about things not working and not being where they were supposed to be.

"Everything is fine," I yelled from the kitchen. "You're all done!"

"What?" came back the alarmed shout. "Who died?"

"Nobody died!" I called back.

"Oh. You said nobody died."

Short length of silence.

"Well, okay. Let's go." His voice drifted down the hall, obviously talking to himself, or, more precisely, to his imagined companions. "Come on, girls. Come on." Brief pause. "Come on, girls. Girls!"

"There isn't anybody, Grandpa," I called out. "It's just you, me, and the trees."

"Yeah. Yeah...I guess that's what I meant, the trees," he said.

"I don't know—" I heard his voice beginning to move down the hall and then caught a glimpse of him crawling past the kitchen entrance on his way to the couch. "I don't know anything," he said. "Money isn't worth anything, [uncertain] isn't worth anything, and I don't think I'm worth anything," he finished.

§§§

WHEN LIFE IS CRAZY

Sometimes Grandpa's confusion could be endearing, but sometimes it was difficult. And sometimes it left us with very unpleasant choices. We faced just such an unpleasant choice when Grandma had an eye exam. Because of Grandma's continuing poor health I drove her to the appointment, and took Grandpa along because he couldn't be left alone in the house. Grandpa and I stayed in the car. This saved him from the stress of going into a strange environment, and the risk of him attempting to disassemble the ophthalmologist's waiting room in an effort to get "things" to work right.

Grandpa didn't mind waiting in the car, so long as Grandma didn't take too long, but his patience lasted only about an hour. After an hour he began to get fidgety. I kept him occupied for a little longer with my MP3 player which had the entire audio Bible on it. I let him listen to that and he remained somewhat content a little longer.

Then came his need for the bathroom.

Grandma's eye exam ended up taking nearly two whole hours. That amount of time was far longer than Grandpa cared to stay in the car, especially when somewhere around an hour and a half into the wait he had to go to the bathroom. He may have needed to go earlier, but it was only then his need made him articulate.

This brought about a bit of a problem. There was no way he could manage walking sensibly into the ophthalmologists office and asking to use the bathroom. And we had not packed the wheelchair because there had been no intention to cart Grandpa around. Regardless, there was the issue of his bathroom trips turning into major accidents. I didn't think the staff would appreciate it if he urinated all over their bathroom—or something worse.

"I have to go pee-pee," Grandpa said.

I wanted Grandma to appear right then so I could take him home. But Grandma wasn't appearing. Grandpa was wearing a diaper, so when he insisted I finally said, "Then just go, Grandpa. You have a diaper on, I can easily change you when we get home. Don't worry about it."

Unsurprisingly, such an explanation wasn't satisfactory. Grandpa and his bathroom needs and usage was no longer much about cognizant rationalization. It mostly consisted in the fragmentary remains of deep seated habits which weren't subject to discussion. He felt a firm compulsion to not soil himself, even when this meant pulling down his diaper and urinating on the carpet, in the sink, or on the table. There was no sense in it, and so no possible way to reason with him about it. He simply had to go, and didn't want to do it on himself.

"I got to find a bush or some place," he said, and started scrabbling to find some way to out of the car.

"Grandpa, you don't want to do that." I tried to explain as gently as possible. "You don't want to get arrested for indecency or something," I said, attempting to jest. "Just let it go. Don't worry about it."

We were sitting in a parking lot right along the main drag with cars whizzing by—not an ideal location for going in the brush. Even if we did seriously contemplate such an idea the only nearby bushes were the landscaping in front of the building, which neither the proprietor or the customers would have appreciated us watering. I felt sorry for him. He must have needed to go very badly, and didn't really understand my answer beyond the fact that I didn't want him to do what he wanted to do. For one second I thought about getting him out of the car and taking him into the office to use their bathroom. Then I quickly played that thought out: "Hi, this decrepit old man I am dragging needs to use your bathroom, or perhaps we'll just end up peeing all over your floor. It happens sometimes, I'm sure you won't mind."

No, we wouldn't do that. Grandpa would have to suffer.

"I *really* have to go," Grandpa said.

It was awful.

"I'm sorry," I said. "You can't get out. It's okay, don't worry about it."

"I'll just do a little bit," Grandpa said, finally managing to get the car door open.

I left the driver's seat and went around to put his feet back in the car, trying to kindly explain that he would have to wait, it didn't matter, and he didn't have to hold it in. Then I climbed back into the driver's seat and electronically locked us in. I tried to not laugh at the absurd stupidity of it all. It wasn't funny, but who would have ever thought I'd be locking myself and my grandfather in the car so he would wet himself? What a cruel sick thing to do, and yet somehow I found myself in the place where it seemed the *least* unacceptable option. How does life get like this?

"How do you get out?" Grandpa insisted, still trying to work the door, and I kept trying to calm him and explain to him why it had to be this way. "Yeah, I understand what you're saying," he finally said. "It's just that I..."

"You don't want to pee yourself," I finish for him.

"Yeah," he agreed, though the thought was probably not so clearly fixed in his mind.

We both lapsed into silence until a little later Grandpa said, "It's strange, I don't know, but the urge to go isn't so bad anymore. I don't need to go, so you don't need to worry about it."

I didn't bother to explain to him that the reason he suddenly didn't need to go anymore was because he had just gone in his diaper. It was sufficient that he was no longer in distress. It was then that forgetfulness was a small blessing.

When Grandma finally showed up and we returned home we ran into more difficulty. Because the house was a split level, with the garage as part of the basement, there wasn't a lot of walking required to make it from the car to the couch upstairs. But when I helped Grandpa out of the car he said, "Boy, my legs feel so weak I don't know if I can hold myself up."

I thought maybe I could coach him into the house since it was only a few steps, but he still wouldn't budge, even with a little forward prodding. When he simply leaned on his cane and looked at the door as if the distance were a million miles I knew getting him to the couch on his own feet would be a huge struggle. I decided it wasn't worth the fight.

"Okay," I said. "I'll carry you." I scooped him up in my arms, headed into the house, and started up the stairs.

"No, you'll hurt yourself," Grandpa protested. "I don't want you to injure yourself."

"I won't," I said. "It's no problem."

Carrying him was almost miraculously easy compared to coaching and assisting him. He was quite light and rested in my arms like a baby, apparently finding no pain or discomfort from the carrying position. Still he fretted and protested. So I said, "Don't worry, I can do it easily. Want me to show you? I can sing and dance while carrying you."

So I sang "La-Da-De-Dah" like some grand opera song and sort of hop-danced the rest of the way up the stairs and over to the couch, where I carefully deposited him. I don't know why I did it. I guess when life was that crazy I had the urge to make it crazier.

§§§

Carrying Grandpa became increasingly common. It took him a while to become comfortable with the idea. Another day I came back from a forty-five minute bicycle ride to Grandpa in urgent need of going to the bathroom. He got all turned around and *insisted* in a desperate sort of way on using the basement bathroom in spite of my suggestions. So I helped him down the stairs, plopped him on the toilet, and then dashed off to my computer to write down some witty dialog that had come to me while out riding. Sometimes the best writing inspiration comes halfway through a bike ride.

It really wasn't wise for me to leave Grandpa unsupervised in the bathroom anymore—though I still did it because it was immensely boring to stand around twiddling my thumbs waiting for him to finish his business. Instead of standing around waiting for paint to dry (I'll use that euphemism), I often put Grandpa on the toilet and then checked back in on him later. Typically this involved the upstairs bathroom which was a lot closer to my normal activity where I could easily overhear him. That afternoon I returned from writing down my literary brilliance and discovered that rather than just urinating Grandpa had pooped—and attempted to wipe his behind. I found him scrubbing the sink with his used toilet paper.

Served me right.

Sometimes something happened that I realized I had not anticipated in the slightest—and yet I should have. This was one of those times. I felt stupid for having not imagined that—of course!—he would forget that he had just used the toilet paper to wipe his bottom and so would revert to his cleaning obsession. Very logical. And yet somehow I had not anticipated it.

At such moments I tried to chant thoughts along the lines of "Bleach cleans everything. Bleach will make it clean."

There was a bit of hasty crises management as I quickly got the soiled toilet paper away from him and into the toilet. I then rushed upstairs to retrieve the box of baby wipes to begin the process of cleaning the sink, Grandpa's hands, and his bottom.

Long before this incident a large bottle of disinfectant had already become my friend. I didn't use it on Grandpa's person because it was too harsh, but for cleaning nearly every other surface the bottle was right beside me. That bottle and I spent a lot of time together.

With the garbage disposed of, and the situation restored to normalcy, I suggested we go back upstairs. He was agreeable, but as soon as he stepped out of the bathroom he slumped slightly and said, "I just don't feel like I have any strength." This would have been one of the many good reasons to *not* go downstairs to the basement bathroom in the first place, but of course he had not understood my reasoning earlier.

"Well, would you like me to carry you?" I said, half joking as I mimicked the act of scooping him up in my arms.

Since he was never exactly agreeable before, I thought it would be the same refusal, but he said, "Well, if you can do it without hurting me and without messing yourself up..." It seemed his level of trust in me had grown, or (more likely) his weakness and inability had reached the point where he saw no other option.

Without waiting for any second thoughts on his part, I scooped him up in my arms and carried him upstairs. I deposited him on the couch and he seemed rather amazed that so much distance had been covered so effortlessly.

At first carrying him was a rare occurrence, but from this point on he offered less and less objections. It became a matter of course, unremarked as though being carried was a normal state of affairs and always had been. The occasions when he needed carrying became increasingly common. Toward the end, a typical evening might include Grandpa crawling off the couch and ending up snoozing on the floor. When bedtime came, rather than going through the hassle of hauling him up into the wheelchair I would simply squat down, scoop him up in my arms, and carry him off to bed. It was a simple solution, but it was also a marker of how far Grandpa's disease had progressed.

When Life is Crazy

§§§

IN THE DARK

Spring of 2008 became early summer. There were good days and bad days, and plenty of just average days. But those bad days were always hiding around the corner, ready to leap on me like some lurking beast as soon as I let my guard down. I had to be always ready for those bad days.

And bad nights. Those bad nights could strike when least expected.

A night in late June 2008 started out okay. In fact, it started out pretty good. I got Grandpa into bed with no unusual trouble, sang him a few hymns and was in bed myself and turning out the lights by 10:30 PM. That wasn't going to bed early, but it wasn't going to be terribly late for my present life. I looked forward to a decent night's rest.

At midnight Grandpa woke up—and I'm not sure he went back to sleep for the rest of the night.

These kind of disasters unfolded slowly. There are many hours in the night, and desperate hope for sleep does not die quickly. At first I wasn't certain how bad it would end up. Minutes ticked by as I tried to wish it all over. Then the next five minutes passed, and the next after that. Eventually the hoping gave out.

Sometimes there was an obvious reason for Grandpa's insomnia—a head cold, or chest congestion. Other times there was no explanation outside of his own broken mind. I don't know why he didn't go back to sleep that night. Maybe I should have changed his diaper. Maybe a wet diaper was keeping him awake. But he had slept with a wet diaper many nights before without the least trouble. Sitting here, looking back, some kind of discomfort with his diaper is the only legitimate *reason* I can come up with. Perhaps it was that, but I don't think there was any reason as such. I think he woke up because he had to go to the bathroom and when he woke up his mind wandered off down a dark path and couldn't find its way back.

This was one of those fateful occasions when Grandpa *forgot* he was supposed to be sleeping.

At least that is my explanation.

In any case, Grandpa didn't quietly go back to sleep. He began to agitate, and talk. I lay on my bed and tried to sleep. He agitated, and I hovered on the edge of sleep, thinking, *Please, let him lay his head down and sleep.*

I tried to pretend it would all go away, but it was not to be. If he lay down for a moment he soon sat up again. He fiddled with his bed and talked.

Seeing that there might be no quick end to the matter, I donned my ear plugs, put a pillow over my head, and struggled to ignore him. I may have dozed. I was aware that he still was not settling down, but I persisted in trying to jump off into the oblivion of sleep. It ended in failure as I was conscious of Grandpa getting more agitated, and sleep fled away. I removed my earplugs and pillow to find him sitting on the edge of his bed with some object of clothing in his hand, and a dresser drawer pulled out on the floor.

I recognized all the signs of a disastrous night. Grandpa was in his "lost" state where it was impossible to speak intelligently to him, or get him to do anything. There was nothing tangible he actually needed. The end result was that he fumbled around doing various fiddly things all about the room, asked questions of thin air, and talked to himself in an attempt to find himself. All of it was futility that only ended when exhaustion overcame him and sleep took him. There was nothing I could do except ride it out, and try to guess when he was finally tired enough that some physical prompting would get him to lay down and fall asleep.

I found it very difficult to deal with this type of situation. In the middle of the night I was not thinking clearly, and desperately wanted to sleep. If I grasped that Grandpa had a need I usually could muster myself up to answer that need and then go back to sleep (or try to go back to sleep). But in such a situation as this, I didn't know what to do. The first impulse was to roll over in bed and mentally will Grandpa into a different world and sleep. That rarely worked for me. I usually ended up lying in a state of dozing, thinking I ought to do something (but what?), and feeling the despair well up as the minutes ground by.

The idea was to get Grandpa back into bed and asleep. But how? The temptation was to sit up and snap, "Get back in to bed, lay down, and go to sleep!" as one would to an unruly child. I didn't do that because it wouldn't work. (An obvious point from this distance, but after several hours of such madness I started entertaining the possibility of just about anything.) Even in my frustration I knew that such a command might make Grandpa angry, it might make him hurt, but it certainly wouldn't make him any more cognizant of where he was or what he was supposed to be doing. Perhaps the ideal thing would have been to turn all the lights on, gently coax him to bed, and then sing him songs until he settled down and went to sleep. That might have been the best thing. But lying on my bed in an exhausted doze made getting up and putting on a pleasant attitude seem like a task beyond accomplishing.

The end result was that I settled for a middle ground. I lay in my bed until I guessed Grandpa might be at the point of exhaustion—and then I gathered up the willpower to get myself out of bed. Then I went and physically picked him up and put him back into bed, hoping that

I was right, and he was tired enough to go to sleep.

If not, in a few minutes he would be up and back at it.

In retrospect I can see the terrible sadness of Grandpa's situation. He was truly and utterly lost—both physically, and in his mind. I can see that now, but at the time it was hard to get beyond his annoying constant stream of dialog.

The dark hours were filled with a rambling Grandpa monologue.

"Hmmm. I wonder if those were the Northern Lights."

"What is this?"

"What should I do with this?"

"Where does this go?"

"What did you say?"

"Are you awake, Ma? Are you there?"

"Answer me. I can't see, Ma."

"Where are you?"

"Ma?"

"Gene?"

"Magene?"

"What am I doing?"

"Where am I?"

"I don't know where I am."

"Oh hum hum hum."

Such would go on *endlessly*, and if I answered one question it would be quickly followed by another. Any parent with questioning young child knows this routine.

If I answered with the least bit of irritation in my voice he would become indignant—that *I* should be irritated over his *most reasonable* activity. Since nothing productive ever came from answering his questions I found it saved my breath, energy, and irritation to simply be silent most of the time and let his words wash over me. Intelligible words mingled with the unintelligible, moaning and groaning. It was as if the stream of noise was there simply to keep him from falling back to sleep. Eventually talking wasn't enough and he would get out of bed and start crawling about the room, fiddling with the floor, fiddling with the dresser, fiddling with the stuff under my bed, fiddling with my bed, and fiddling with my blanket.

Knowing what is the right thing to do, and the wise thing to do, and acting upon it is hard at 2:00 AM.

On this particular occasion at 4:00 AM I put Grandpa back in bed for the second time in those fours hours since midnight. I'm sorry to say I didn't do it with gentle affection. I roughly deposited him in bed, and he started to struggle. Which was to be expected. One thing is sure in midnight watches: I don't know what I should do but I *do* know what I shouldn't do—and somehow I do what I know I shouldn't do, ending up with the bad results I *knew* would happen. I didn't know if I was more mad at Grandpa or myself. At least *I* should have known better.

So it was 4:00 AM and after spending four hours keeping himself awake Grandpa was still going just as strong as he had been at midnight. As best as I could tell he only had two hours of sleep for the entire night (and myself no better). Sometimes I wondered how an eighty-year-old man could do it. I would have thought sheer exhaustion would set in after two hours, and certainly after four. But at this point it was clear the night had become a complete and unmitigated failure, and there was no possible way I could remedy it. Not only was the night shot, but it was now guaranteed that Grandpa would be a wreck for the following day, which meant I had another 12 hours or more to slog through before I had any chance at recuperation. Bad nights were followed by bad days. Exhaustion ravaged Grandpa's ability to function, and all the more so as he declined. It was a terrible thing to be in the middle of a bad night, hours on end spent sitting up with Grandpa in his lost rambling, and *know* that the next day would be even worse. The knowing was horrible. I knew there would be no respite, no mercy, and the hours stretched on interminably long. I sat in the dark, listening to

Grandpa, and half thought, half silently pleaded, "How am I going to make it through? How am I going to hold on?"

I could leave Grandpa in the bedroom and get maybe two hours of peace and quiet—if not sleep—somewhere else in the house before the next day started. Or else I could stay with him and listen to his monologue until dawn broke.

There didn't seem to be much of a choice.

I left and went downstairs to try to get what sleep I could. I slept maybe two hours. When I woke I went back to check on Grandpa and found him sitting on my bed, still fiddling with things and muttering to himself, the room in even greater disarray than when I had left. By all appearances he hadn't slept in those two hours. It was amazing.

Thus began the bad day.

Lack of sleep rendered Grandpa mindless. A particularly bad night would render him incapable of eating, drinking, or moving himself about the house. Each meal became an effort to get him to eat *something*, however small the amount. At breakfast he drank half a cup of coffee and dumped the rest on the floor. He was not even able to get a spoon into his mouth, so I had to feed him breakfast. He only ate half a bowl, and refused any more. Afterward I carried him into the living room and put him on the couch. He got off the couch and spent most of the morning on the living room floor, sleeping some. At lunch I wheeled him to the table in the wheelchair and laboriously managed to coax him into eating most of a small tub of pudding and a small tub of chicken stew. He paid no care, or attention. Every spoonful I managed was a victory. At supper I convinced him to eat a few spoonfuls of spaghetti and meatballs, a few sips of coffee, and a few bites of cake. That was all. I took him back to the couch, which he determinedly left and spent the evening sleeping on the floor.

If I was lucky, I got 500 or 600 calories into him all day and maybe 8 or 12 ounces of liquid. This was all expected—the day didn't turn out one bit different than I anticipated after Grandpa slept only 2 hours the night before. After a while I knew how some things would go. All I could do was soldier on, and hope he would eat better the next day and make up for what he had lost.

I survived that day. It was the second day after a bad night which felt like it would kill me. Then all my lack of sleep and exhaustion caught up with me. The second day was always tough.

The silver lining to the cloud of these miserable days was Grandpa's inability to do two bad nights in a row. That was one thought I tried to console myself with when a sleepless night turned into morning, and a bad day dawned. I told myself the next night would be better. Day by bad day, that was the most I could hold on to.

§§§

Still, the bad nights kept coming. The night are the lost time. In darkness, nothing has meaning.

Dragged to wakefulness, I glanced at the clock.

It said midnight, or close enough.

I rolled over, trying to will myself back to sleep. But sleep wouldn't come. The talking time had begun.

It came in the darkness, a low disembodied voice. The words were slow, weary, and sad.

"I don't know," he said, but he wasn't talking to me. Not really.

The words went on, rambling, running together, sometimes slurred. He was exhausted, but it did not stop.

What was the need? What was that question he had? It slipped his mind, but he knew it was there. If only it would come to him. I heard his words as I lay in the darkness, but no answer I gave was ever enough.

"I can't," he said, but he didn't even know what he wanted to do.

It was that nameless hour. In the darkness he was lost, lost in his own thoughts and the forgottenness that dogged him for every waking hour. I could not find him to bring him back. He sat there on the edge of his bed and talked, and I laid in mine and listened.

We lived that vigil together, in the hours when the world slept.

If only the words had meaning. If only they formed some request I could have answered, some need I could satisfy. If I could have fixed it, I would have. But there was no fixing, so I listened.

Maybe his back was bothering him. There was nothing I could do. All I could do was listen, and wait for it to end. Utter exhaustion would come, or morning, eventually.

His words rambled on from incomprehensible statement to half formed question. A question became a complaint which then was a request, ending as a prayer. "In Jesus name, amen," he finished.

The words went on. "Oh, Ma," he said. "Oh, Mother." Then, "What did you say?"

He listened for an answer, an answer to a question beyond his grasp. "Oh, God," he groaned.

I wished I could fix it. I listened to him stir restlessly on his bed. The bed springs creaked and I knew he was getting down on the floor. He would crawl in the darkness like a blind man feeling his way around the black room, but more than blind because nothing had meaning. He was searching, for something. He was lost in the bedroom, lost in the night, lost in his own mind, beyond the reach of any help to bring him back.

He wanted help.

"Do you need something?" I spoke into the darkness.

"Yes, yes," he said.

"What do you need?" I said.

"I'm trying to say the words," he told me. "But I can't do it."

He couldn't say them, and he couldn't think them clearly either. The thoughts were half formed, and they tormented him at the edge of his mind.

He returned to his mumbling. The garbled words came, the weary moans of an old man lost in the night.

It would be a long night.

In the Dark

§§§

No Going Back

The morning was cool, even cold, when we climbed up onto the roof of the small garage addition. This was a long time ago, and it was my first roofing job. I was a small boy and to me it felt dangerous and scary up on the roof of a one story garage. In reality, there was little danger, and I had little to do with the roofing. It was Grandpa's garage, and my Dad had come to help him re-shingle the roof. My older brother Teman and I might hold some nails or other tools for the men, but mostly we were simply tagging along for our first supervised introduction to the home repair task of roofing.

The day warmed as the morning passed, and my fear of heights faded. Soon enough I felt like a seasoned professional, holding things, carrying things, and fetching for the two people doing the actual work. The roof was a small job, and at supper time we finished up for the day. To the little me, it felt like we had accomplished great things.

Some eight years later I was back on a roof with Grandpa. This time it was the front of Grandpa's house that needed shingling. I was about fifteen and Grandpa had reached his late sixties. Now I truly had become experienced in all the vagaries of home repair, and Grandpa was getting old. Late sixties is an age by which most men would have long ago given up climbing on the roof, but Grandpa was there, taking the lead. He had started the project alone but had soon discovered he was no longer the man he had been. With great reluctance, he was forced to concede that—at almost seventy years of age—he needed help roofing.

It was a Friday in early summer. Teman and I had been picked up by Grandpa in the morning for a day of roofing. Tomorrow Dad and his brothers would show up—the full crew to finish the job. Much as Grandpa needed the help, the prospect of so many people helping put him in a bad mood. He didn't like needing help, or accepting help. He wanted to get as much done as possible before all the help arrived on Saturday. Trying to complete all the work before help arrives might seem contradictory to the whole idea of help, but that was Grandpa.

The day turned out very hot for early summer. We worked and sweated under a blazing sun. Progress went slowly. Grandpa's back bothered him, and with that heaped on the frustrations of work I sensed it took all of his effort to keep from descending into a very foul temper. I felt bad for him, but also a little concerned. Teman and I were drinking plenty of liquids to compensate for the water lost through sweat while working on the hot roof, but Grandpa continued in his usual habit of drinking a few cups of coffee and smoking cigarettes. I worried that he would keel over from heat stroke.

Grandpa didn't collapse from the heat. One of my lasting memories from that day is the image of him working on the roof: smoldering cigarette tucked between his fingers, hammer in hand as he stooped at his labor. We persevered through the afternoon, but didn't make much progress that day—mostly because Grandpa had a particular idea of how the work should progress which wasn't the most efficient or speedy. The roofing project was finished later, after a swarm of additional helping hands overwhelmed Grandpa, working everywhere at once and doing the work faster, and differently, than he wanted it done.

What didn't occur to me then, but does now is Grandpa's toughness. Few men in their late sixties would be willing to get up on a roof—even less would have the strength or endurance for a day of roofing work. Rare indeed is the man today of that age who is capable, much less insistent, on working under the hot sun. Grandpa was a tough old man, but it was a quiet toughness that you often missed.

§§§

Some things change, others remain. Grandpa never stopped being that tough independent man, but where disease sapped strength and ability his toughness and independence showed in different ways.

On the 4th of July 2008, the extended family returned to Slumber Valley. A pavilion was rented at the camp ground for the family reunion, and food contributions were lined up. Then the day arrived.

Grandpa wasn't really fit for traveling. I don't remember why that location was chosen for the summer reunion. Perhaps it had been Grandma's idea because she wanted to visit her old haunts, or maybe someone else felt obligated to host the reunion and thought it a good location. Whatever the reason, it didn't have a sick man foremost in consideration.

It would have been easiest to keep Grandpa home. He hadn't been out traveling in a long time, and we were using the wheelchair regularly to get him around. He couldn't use the bathroom alone, and he struggled to eat. There was no reasonable reason to take him. But I wanted him to go.

Those many years ago Grandma and Grandpa had the camper at Slumber Valley, where for two or so summers they took us grandchildren to visit. I remembered the dirt paths, the swimming pool, the creek, and the waterfall. Those years were gone, long gone, but I wanted to go back. The place held memories for me, and if there was going to be a last time I wanted to make this the last time.

So I took Grandpa. I didn't know if it would be a disaster, or if we would be able to stay more than a few minutes, but I cleaned him, dressed him, and loaded him and his wheelchair into the car. Now, years later, we were returning to that place of memories. The journey seemed so familiar, and yet vague, as I made the last few turns. Then the campground came into sight, and the memories came back.

Everything looked the same, and yet it was not. A few years earlier a massive flood had swept through the area, scouring the creek, eating out embankments, washing up boulders, and knocking over trees. Much escaped the water's ravages, but some things did not. And more than the land had suffered in time's passing.

It had been nearly two years since I began caring for Grandpa, and watching him succumb to the ravages of Alzheimer's. A decade more at least since I last visited the campground. Those many years ago Grandpa could walk. He could run, he could ride a bike. I have a memory of a summer day, Grandpa seated straddling a bike, parked under the shade of a vacant pavilion. Now I pulled the car up to a pavilion teeming with relatives, and got the wheelchair out of the trunk. I helped Grandpa into the chair, and took him to the party.

We arrived late, because Grandpa couldn't stay long.

Alzheimer's drives its victims to their knees—figuratively and literally—as inch by inch, day by day, the battle is lost. At first, Grandpa staggered and stumbled as he tried to walk. Now he crawled aimlessly about on the floor unless I pushed him in the wheelchair or carried him, feeling so light in my arms.

Before, he struggled to get to the bathroom in time and use the toilet properly. Now I changed his diapers.

In the early days he couldn't remember the last time he had taken a shower, and struggled to shave himself. Now I bathed him, and shaved him, and dressed him.

Before I cut up his food so he could feed himself. Now that was failing, too. His hands would shake and jerk clumsily as he tried to bring the spoon to his mouth. He grabbed imaginary implements and food and wondered why nothing reached his mouth. His mind wandered as he played with the folds in his clothes, the food in front of him forgotten. It was a battle to eat, and one he was slowly losing, but which he desperately wished to fight alone.

I parked him in front of the picnic table and took a plate to the food buffet, looking for things he could eat. With a careful selection of food placed in front of him he did well enough for the meal, but his energy began to fail with dessert. His determination to eat the meal by himself gave way and he consented to someone else feeding him the chocolate cream pie—some things he wanted more than his dignity, or independence.

After the meal, I went to the falls again. Last time Grandpa had run on ahead, racing. This time I went without him, following the path among the trees. The falls were still there, much the same. Perhaps they seemed smaller than before, less threatening and less majestic. Time will sometimes do that. Still, the water cascaded down, loud and uncaring, as if it thought to drown out the world's sorrows.

The end was coming. Slowly, perhaps, but inexorably, as every little loss brought us one step closer to the final defeat. But perhaps the battle should not be considered as lost. Maybe it is better to say that the battle was won, day by day, as with love he was helped to the end. Helped with what dignity and grace we could muster. If it is *how* we live that matters, then each day can be taken up daily in the victory of living out love, or given up daily in the defeat of an empty heart.

I left the falls, the roar of the water quickly fading away. Back at the gathering, soon Grandpa wanted to leave. Two hours was an amazing length of time for him now. By determination he had made it that long, but it was all he could take. So we left. I drove the rutted dirt path, taking it to the highway, and then home.

Ten years had passed. It felt like nothing had changed, and yet everything had. And there was no going back.

§§§

GONE TO PIECES

Up until the summer of 2008 Grandpa remained generally continent of bowel—a contrast to his utter urinary incontinence. There were exceptions to this normal bowel continence —the exceptions being messy and nasty—but those infrequent occurrences did not, at first, bring a precipitous decline in that area. But in tandem with Grandpa's increasing difficulty with mobility came increased problems with defecation.

All his life Grandpa had issues with constipation. These problems grew worse with age. During the years I cared for him, his normal habit was to have a very large and exceedingly firm bowel movement only every few days. I fretted over the possibility of this habit taking a turn for the worse. There existed a thin line between passing a large constipated bowel movement and becoming completely impacted. I feared we were very close to crossing that line.

In spite of my fears Grandpa continued to have his regular—if not as frequent as I wished—bowel movements, and all was well. This changed early in the summer of 2008. Grandpa's failing diet and decreasing mobility finally caught up with him.

Over the months of caring for Grandpa I developed a sense for his bowel habits, and so had a pretty good idea when he was due to pass something. Mindful of this, and still ever fretful about the possibility of him becoming impacted, I would watch the toilet after his trips to the bathroom, waiting for signs that he had voided his bowels. Sometimes I was off by a day and there was nothing, and I would worry. But then the following day he would pass a stool and all was well again.

Time passed, and Grandpa grew increasingly unable to understand *intelligently* when he had to produce a bowel movement. In a way his constipation put off the day of his bowel incontinence because moving his bowels became such a procedure it usually couldn't just "slip out." The rare time it could, and did slip out, was the rare time we had some fecal incontinence.

I knew it was nearing time for a bowel movement when he started having unaccountable agitation and a particular restlessness that were the signs of an old man needing to (in Grandpa's words) "take a crap." I could see it, but he couldn't quite remember it himself anymore.

When that restlessness came I would prompt him, "Do you need to go to the bathroom? How about we go to bathroom?" If not at first, eventually he would agree.

Then the summer of 2008 came. It was a day for Grandpa to have a bowel movement and he showed the normal signs of agitation indicating it was time. I took him to the bathroom—and he did nothing.

"Wouldn't come out," he said. Okay, I thought, maybe he wasn't *quite* ready. Maybe in a few hours he would go, or tomorrow at the latest. There had been a few times before when this had happened. No need to get all uptight about it, I told myself.

His agitation persisted. I took him back to the bathroom again. Still nothing came.

By this point Grandpa was *very* agitated and clearly uncomfortable. He sat on the couch, then got up. He moved about, then sat again. Then got up. He was beside himself.

I had the dawning realization this wasn't like the other times.

"It's stuck, isn't it," I said.

"It feels like I'm sitting on a stick," he said.

Unfortunately, this was a little too literally true. A quick check revealed that indeed "it" was stuck, euphemistically right in the doorway, and not coming out.

Great.

It was grocery day. My sister Titi had just arrived to stay with Grandma and Grandpa. I was supposed to head out the door to pick up the week's supply of food. Suppositories and fleet enemas were added to the list. With the promise that I would return as soon as possible, I left.

I typically picked up a few items at the nearby Walmart, and then did most of the shopping at a local grocery chain. With the present crisis still in progress I decided that I would pick up the suppositories and enemas at Walmart and circle back home to resolve Grandpa's problem before going on to finish the rest of the shopping.

But it wasn't going to be an easy day. As I drove through the Walmart parking lot my car was T-boned by a driver blindly taking a short cut crossing through the parking spaces. She smashed the side of my vehicle, but it remained (just) drivable. The day was rapidly growing worse. I had to wait around in the parking lot for a police officer to arrive and write a report. While I waited, poor impacted Grandpa waited back home.

When I finally made it home I found the situation with Grandpa hadn't improved, and I quickly discovered that the suppositories were completely ineffective. Our only hope was the Fleet enema and if that wasn't successful we faced a trip to the hospital emergency room. Somehow, it didn't occur to me to attempt digital extraction. (What a term!)

By this point it felt like life had come unhinged from reality. I read the instructions on the Fleet enema bottle, and it had nothing to do with my situation. The directions talked about lying on one side and holding the enema liquid inside for as long as possible. It said nothing about dealing with an elderly Alzheimer's man who would fight you tooth and nail if you tried to make him lie down and who couldn't possibly understand the concept of retaining the enema in his colon. It said nothing about what to do if the person was so impacted the feces was stuck halfway out. Grandpa was bound up so tight I didn't see how there was any place for the enema fluid to go.

I had no directions on how to handle the situation. I wanted someone to come and take over. I wanted someone there who had done it all before, knew what to do, and could make everything right. Too bad. There was nobody around to tell me what to do, and I was on my own. I had an old man with Alzheimer's who was completely impacted, and I had a Fleet enema bottle.

What was I going to do?

I decided all I could do was make my best attempt. It would be messy, and ugly, but I saw no other way.

I took Grandpa into the cramped bathroom where I hoped to contain whatever mess developed. By this point he was so exhausted from all of his agitation he couldn't stand, but he wouldn't be still and lie down, either. Taking the path of least resistance, I had my sister hold him up while I got on my hands and knees to work on his bottom.

I tried to explain in advance what we needed to do, but of course Grandpa didn't understand what I said and had no idea what was happening.

"Hey. Hey! What are you doing? What are you doing there?" he said as I began. "Hey! Stop that! You hear me? You stop—Ahhhh, shit! Stop that, it's all over the place!"

The last comment came as I squeezed the fleet enema bottle and— much as I feared—he was so impacted that the fluid immediately back-washed, blasting out of his rectum at high pressure, sending fluid and chunks of feces everywhere.

"Shit! Aw, God damn it! What are you doing? Shit! Stop!" He

fought as best he weakly could and my sister struggled to support him.

"Hang on, Grandpa!" I said, trying to coax him through. "I'm sorry, I'm sorry we have to do this, but it has to be done. We're almost done! Just hang on!"

For a moment I thought it wasn't going to work. But it did. It took the entire bottle before the complete blockage finally moved. In the struggle it was futile to hope any of the discharge would be caught in a container. The bathroom was a mess. When the blockage came free Grandpa deposited the largest bowel movement I have ever seen directly onto the floor in one big heap.

We had done it.

To say we all felt immensely relieved seems like an understatement. We had just averted a nightmarish trip to the emergency room with Grandpa going ever more out of his mind, and who knows what else.

There was a lot of cleanup. The pile of feces on the floor was the first thing to go. Then I bathed Grandpa, who was nearly limp with exhaustion, and carried him to the couch where he promptly fell asleep.

Then, after all of that, I had to finish the grocery shopping. There was no break.

This event was a turning point. Not only was such fecal impaction traumatic for all of us, but it also was dangerous to Grandpa's health. I had to do something about his chronic constipation or else the cycle would simply repeat itself until something worse happened.

It was time for a trip to the doctor

In the examination room I explained to the doctor Grandpa's situation of diet and exercise (more precisely, the lack of either), and stressed the fact that nobody could convince him to swallow a pill. What were we going to do? The solution would have to be something else.

"The constipation is getting worse," I said. "We need something to control it, or he will end up in the hospital."

The doctor wrote a prescription for a powder laxative—polyethylene glycol 3350—that was administered by dissolving it in a drink. She said, "I'm sorry. It typically comes to this. There is no perfect dosage of laxative. You will have to adjust the amount depending on how he is eating. The results are often messy."

She was right.

I spiked Grandpa's morning coffee with the powdered laxative and tried to fractionalize the dose based on his eating. Sometimes I got the dose perfect and we ended up with a nice but softly formed stool. I say sometimes. The laxative was potent, and too often we ended up with very messy diarrhea that overflowed Grandpa's diaper, and all over him. This was the beginning of Grandpa's final descent into complete incontinence.

Of course the idea was to avoid giving him diarrhea. The ideal was to simply make his stool loose enough, and regular enough, that there was no impaction. But how much laxative he needed depended on how much he had eaten and drunk, and that was a moving target from day to day. If I wanted the perfect poop I had to continually adjust the laxative dosage to meet some unknown balance. In the laxative dosage game failing to give enough meant impaction, and giving too much meant dealing with a watery soup of diarrhea.

Rather than attempting to adjust the laxative dosage amount on the fly, and ending up in some situation where I was too clever by half, I settled on giving him a dosage every other day. This was not perfect, but it seemed to end up with the best average in frequency and consistency. Some bowel movements were a little on the hard side, some were soup, and some were just right. It was messy. It was imperfect. But at least we had no more impaction. With a regular schedule and dosage I wouldn't forget when I was supposed to give him laxative, or how much he needed—two things which were a big problem if I was constantly adjusting things in the moment.

I was not happy about this change because it felt like I was the one making Grandpa incontinent of bowel, which I did not want to do. But there was no escaping it. There were no good options. This was the future.

It felt a bit like the last straw—not so much because it was nasty, but because it felt like we had reached the point where *everything* was broken beyond repair. Grandpa couldn't walk right, he couldn't eat right, he couldn't urinate right, and now he couldn't defecate right. There was nothing normal left.

I began to feel increasingly alienated from normal life—all life outside my little world. All normalcy had left my life. I was living in a bubble, a bubble where eating and going to the bathroom were a struggle, and sometimes I mindlessly stayed up all night. People were sympathetic, especially family, but it felt like nobody could understand. There was nothing normal about it, and nothing left to compare with normal life.

Some days I would sit by myself out on the front stoop for a moment of sunshine and there watch people walk by. It seemed their lives were a million miles away from mine. They lived in their happy little worlds, walking carefree on the street while they talked and laughed with their friends. I sat and watched them, and soon I would go back into the house where eating, defecating, and living were all a struggle.

When I went to the grocery store it felt as if a glass box surrounded me. Everyone else went on with their regular daily life shopping for meat and vegetables and perhaps something for the weekend party. I lived in an entirely different world. I walked by them and among them, but I wasn't one of them. I never touched them with their normal lives and normal parties. In my world I bought baby wipes, adult diapers, junior food, laxatives, latex gloves, and nutrient drink. In my world eating wasn't about having a good time, it was about trying to keep someone alive. Using the bathroom wasn't something kept out of conversation—it consumed half my time. I emptied my cart onto the checkout line, watched the supplies ring up, wondered what the cashier thought, and knew they had no idea what my life was like.

Nobody knew. Nobody understood. And nobody out there in the world cared. That's what it *felt* like.

"You really into the fitness drinks?" The clerk asked, picking up the six-pack of nutrient drink. "You use them for body building? Are they any good? You drink them instead of a meal?"

There was the urge to burst into an absurd laugh. Body building?

"No," I said. "They're for my grandfather. He has Alzheimer's and won't eat very much anymore."

"Oh," the cashier said.

That was always a conversation killer. It was awkward then, and usually they tried to say something about how what I was doing was so wonderful, but I could tell they wish they hadn't opened their mouth. I knew they didn't understand, and didn't want to.

I tried to cope like I always had—exercising. I lifted weights in the basement, even when I already felt exhausted, even if I had to do it at night because of caring for Grandpa. I went on bike rides, even when I couldn't get it in until after dark. I rode, the countryside slipping by, and for a few minutes I felt relief even while I felt so alone. There was me, and the silent houses that passed by, the houses and people and families who did not know my troubles, my sorrow, or the place I would return to when the ride was over.

And I wrote. I was always writing.

In it all there was no escape from what was happening. I was caught in the final trap of caregiving. I couldn't separate myself from Grandpa's needs. They had become the sun around which my personal world orbited. It was my duty, and my obsession. No matter where I went, the needs of Grandpa were never far from my thoughts. There was no vacation—the idea both unthinkable and impossible.

His needs had become my life. Whenever I was away, I thought about Grandpa—what he was doing and what he might need. I never felt completely at ease away from the house as my mind hovered on what might be happening in my absence. I always felt like I needed to get back.

People said I needed a day off, and it was true. But somehow I felt more relieved when I came back than going away because when I was with Grandpa I knew I could handle any problem. It felt like I never had a break, even when I was away, because I knew Grandpa needed me. He never stopped needing me, and no one could replace me because by now no one understood him and his needs as well as I did. We were two peas in one pod, two halves of one whole. He needed me, and I could not escape. It got into my bones, and would not leave. Everything was going to pieces, and there was no putting it back together.

§§§

INVALIDS

Life at Grandma and Grandpa's house continued to change in big ways and small. A major change came about a year after I moved in. Then my brother Arlan and my cousin Melinda both moved out, each taking a new path in their lives. Arlan moved closer to his job out of state, and Melinda began her independent life in an apartment downtown.

Fewer people in the house meant less interpersonal drama, but it also meant fewer people around to help. I had always been the person who did nearly everything for Grandpa, but the little things were important too. Simply knowing there was an extra person in the house to keep an eye on Grandpa if I decided to go on a bike ride made me rest easier. When Arlan and Melinda left, I had to work things out for myself.

When Melinda left, her spacious bedroom became available. Grandma immediately suggested that I move into the room—with or without Grandpa. I declined, at first. My reasons for not leaving Grandpa alone I have already mentioned, and moving us both into the bigger bedroom had its own problems. Grandpa had become accustomed to our current tiny bedroom. When I began living with Grandma and Grandpa the recent rearrangement of sleeping quarters was still so fresh Grandpa had a hard time remembering where he went to bed. A year later his rightful bedroom was firmly fixed in his mind. He knew where he was supposed to return after a midnight bathroom trip. It was comfortable, and comforting, for him to have the same familiar four walls around him when he went to bed. I was loathe to disturb all of that for a little more space.

Based on that judgment, the larger bedroom remained empty and Grandpa and I continued in our cramped quarters for many more months. Eventually Grandpa's decline reached the point where I decided it was time we moved. The final impetus was Grandpa's cessation of walking. Carrying him to bed in the cramped bedroom was difficult, maneuvering the wheelchair into the room downright impossible. Since he was no longer walking to bed at night, or getting up in the night to use the bathroom, there was no longer any concern about upsetting his habits of travel. Lastly, I concluded that Grandpa's awareness of his surroundings had deteriorated to the extent that he no longer would appreciably notice a room change. I judged that so long as I still put him to bed, and it was his own bed, going three feet through a different door would not upset him.

We made the change, and my judgment proved correct. The new room was spacious enough to provide access to both sides of Grandpa's bed. The extra space also allowed me to drive the wheelchair into the room and right beside the bed, which made transferring Grandpa much easier.

All was good, but Grandpa *did* notice the change in rooms.

"Huh," he said, and looked around curiously the first day I wheeled him into the new bedroom.

"We switched bedrooms," I said, matter-of-fact. "This will be easier for us, and nobody else needs the room."

"I wondered," he said. Though he noticed the change in passing, it did not seem to bother him. He settled down without complaint (my big concern), and never mentioned the change again. The new bedroom space made it much easier for me to care for him, and afterward part of me wished we had moved earlier. But in spite of that second guessing I think the move happened at the right time in Grandpa's decline—where he would no longer be upset or frustrated by the move.

There were other changes as health problems grew worse. When Grandma's own ailments began to seriously impact her life, she found herself unable to eat regularly. Exceedingly high blood pressure at the end of the day, and a sense of stomach distress, meant that a normal supper became out of the question, and sometimes any supper was impossible. Retreating to her bedroom, she rested there in the hopes that her blood pressure would come down and her chest pain stop. If she felt she could tolerate some light food for supper she would take yogurt or something similar to her bedroom.

Then one day she took her breakfast back into her bedroom to eat. And her lunch. After that, she kept doing it every day. She was withdrawing from Grandpa's life. This did not come as a surprise to me. I foresaw the change coming, eventually. But it was a big change nonetheless.

Grandma had long manifested difficulty tolerating Grandpa as Alzheimer's altered his behavior. As Grandpa grew increasingly unable to understand his surroundings, or whether Grandma was even present or not, it became clear to me that little was gained by having Grandma and Grandpa in the same room all day. At least half of the time Grandpa didn't know if Grandma was there or not. When he did know she was there (and sometimes even when he wasn't sure) he would harass her with attempted, incoherent, conversation and questions. He meant well, but when she was trying to nap he would make it difficult for her by poking at her as she reclined in her easy chair. If not that, he called loudly for various people from his spot on the couch, which made it impossible for her to sleep.

Grandma had little she could offer Grandpa, and he usually irritated her. The end effect of having them both in the living room was that I had to constantly run interference between the two of them in an attempt to keep the peace. And being the peacemaker strained *my* patience.

It came to the point where I couldn't wait for Grandma to conclude she had enough of Grandpa and decide to relax elsewhere. I had to restrain myself to keep from telling Grandma, when she became caustic toward Grandpa, that if she couldn't stand him she could always go back to her bedroom. Instead of such commentary, I quietly helped make her bedroom more attractive.

When the TV in the living room died (a great blessing in my book) I rearranged her bedroom so she could easily watch TV on her computer from her bed. I also moved a spare easy chair into her bedroom so that if she wished she could sit and watch TV or read her newspaper. With bed, nightstand, easy chair, computer/TV, and the adjoining master-bath right off her bedroom, Grandma had everything she needed for a comfortable secluded existence away from the reality of Grandpa.

After I had everything set up I knew it was only a matter of time before Grandma realized the advantage for herself. As she began feeling worse and worse with her own sickness, what little ability she had left to cope with Grandpa vanished entirely. Then the more she distanced herself from Grandpa, the more she found she liked it. As soon as Grandma started spending time in her bedroom, it quickly escalated to the point where she was spending just about *all* of her time there. Since Grandma couldn't cope with Grandpa, I found this degree of separation a preferable progression to some other more permanent rupture in their relationship.

With Grandma and Grandpa now effectively living on opposite ends of the house, keeping peace was much easier for me. This was a great relief which offered some balance against how things had become *harder* for me as Grandma and Grandpa both grew more ill. I no longer found myself under the stress and obligation of trying to modify Grandpa's behavior for the benefit of Grandma. It was now just me and Grandpa, and I was *highly* tolerant of his quirks—when it wasn't the middle of the night, anyhow. If he wanted to sit on the couch and call for Gene, Doug, George, Jenny, Jean, Jacob, John, and any other name that came to his mind—I let him. If he wanted to drag chairs around the house, I let him. If he wanted to moan and groan, I let him. If he made a mess dumping out the kitchen garbage can, I had the luxury of cleaning up without having to worry about Grandma becoming upset. In short, I now had much more freedom to tend Grandpa as I felt was best instead of tending him in a manner that pleased someone else.

Grandpa's decline had reached the stage where much of his activity was almost startling in its close similarity to the behavior of a toddler. Having grown up in a very large family, I found that dealing with the activity of a toddler came to me without thinking. I picked up the messes made, kept things out of reach, ignored the noise and activity, and answered incomprehensible questions and conversation with vague answers that popped out without even thinking. Grandma couldn't fathom how I could stand to deal with him.

Grandpa, for his part, was far enough gone that he wasn't able to fully grasp the change—which was good, because if he had understood the absence he would have been deeply hurt. As it was, he sometimes faintly realized that Grandma wasn't around as much as she was before, he didn't like it, and on occasion he might wonder if she was mad at him or something. But mostly he was so lost in his own very tiny world that her absence away in her bedroom was no different than her presence in a chair across the room. In either case he was still lost and alone in his little spot on the couch, unable to remember where anyone else was, much less himself.

His obliviousness saved him from a lot of stress and grief. In the early months of my caregiving, the idea of Grandma going for a regular doctor's visit made him agitated. Now two years in he would sit on the couch, carefully folding and stacking his magazines while I led paramedics up the stairs behind him to fetch Grandma who wallowed in her room in the midst of heart pains. Those paramedics didn't enter his small world, and so it was as if they didn't exist. For all the cruel things Alzheimer's did to him, I was glad it left one small benefit in its wake.

In the confluence of all these things the dynamic of the house had become very much *not* normal. We were in full blown dysfunction. In the first medical ward on the couch we had Grandpa. In the second medical ward in the master bedroom we had Grandma. Then there was me, the overseer of this sick house. Since Grandma at that time couldn't stomach much more than a liquid diet, and the range of food Grandpa could eat was rapidly shrinking toward only canned mush, I was reduced to cooking only for myself.

I discovered it was very uninspiring to cook just for oneself. Grandma never had broad culinary horizons, and was always impressed and very appreciative of what I could cook without even straining myself. Now, with no one to appreciate what I made, I found the act of cooking very underwhelming. I had many things I wanted to accomplish in any given day, and taking time out of my day to cook seemed rather pointless. I ended up sitting at the table looking at one plate. Why bother? I wasn't going to complain if I had cold cereal three meals a day. I would have preferred to forget about eating altogether if my body didn't rebel at such a venture. Eating alone is boring, if not downright discouraging, verging on depressing. If there is no one to sit down and eat with you, there doesn't feel like much reason to sit down and eat—you might as well grab something while on the go between activities.

My previously faithful supper menu gave way and I wasn't entirely sure what I would do. Some days I still cooked a full supper. Some days I made a light meal. Some days I ate leftovers. Any semblance that we had a normal life was gone. It felt as if we had crossed a line. This was a house full of invalids.

It felt like a very bleak house indeed.

§§§

HOW TO CLEAN THE CARPET

One early morning in mid November 2008 Grandpa was wildly agitated. I suspected he needed to use the toilet for a bowel movement, but he refused to admit as much. Instead of eating breakfast he bellowed at the top of his lungs for "Ma!" and wrestled with the kitchen table. He was in such a fit that I wasn't going to man-handle him down the hall to the bathroom unless he agreed it was where he needed to go.

Finally he stood up and declared, "My asshole hurts so bad!"

I said, "Well, maybe we should go to the bathroom then."

He looked at me questioningly and said, "You think so?"

"Yeah," I said. "I think we should."

So we started toward the bathroom, Grandpa tottering and me at his side. After maybe two steps he exclaimed, "Oh, shoot! I just did something! I don't know what it was, but I did it!" I propelled him—pronto—into the bathroom and got him onto the toilet. He had done a portion of his business in his diaper, but he did a lot more in the toilet.

This was the confused and disconnected relationship he now had with his own body. Sometimes he understood that his body was telling him *something*, but couldn't make sense of what it was saying. Sometimes, he didn't understand his body at all. Success in avoiding a loaded diaper was erratic at best. There were days he didn't even agitate before soiling himself, and so there was no hint before it happened. Other days I had warning but he soiled himself too quickly for us to reach the toilet in time. And then some days he agitated, but I simply mis-guessed the source of his agitation. In the end I had to realize there were bigger problems in life than getting Grandpa to defecate in the toilet. It was better if I didn't become obsessed with attempting to avoid a dirty diaper.

Not only did Grandpa sometimes have difficulty understanding what his body was telling him, but the problem was made worse by the fact that I was giving him the doctor-prescribed laxative to make him go. If we had a day where the dose was a little high for the amount of food I managed to cajole Grandpa to eat that day, the bowel movement coming through afterward would have made a normal man struggle to reach the bathroom in time, much less Grandpa.

I simply couldn't win.

My greatest fear was Grandpa taking an unsupervised minute to drop his pants and empty his bowels in a most inappropriate location. We had some near misses of such a fateful event. Then, two days before Thanksgiving in 2008, it finally happened.

I was preoccupied at my computer, and didn't register anything unusual coming from Grandpa in the living room. My first hint that something was wrong was the exclamation from Grandma. It was the sort of gasp that had me immediately out of my chair and down the hall.

Then I saw it.

Evidence showed that Grandpa had walked to the middle of the living room, dropped his pants and went poop. Judging by the state of things, he had then walked back and forth through the mess, smearing it across a ten foot stretch of the living room carpet before sitting his bare soiled bottom on the couch. On first sighting the disaster area, I felt overwhelmed with dismay.

It was gross. I was also thinking, "How on earth am I going to get that cleaned out of the carpet?"

I had dearly wished to avoid this kind of incident, but given the number of times I had stopped Grandpa from dropping his pants in various other inappropriate places in the house I knew this possibility was a continuing danger. I guess we couldn't be lucky all the time, and I suppose part of me suspected it was inevitable, given the fact of Murphy's Law. Nonetheless, a soiled ten foot stretch of the living room carpet was a house-keeping nightmare. Being two days before the entire extended family was scheduled to come over for Thanksgiving didn't help, either.

Grandma later admitted that she had wanted to faint at the sight. Instead, she rose to the occasion and did the best thing she could under the circumstances—she retreated to her bedroom, shut the door, and left me to deal with the situation.

Cleaning the carpet involved plenty of scraping to remove as much of the initial material as possible. Then I advanced to scrubbing, along with the application of very small amounts of ammonia and hydrogen peroxide, prodigious amounts of baking soda, laundry detergent, and plenty of water—though not all of these things at once. I spent about two hours cleaning on the day of the disaster. I did not apply any hydrogen peroxide or ammonia the first day. I ended the first cleaning session by liberally sprinkling baking soda all over the carpet and working it in with a scrubbing brush. This was suggested to help eliminate odors, and it did seem to help a lot. The next morning after the carpet had dried somewhat, and with fresh daylight, I saw the stain was still quite visible. For round two I vacuumed up the baking soda and moved on to hydrogen peroxide.

It was very important to soak as much liquid as possible out of the carpet with fresh paper towels after every cleaning pass. This was key for lifting away the offending material and stain. The rule of thumb I followed was to keep cleaning until the paper towels no longer came away discolored.

After another two hours of cleaning the day before Thanksgiving, the carpet looked pretty good. I decided it would have to be good enough. On Thanksgiving day when the carpet had again dried I could still see a faint stain, but because I had scrubbed so hard and used so much cleaning solution the surrounding non-stained carpet was beginning to look faintly pale in color. Any further cleaning was likely to end up with a noticeable pale strip running through the carpet, even if I managed to remove the last traces of stain. The discoloration was faint enough that people might not even notice—and after prodigious amounts of detergent, hydrogen peroxide, and ammonia, it was pretty benign in any case.

I decided to let it rest.

Thanksgiving was saved. Grandma wanted to keep the whole incident hush-hush, but I wanted to greet every arriving relative with the salutation, "Who wants to lick the carpet?"

No point in letting all the hard work go unappreciated, right?

Thanksgiving was a balancing act with Grandpa. There remained the ever-present thought that this holiday might be his last, and so there was the desire to have him where everyone could see and enjoy him as much as possible. Everyone wanted those happy final memories. But then there was also the reality that Grandpa could not cope well with large gatherings. The bustle was utterly overwhelming to his crippled mind. Anything more than a slow, nearly monosyllabic, two-way, or one-way, conversation was more than he could grasp. A room packed with people noisily talking and laughing was unbearable.

The balancing act on Thanksgiving meant that Grandpa was very happy to see everyone arrive (he knew they were family, even if he didn't remember exactly *who* everyone was), but after fifteen minutes —about how long it took the majority of guests to appear—he had experienced enough. He crawled across the living room floor to poke and prod and examine a strange object in a chair (said object happening to be a very awkward grandson) only to give up in perplexity. He was then helped back to the couch, where he promptly fell asleep propped up in the warm crook between two relatives. The solution to being overwhelmed was to either shout and agitate, or else shut down and fall asleep—and he chose the latter.

Lunch followed shortly thereafter. I moved Grandpa to a location with only a few dinner companions who knew enough to not distract him from the difficult task of eating. After lunch I wheeled him back to our bedroom and shut the door. In this manner he survived in decent fashion. As the afternoon went on he agitated some over the loud talking that drifted through the door, the strange thumps, and the baby cries, but it was not enough to work him into a fit. Any relative who wished to visit could come in and sit with him, but basically fifteen minutes of everybody was all he needed, or could handle.

I was pretty pleased with the success. There was no dirty carpet, everyone enjoyed themselves, and even Grandpa had as good a time as he was able. Even more importantly, the excitement did not end up making a very bad day for him, or a bad night.

But the flush of that minor victory did not last. Promptly following the Thanksgiving holiday, Grandpa became sick.

He caught a mild cold from me. I had suffered with a bit of a sore throat, and some slight congestion. Physically, Grandpa did not appear to suffer any worse than I had—and in fact his chest congestion was nowhere near as bad as it sometimes became during a fit of emphysema. Nonetheless, his cold turned into a string of very bad days. By this point in late 2008 Grandpa was at the state in his Alzheimer's where even a little bit of sickness, tiredness, or both, had a dramatic, even frightening, detrimental effect on his cognitive abilities. It made me realize how thin a mental thread still kept him anchored to life.

The sickness started in earnest on Friday, the day after Thanksgiving. Grandpa's nose began running like a faucet, and he was cranky. By supper time he was slouched over sideways in his wheelchair, snot making a regular appearance at the end of his nose. He muttered vaguely dissatisfied things at the world at large, struggled irritably with his wheelchair, and didn't eat his supper.

This was not good.

"Looks like tonight is going to be a bad night," I commented to Grandma. Grandpa was clearly out of sorts, and when he felt out of sorts that often translated into a very bad night. I had developed a sense for these sort of things.

Unfortunately, I was quite accurate in my prediction. When I put him to bed that night he immediately began to fuss. This was another bad sign—his Alzheimer's now made him so exhausted he would typically fall asleep almost instantly on lying down. When he didn't it meant something was wrong.

I was exhausted myself, so I tried to ignore the signs of a looming bad night. I was so tired that I put in my ear-plugs, pulled a pillow over my head, and managed to fall asleep in spite of Grandpa's activity. About midnight Grandpa's low grade muttering and fussing with his blankets escalated to the more insistent calling, "Ma? Hey, Ma?" at which point I woke and knew for certain we were in for a very *horrible* night. Grandpa had an undefined vague state of miserableness which kept him from sleeping, and once he got the ball of sleeplessness rolling it snowballed from there.

It was a bad night to match any other bad night. The fussing dragged on, and at about 1:30 AM I decided to cut my losses. I moved Grandpa to the overstuffed chair beside his bed where he could sit more comfortably—and hopefully fall asleep. Then I left the bedroom and laid on the couch where I hoped I could sleep, or at least rest better in the absence of his insistent noise-making.

The situation continued downhill. By the time I had finished rearranging Grandpa in the bedroom and settling myself on the couch

I had been thoroughly awakened. It took some effort for me to fall back to sleep. Eventually I did, sleeping fitfully for maybe an hour. Only an hour. I woke and went to check on Grandpa. I found he was still agitating, and in fact his volume had increased. He still had no apparent need which I could address so I went back to the couch again.

His volume continued to increase. At this point we had passed 3:00 AM. I lay on the couch and thought, "He will be terrible come day time. This is really bad. I wish he would sleep." Meanwhile, Grandpa kept up his litany—not incessantly, but erupting at probably precisely the moment when he began to feel tired so as to make *sure* he wouldn't fall asleep.

"Ma? Hey, Ma!"

Then again, "MA? HEY, MA!"

Finally, "**MAAAAAAA! HEEEEY MAAAAAAAAAA!**"

The bedroom door was shut, and I was down the hall in the living room wearing ear-plugs. It didn't matter. I could *still* hear him clear as day. For a man nearing his eighty-first birthday and growing rather frail he certainly wasn't lacking in vocal power. I got back up and went to check on him, wishing I had some brilliant and easy solution that would make him settle down long enough to fall asleep. It was heading on toward 4:30 in the morning and if he had slept at all during the entire night it was probably for no more than an hour. You would have thought someone sick, and that old, would have run out of energy a long time ago.

"Grandma's asleep," I said grumpily to Grandpa. "What do you want?"

"Well, uh, I'm feeling nervy," he said, perhaps making the understatement of the night.

I felt at a loss about what to do. For a moment I considered leaving the bedroom light on in the hopes it might make his "nervy" feeling go away, but I knew the chance of that helping was almost nil. The nervy feeling was coming from within him, a vicious self-feeding cycle of unease that came from sitting up in the middle of the night for hours on end. The best solution would have been to sit down with him and hold him in my arms until he relaxed and fell asleep. But I was feeling too grumpy and tired. So I mumble something about going to sleep, and left again.

I lay on the couch, wishing I had the ability to sleep like a rock. Sometime later Grandpa finally fell asleep. when I next checked on him I found him resting quietly and so I went back to my own bed. By 8:00 Grandpa was awake for the day.

He paid for his little stunt, as he always did. I was still young and could bounce back from a bad night pretty quickly. Grandpa couldn't, and his all-nighters were perhaps the most self-destructive thing he did (but try explaining that to him). What followed was three days where he hardly ate or drank.

He was like a man stupefied. He sprawled where he sat. He drooled. He stared blankly. What strength he had was spent, and like a druggie coming off a trip the next several days were nearly hellish. We had no repeat all-nighters—he hadn't the strength—but during the day he was in mindless shambles. When he wasn't a nearly comatose sack sprawled on the couch, he was shouting for people living and dead, real and imagined. He wouldn't eat or drink at meals. It was exhausting for me. Not so much physically—because there was practically nothing I could do for him—but emotionally and mentally it was very hard. I was afraid he would never recover.

The experience sucked all the energy out of me.

How many days could this go on?

That Sunday was my dad's birthday, so it was arranged for my Uncle Kevin to come down and watch Grandpa so I could attend the party. When I came back from the party I found a tale of woe. Grandpa had eaten and drunk nearly nothing (yet again), and had been unable or unwilling to stand for his diaper changing, a problem I probably could have handled much better than Kevin. I returned to find Grandpa sleeping on the living room floor, looking terribly exhausted. I think everyone was exhausted.

On Monday Grandpa was better. He was much calmer and more mentally collected, but still he was not very interested in eating for a man who had consumed little in the last two days. Late in the morning he sat on the couch, his hands clasped in his lap, his eyes closed. I don't know where his mind was, but twice he began to sing snatches of song. The first time it was some line from a traditional Christmas song, his voice slowly picking out the words until he trailed away. The second time he suddenly began "Jesus Loves Me" in a halting faint voice, his eyes still closed.

"Jesus loves me...this I know...for the Bible tells me so..." The careful plodding words were endearing and made me want to laugh like one does at a little child who does not realize how cute he has been. But at the same time it was almost heart-breaking, enough to make me want to cry.

I can know in the abstract why I do something, and that knowledge can set my course of action. But in the day-to-day living it can get hard, very hard, and somehow the knowing starts to feel dry and empty. Then in the flash of some everyday moment I see something, and feel something, that reminds me of my reasons in a way I can't describe with words.

Grandpa did bounce back this time. It was not the first time he had a bad spell, and so through the whole experience I told myself, "It's happened before—Just hold steady and it will pass." But at the same time there was a voice in the back of my mind which whispered, "Oh God, he isn't eating or drinking. What if he doesn't snap back? What if this is it?"

Monday morning Grandpa got out of bed with a diaper full of soupy poop. I had stopped the laxative when he stopped eating, but it wasn't soon enough. Thus the liquid emulsion in his diaper. He wasn't *entirely* back to his normal self, so he wasn't accepting my usual explanations as to why he had to stand still so I could clean him up. As soon as I peeled the reeking diaper off his bottom, he decided it was indecent for his pants to be down and tried to pull them back over his soiled bottom. He tried to pull up the front of his pants while I tried to keep the back of his pants pulled down with one hand and wipe him with the other. I had to keep my eyes on several things at once while he lurched around the room—for some reason bound and determined to get out—as I continued to clean his bottom. Unable to stay on his feet he quickly went to his knees and started crawling from the room and off down the hall, pants bunched around his thighs. I crawled after him, wiping all the way.

Grandpa was being anything but helpful, but thanks to some dexterity and quick work on my part nothing besides his bottom ended up soiled. Rather than losing my temper as he crawled off down the hall I simply followed after him and amused myself by thinking how life could hardly get more surreal than crawling down the hall trying to wipe my grandpa's bottom.

In five minutes I had him cleaned up. I put a fresh diaper on him, loaded him into his wheel chair and moved him to the kitchen table. No harm done.

If Monday started a little crazy, Tuesday was better. He rose like it was any normal day and ate like he had never been sick. The same for Wednesday, and Thursday. So life returned to normal. At least, as normal as life ever was anymore.

§§§

- 2009 -

GRANDPA'S GUITAR

G...F...E...D...C...E...A...G. The notes slid down the scale, clear and sharp, except when I flubbed it.

This was January 2009, and I was learning to play the guitar. If you had asked me four, or maybe even two years ago if I was going to learn the guitar I would have shook my head in disbelief. This was something of a turn-about for me. I admit I was a bit surprised at myself, but maybe I shouldn't have been.

There is some musical talent on both sides of my family. On my mom's side of the family my Aunt Marianne plays the guitar, and on my dad's side Grandpa played the piano, guitar, and mandolin. His father played the cornet in a band. I have two cousins who can play more than one instrument, and I don't know how many relatives can play at least *some* instrument. So there is a definite musical lineage in my family, but until I picked up the guitar that year I had been a wasteland of that particular talent.

When I was a child my parents tried to encourage me in musical directions. They sunk hard earned money into an electronic keyboard and music lessons, but I partook of them with tepid interest at best and pretty much leaped at the chance to give it up. Not only did it require diligence to practice but it was boring and I really had no appreciation for the music. It had no relevance to my youthful life and interests—if I was going to do something creative I would draw a picture or tell a story or make something. Music, apparently, wasn't my natural outlet for self-expression.

My first experience with a guitar was as a little child. My mom's sister Marianne, being a generous aunt, gave us kids an old practice guitar to play with. I wish I could say that sparked my musical interest, but it didn't. It didn't even leave me with a positive impression of guitars, though perhaps through no fault of its own. It was a classical, nylon string, guitar. It may be that I don't care for the sound of classical guitars. It was certainly not a quality guitar (hence, children playing with it), and it was surely out of tune. But as a child I didn't account for all those facts. To me it simply sounded bad, and I couldn't figure out what anyone would like about a guitar. The impression stuck with me, even though I had the chance to see other people properly play steel-stringed guitars. For me, the first thing I thought of when someone mentioned a guitar was a dull sounding instrument, not pleasing at all.

For many years the guitar remained unfairly stereotyped in my mind, but as I grew older my opinion of music as a whole changed. I began listening to music (certainly the first step one must take if one is going to have any interest in things musical), and I grew to enjoy a variety of music. Sometime in my teens it occurred to me that it would be enjoyable to know how to play a musical instrument. But at that point in time money and space were constrained. If I was going to attempt to learn any musical instrument I would have to consider it as something more than a "nice idea." So my musical ambition languished.

Then sometime in 2007 or 2008 I decided I wanted to learn how to play the guitar. Caring for Grandma and Grandpa had changed the situation in my life and learning a musical instrument seemed a good way to keep myself occupied, engaged, and learning something new. It seemed, at least, like a symbolic way of saying I wasn't stagnating. It helped that I discovered a basic guitar for learning was (as far as musical instruments were concerned) quite cheap. The idea of sinking a large amount of money into something that would turn into a fantasy after six months was possibly more intimidating than the idea of attempting a musical instrument itself.

For a while I played around with the idea of purchasing a guitar, and finally in 2008 more definitive intentions began to coalesce. In the fall Grandma heard of my interest in learning the guitar, and immediately suggested my uncle Kevin could give me Grandpa's old guitar. "It's just sitting in his attic," she said. This was news to me. I had been under the impression that Grandpa had sold off his guitar many years ago, and its presence in the family was nothing more than a dim memory. It was with some bemusement, and a bit of excitement, that I received a battered guitar case from my Uncle Kevin in the middle of October. Already Grandma had dug up Grandpa's old guitar lesson books. Everything was falling into place.

Part of my mind knew that the reality of guitars was not represented in the out-of-tune and abused object we had played with as little kids. But some part of me still had not shaken those deep-seated memories. When my fingers brushed across the strings of the guitar they twanged with a clear sweet sharpness that surprised me. *Wow,* I thought, *that sounds nice.* Somehow, learning an instrument didn't seem like that dull and tiresome duty of my childhood memories.

So I began learning how to play Grandpa's guitar. It was a bittersweet experience, in a way. What I had was a piece of history, a piece of Grandpa's history from a long time ago.

I know very little about guitars, but I am sure Grandpa's Silvertone guitar was not a very good one. Grandpa would not spend a lot of money on himself. The guitar lesson books he bought were used, and I'm pretty sure the guitar was also second-hand and second-rate when he bought it. Still, I liked it. By the time it came to me it had sat for years in an attic. The guitar case was worn and stained, and the guitar itself showed many signs of age. The tuning keys were stiff, and grooves were worn into the fretboard where the strings had been pressed against the frets. The body of the guitar itself was cracked in both the front and back (from excessive drying in a very hot, dry attic, I suspect), and the wood of the body felt slightly punky in places. But the instrument could still tune and play. It was surprising the guitar sounded as good as it did. It was good enough for me.

The guitar was old, made before I was born. It was history from before my time. Grandpa's lesson books sat on my shelf, the worn covers stating, "The New Mel Bay Modern Guitar Method." Inside the front cover the names of two previous owners were scribbled out. The completed date scrawled beside the early lessons was from June 1974, seven years before I was born. Flipping through the old lesson books, and pulling out the guitar with its strap and the spare strings still carefully coiled in their packages at the bottom of the case, was like rummaging through a distant part of Grandpa's life. When I brushed my hands over the strings, touching what Grandpa played decades ago, the notes thrummed out and it was like I felt and heard Grandpa's past—a part of his life I had never seen or heard before. This was a part of his life from long before he became what he was now. A time when he learned something that I struggled to learn. It was somehow quietly sad, and when playing the guitar it was hard not to think about how time marches on, leaving so many things behind.

I was hesitant to practice in front of Grandpa. From my past attempts to share recorded music with him, I knew he had very particular opinions about what he liked. One song he might enjoy very much, and the next he would proclaim as "terrible" when I might find only a trifling difference in quality. Even more than that, his Alzheimer's had made him increasingly sensitive to the mood of music. A long, slow piece of cello music would make him feel terribly sad and afraid, and he could not abide listening to it. Further, since he was someone who had learned the guitar I suspected he might be particularly sensitive to someone playing it poorly. All things considered, I didn't want to torment him with my attempts.

I waited until I had mastered something resembling a song before I tried playing in front of him. It was then I discovered that I was wrong. He enjoyed listening. Not only did he enjoy listening, but he was highly approving of my learning. I don't recall having ever discussed learning musical instruments with Grandpa, but for a man typically dour I found him surprisingly positive on my learning how to play. Then I realized that I had touched on something near to his heart.

"That's a nice guitar," he said, brightening at what was perhaps my first appearance with it. "Where did you get that?"

"It's your old guitar, Grandpa," I said. "Do you remember it?"

"It is?" He sounded half uncertain, half confused. "Well, I think it is good," he said.

And so I played for him. I was learning, slowly, and I had much more to learn. Two months in I had no expectation of becoming a great guitar player. I told myself I would be happy if I eventually became able to play average songs with average ability. But that was only later, maybe. Right then I had finished learning the first position and I was beginning the process of learning chords. I hated chords, especially the F chord.

The real problem with the F chord was holding down two strings with my first finger. I found I could easily hold down one string with my first finger, one with my second, and one with my third. But holding down two strings with my first finger while holding down one with the other two was just about agony to pull off—and we're not talking about in a musically successful fashion. I'll never be able to do it, I thought. But I was old enough, and mature enough, to recognize the source of that feeling. I felt it every step of the way in any learning process and each time I managed to overcome.

It was enjoyable to play guitar music. But I also found the simple learning itself to be a pleasure. It had been a long time since I had learned something so completely new. The struggle, the dawning understanding, and the opening of a new world was something good in itself. It reminded me of the newness in life, when during my present situation everything could seem dull and repetitive.

Grandpa listened when I played for him. It would be untrue to say that he listened with constant attentiveness. I sat in the middle of the living room and played. Grandpa sat on the couch. Sometimes he listened while he messed with his magazines, idly folding and tearing sheets of paper. Sometimes he fell asleep as I played. Sometimes he just sat quietly and listened. And sometimes his mind wandered off, perhaps carried by my music to distant memories. There were days when it seemed like my music dredged up thoughts. He would interrupt and say, "But what about...what about..." but then he couldn't remember what he was going to say, or ask, and I hadn't a clue. Then there were the times when he forgot what he was doing. One evening while I played he loudly announced, "Where am I and what am I doing?" To which I blandly replied. "You're sitting on the couch listening to me play the guitar."

Sometimes he didn't know I was playing the guitar, and perhaps wasn't even aware of the sound. But other times I knew he was. He would say, "That sounded good" when I finished a piece. Or if I hit a string badly he would quite seriously (and innocently) say, "Did you hear that? It sounded like there is a goat calling downstairs!" One time when I finished playing "Michael, Row The Boat Ashore" he spontaneously burst out in the last line of the song, without me having told him what I was playing. Another time when I finished playing "Tom Dooley" he asked me what song that was, and when I told him he said, "Ah. I knew it, and I just kept trying and trying to remember."

Along with remembering songs, Grandpa still remembered some things about his own time learning the guitar those many years ago. Sometimes when I was muttering or gasping in frustration at some difficulty he would make a comment. One day he gave a little laugh and said, "Got grooves in your fingers, huh?" (Which indeed I did.) Another time when I complained about how difficult it was to learn the chords he gave some garbled statement of agreement. It sounded like he made some comment about the D chord, but I couldn't decipher his words. However, when I looked up the D chord later I saw it did indeed look like a doozy, so it appears that while Grandpa's mouth hadn't cooperated, he had tried to express a valid statement.

In spite of all that was confused for him, guitar music was something he hadn't entirely lost. It was something he could still enjoy. One day halfway through my lesson I stopped for a break and he said, "What, are you done already?"

In the end what he wanted most was for me to be there with him. Sometimes he expressed it in a way so poignant it was almost painful to see. One day I had finished up my playing and began to take my stuff back to the bedroom. Grandpa looked up and saw what I was doing, and his face became sad. "Don't go. Don't go," he said earnestly. "Sit here with me." He patted the couch beside him, and looked so hopeful and *wanting* that I couldn't help feeling a stab of awfulness that he could feel so terribly lonely and in need of company in his own living room. So I left my stuff and just sat there with him for a while.

§§§

FAILURE TO THRIVE

Grandpa was never much of a cook. In all the time I knew him he didn't care to make anything, except two things: fudge, and peanut brittle. He liked sweet things, and those two simple recipes were as far as he would venture into baking. It was enough to satisfy his cravings. I remember as a boy walking into Grandma and Grandpa's kitchen and being met by the heavy rich aroma of peanut brittle wafting from the stove.

For a man who loved his sweets Grandpa also had a secret (or not so secret) fear of becoming fat. The idea was laughable—even in his prime he was a skinny that verged on scrawny, and that was before old age shriveled him.

One of the few pleasures I had was supplying Grandpa with desserts. I knew he enjoyed eating almost any kind of baked goods, and so I scoured the store for new treats. I would ply him with whatever tasty things I found, but he held onto an abiding self-restraint. No matter how much he liked dessert, his guilty conscience about "getting fat" would restrain him from indulging too much.

"Grandpa, would you like a piece of cake for dessert?" I would ask.

"Yes, that would be good," he would say. "But make it a small one." Such a statement would be followed by him holding up two fingers, not even an inch apart. "I shouldn't be having too much. I don't do anything around here. You get fat if you just sit around and eat."

Only when he had the rare strong hankering, or I found something particularly good, would his moral fortitude fail him, and he ended up indulging in a little extravagance. Sometimes fudge was that extravagance.

The days of making fudge for himself were long gone, but my sisters could make a killer batch of fudge, thick and smooth and ready to melt in your mouth. The fudge was cut into little squares about the size of the end of my thumb. Grandpa usually declined to go beyond one piece, but some days he couldn't help himself and would agree to a second. On rare occasions I managed to goad him into eating a third. Eventually it always came down to, "No, no, I better not eat any more. It's very good, and I like it very much, but it is rich. I've had too much already."

One day Grandpa proclaimed, "I'm getting fat, you guys are feeding me so much dessert."

The opposite was true.

When I first came the influx of my better cooking and my attention to Grandpa's needs—constantly offering him snacks and desserts—brought his weight from 125 lbs. to 135 lbs. I was proud of this achievement. The height of my success did not make him fat—in spite of his paranoid conviction. If I was lucky the gain may have brought him up to what was medically considered an acceptable weight. But this didn't last. Subtly, the situation began to change.

When I first arrived Grandpa was eating like anyone else. I quickly realized that he was a picky eater and didn't *like* a lot of foods—but he ate whatever the rest of us ate, even if he didn't care for much of it. There was no question about whether he would eat the same meals as the rest of us, and he would have been *deeply* insulted if someone had tried to offer him different food.

From that place of normalcy everything began to fail. In the first few months he could mostly still manage to eat without assistance.

His regular problems were minor—confusion about where to throw his garbage. Often the little bits of food he couldn't eat were thrown onto the floor right next to the garbage can instead of in it. Or, if not that, he would become distracted into carefully cleaning his plate with a tissue instead of eating his food.

Then he began having trouble with his dinnerware. It started with a bit of trouble *getting* food onto his fork, then progressed to difficulty *keeping* food on his fork for the entire journey to his mouth. Half the time everything on the fork fell off before it reached his mouth. The time came when I removed the fork from his place at the table and limited him to a spoon to decrease his difficulties.

It began with the fork, but his troubles quickly extended to the entire dining experience. Eating became an activity fraught with difficulties that could be humorous or frustrating in turns. Tissue paper became crackers. These 'crackers' were torn up and thrown into his soup. Or else tissue paper became bread, carefully folded and stuck in his mouth. If I didn't catch him before the tissues made it to his mouth the expression of astounded perplexity which appeared on his face made it nearly impossible to keep from laughing. Often enough, he tried to dutifully chew up the paper.

"You don't want to eat that, Grandpa," I would say, as kindly as possible.

"I don't?" He looked at me, puzzled, uncertain.

"No, how about you eat this instead," I said, and swapped him a slice of bread for the tissue.

"I don't understand," he mumbled, but went back to eating his supper.

Eventually, we had to take away the tissue paper and his place mat because they both became such a distraction from the real food.

It was difficult to watch him struggle with feeding himself. He would go through all sorts of contortions in an attempt to get the spoon to his mouth, only to have the implement list at the last second, two inches from his mouth, and dump its contents down his front.

"Awww, damn it!" he would say, and then try again. I felt his dismay and frustration that grew to desperation as every spoonful failed to reach his mouth.

"Jeepers!" he exclaimed after yet another lurch sent his spoonful of cereal onto the table. He raised the spoon—for a moment contemplating slamming it down on the table. Then he lowered his hand. "I'm making a mess of things," he complained, trying to scrape cereal from the table. "I'm a slob. Why can't I do anything?"

There were many times my primary task during Grandpa's meal was wiping up the messes as he ate so that he wouldn't be distracted from eating by his own futile attempts at cleaning up his mistakes. Those drips of milk and bits of food were important to him.

On top of his difficulty using his implements and recognizing what he was supposed to eat, he was also spitting out more and more of his food because he felt he couldn't chew it. Then, as his attention span shortened, he had difficulty maintaining focus long enough to finish his meals. The Alzheimer's continued to progress and not only did feeding himself become difficult, but food increasingly lost its appeal. Between the two problems, Grandpa's food consumption began to decline.

I tried to use his love for sweets as a means to keep up his dwindling weight. I made certain that we had a constant supply of desserts in the house—cakes, brownies, cookies, candy bars, fudge, sweet rolls, and anything else I thought might catch his interest and keep him eating. I offered them for snack in the morning, after lunch, for snack in the afternoon, after supper, and for snack at bedtime.

Plying Grandpa with desserts worked for a while, but the eating problems progressed to the point where I found his deficiency a bit alarming. It was one thing for him to struggle to eat and make a mess in the process if in the end he still consumed all he needed. It was another thing entirely if in spite of all my efforts he was no longer eating sufficiently.

It reached the stage where a large supply of patience and continual prompting were necessary to help him through a meal. At first his problems with feeding himself, and disinterest in food, were only severe when he was mentally in a worse state than usual. When that happened I could shrug it off and tell myself he would make up the difference the next day. Then it grew worse, and by the summer of 2008 his failing ability to eat had become a serious and chronic problem. My concerns were confirmed when during that summer my sister Titi commented that it looked like Grandpa had lost weight. A weighing confirmed the fact—he was back down to around 125 lbs.

He was starting to waste away. There is a name for this. They call it "failure to thrive."

I decided it was time to change Grandpa's diet. Pondering what I saw when Grandpa ate, I concluded that he now spat out anything of differing texture in his food. My first thought was that I should begin feeding him pureed baby food, but as I stood in the grocery store aisle I had second thoughts. My instincts told me he wasn't quite so far gone that he would find eating the bland puree of baby food acceptable. Though chewy things, crunchy things, and any other noticeable lumps were now spat out, he still wanted taste and substance.

Instead of baby food I went to the halfway point of junior food which I found fit him just about right. A junior food meal of chicken and potatoes with a cheese sauce had taste and substance without anything standing out enough for him to think it needed to be spat out. He ate it because nothing felt too difficult to chew or swallow, but he wasn't thrilled. The stuff did not taste like home cooking. In retrospect, I wish I had tried pureeing more of my normal cooking in the food processor so that Grandpa could have continued to enjoy the taste of home cooked food.

I fed him the junior food but for variety I also served him canned ravioli (which he liked but I loathed), and "select" brands of canned soup which were substantial enough with meat, potatoes, and vegetables to be more stew than soup and constitute a solid meal. This provided enough variety so that he didn't have to eat the same thing over and over again.

The change in diet helped because it meant he was no longer spitting out his food, but having the right food didn't solve all the problems. There remained the issue of Grandpa knowing how to feed himself, and being *willing* to eat.

As his ability to eat continued to worsen I became very worried. I began to face the possibility that Grandpa might eventually starve himself to death, and I devoted increasing amounts of time to fighting this possibility. The battle was not just feeding him, but convincing him that he wanted to eat and that there were things he would like to eat. Toward this end, I developed a list of the things he would eat so I would have a ready supply of alternative choices.

I was worried, but I tried to put the problem in context. It looked like he wasn't eating much, but how many calories was he really consuming each day? To answer that question I tracked the exact number of calories he consumed over several days. With such facts I thought to objectively determine how poorly he was doing.

For a few days in the summer of 2008 I kept meticulous records of all he consumed but this type of record keeping (on top of caring for Grandpa) quickly became too much, and I stopped. A short record was enough to lay out the stark facts. The situation was not good, but not so bad that he was in imminent danger of dying from starvation. I found some comfort in that realization.

§§§

As 2008 moved into 2009 the great struggle for Grandpa was learning how to deal with the fact that he couldn't feed himself. Of all the things he had to learn to accept, this was perhaps the hardest. There was little I could do to help except be there to offer my assistance. With all of his being, Grandpa wanted to feed himself. But the cold fact of reality was that he grew increasingly incapable. When he couldn't scoop food from his bowl, or couldn't bring it to his mouth, or couldn't even grasp the spoon—then he couldn't feed himself no matter how hard he tried.

On a good day in February of 2009 it took all of Grandpa's mental ability to eat lunch—and he couldn't do it alone.

"Would you like some lunch?" I asked him after I came back from my bike ride. "Are you hungry?"

"Are you hungry?" he repeated back to me.

"Would you like something to eat?" I asked, rephrasing the question.

"Yes, I would," he said. "But not just anything. What do you got? Some of the stuff you feed me I wouldn't give to a cat." He didn't get that last sentence so clear, but I managed to decipher the gist of what he meant.

"All sorts of stuff," I answered evasively. "What do you want?" I tried to avoid giving him a run-down of choices because he could never remember them all, and often if given a definite selection he simply decided they all didn't sound good enough and he would just go without eating.

"Well, I don't know," he said. "What have you got?"

"Lots of stuff," I said. "Imagine that you could have whatever you want—what would you pick?"

"Well, that's not very nice," he said.

"Okay, would you like soup or sandwiches?" I said, trying a different approach. It was key to keep the question always an either/or and work down to a final selection through a process like twenty questions. I did the same with breakfast, where the first question was hot or cold and then we worked from that point. This helped eliminate confusion by limiting his choices, and what he had to remember. It also reinforced a sense of inevitability.

"Yeah, I guess I'll have that," Grandpa agreed, failing to specify which.

"Soup or sandwiches?" I repeated.

"Sandwich sounds good," he said.

"Would you like tuna fish or grilled cheese?" I asked

"I'll have the Dur-guh," he said, pointing at a spot on his pants.

"Grilled cheese?" I prompted, not missing a beat.

"No, the other one," he said.

"Tuna fish?" I offered.

"Yeah, that sounds good," he said.

"Okay, I'll get you a tuna fish sandwich in a little bit." I turned to go.

"Now wait a minute," he protested. "I also want a...I want...some nu-hunn and...and..."

"I'll get you some drink too," I assured him.

I knew that in a muddled way he was trying to express a request for coffee—it was always what he wanted to have with his lunch—but I tried to get him to drink as much of the nutrient drink as possible because it was rapidly becoming his largest source of calories. I bought the "plus" variety of the store brand which meant in 8 oz. there were 350 calories. A few cups of that stuff could make up for a lot of lost food.

I made the tuna sandwich and cut it into quarters and stood the quarters up on their ends on his plate so they were easy to see and pick up. As his ability to eat deteriorated I had to alter how I presented his food. By this time in 2009 he had progressed to the point where he was having difficulty figuring out how to use *any* implement, so finger food was best. But nothing was working well for him anymore—not his head, his hands, or his mouth.

Eating the sandwich started with difficulty. First he thought to pick up the entire plate. I prompted him that it might be better to pick up the sandwich instead. Then he moved to pick up several quarters at once, and I suggested it would be better to take one quarter at a time. I rearranged two quarters of the sandwich, demonstrating. Finally, everything clicked together in his mind and he picked up a quarter of the sandwich and started eating. He finished off the sandwich haltingly, but without any further trouble.

"Would you like some potato chips?" I asked after he finished the sandwich.

"Yeah, I guess that sounds good. I would like that," he said.

I pulled out out the nearly empty bag of potato chips.

"But only...only give...just a..." he said, struggling.

"You only want a little bit?" I said.

"Yeah, the bag is almost...not much."

"Oh, you don't need to worry about using them up," I said. "There is another bag."

"Oh, okay," he said, visibly relieved.

He started out eating the potato chips, but things quickly went south. Perhaps he muddled up taking a drink from his cup with eating the chips, or maybe he just forgot what he was doing. The end result was Grandpa reaching down to the table top, pinching his fingers together and lifting his empty hand to his mouth, studiously holding them to his lips, and gently blowing on them. Befuddled, he realized this wasn't accomplishing anything, and returned his concentration to the table. After a little bit he rediscovered his cup and picked that up for a drink. Then he set the cup back down—this time directly on his plate of chips—and began pushing the plate and cup around the table.

He finished pushing his plate and cup around and returned to pinching his fingers together and lifting the empty hand to his mouth, saying, "Awww, shit," every time the movement didn't result with food appearing in his mouth. This did not improve, even after I suggested he needed to pick up a potato chip. After several such failed suggestions I realized that he had (for the moment) forgotten how to eat.

For months he had done a lot of "ghosting" where he very convincingly used an imaginary implement to eat. When ghosting he could be amazingly accurate in his movements—scooping from the bowl and pretend inserting into his mouth—except all was for naught because the spoon he was using didn't exist. At first I fixed this by inserting a spoon into his hand. The ghost eating then became real. But as he grew worse there were times when it went beyond ghosting to the point where he was no longer entirely sure what needed to be done to get food into his mouth. He would clench his fingers and lift his hand from table to mouth in the vague memory that such was how food appeared in his mouth. But it was the faint memory of a once remembered habit, not something that could turn into the actual deed.

"I guess you forgot how to eat," I said.

"I guess," he said. "Something like that. I don't know what's going on."

I fed him the rest of the chips, and he was agreeable to opening his mouth so I could stick them in. Halfway through the process he dumped the rest of his chips on the table. When he didn't remember what to do with his meal anymore he dumped it on the table if no one was quick enough to stop him. This meant that we often ended up with a lot of food and drink on the table.

I picked the chips off the table and continued to feed him while he continued to "feed" himself imaginary things. He had his cup in his other hand, but wasn't paying any attention to it and the cup continued to list further and further in his hand until he started unconsciously pouring his drink on the table. I rescued the drink from him and cleaned up the mess.

Betwixt and between all of this I was also eating my own lunch. It was something of a project, but this was a *good* day. Sometimes he had a much worse lunch.

Once we were finished I wheeled him to the living room and moved him on to the couch. Then I went back to the kitchen and began working on a roast for supper. From the couch Grandpa began calling for my Uncle Joel.

"Joel? Hey Joely! Joel!?"

"Yeah, what do you want?" I said from the kitchen.

"Is that you, Joel?" he called out.

"It's me. What do you want?" I called back.

"I want you to say, 'Hi, Pa,'" he said.

"Hi, Pa," I dutifully said, moving about the kitchen.

"Good. How are you doing?" he said.

"Just fine," I said. "Everything is good here."

There was a little more disjointed conversation as Grandpa fretted in a muddled sort of way about the general woes of Joel's life until he went silent again. Then:

"Gene?"

"Yeah?" I said.

"Go lay down," he said.

Then a little later: "Ma? Hey, mother? Ma?"

"Yeah?" I said.

"I just want you to know I love you very much, and I wish..." he trailed off into incomprehensibility.

I decided what he really meant was that he was very lonely, so I went out to sit with him. We just sat together, two lonely souls living out the last months of Alzheimer's end.

§§§

BATHING TROUBLES

I have a clear memory from my childhood. It was a summer evening and I was a little boy, maybe six years old. I had stepped outside at Grandma and Grandpa's house to see Uncle Kevin in the garden. Curious, I went over and watched him chop up the ground with a hoe. I asked him what he was doing.

"I'm weeding the garden for Grandpa," he said, drops of sweat flying from the end of his nose as he worked. "Now don't you tell him what I'm doing. He won't want help with his garden, and I want this to be a secret."

Secretive garden weeding done on the sly without Grandpa's approval? I took off back for the house so I wouldn't be caught anywhere in the area when Grandpa found out. Of course, just as I dreaded, Grandpa came out as I went inside and met me at the front door. "What's Kevin doing?" he asked.

I felt myself grow hot. Honesty compelled me, but Kevin's command restrained me. What to say? I settled for muttering, "You'll have to see for yourself," not meeting Grandpa's gaze like some guilty criminal.

One step outside was enough to give Kevin away. Grandpa crossed the yard while I stayed at the doorway watching and realizing it looked like I had run off and tattled to Grandpa, even though I hadn't.

"He ran off and told you, huh," I heard Kevin say, continuing to hoe. "I told him not to."

"No, he didn't," Grandpa said, and I felt better. "I was coming out anyhow. What are you doing? You shouldn't be weeding the garden. I can do that."

"I don't mind, Pa. I'm glad to do it," Kevin said

"Well, you shouldn't." Grandpa said. "I don't want you coming over here to weed the garden for me."

"I don't mind, Pa." Kevin insisted. "I'll do just a little more."

Grandpa didn't like people helping him. He didn't think it proper for guests to work when visiting, and he didn't like the idea that people thought he needed help. This was true all those years ago, and it was still true when I cared for Grandpa. Often I felt caught between Grandpa and his dignity, not knowing what to say or do. I tried my fumbling best, and like Kevin I helped as much as I could on the sly.

As the Alzheimer's worsened Grandpa grew increasingly unable to keep track of time and dates. As it became increasingly difficult to wash himself he came to dislike and avoid bathing more and more. I had to start suggesting that it was time for a shower or bath. Grandpa began insisting, "Didn't I just have one?"

"That was last week, Grandpa," I would remind him.

"Well, I can't be that dirty. It wasn't that long ago," was his reply.

This was an opportune time for argument, as he was legitimately intimidated by the prospect of bathing himself, and honestly felt in his mind like he had just done it "yesterday." To him it seemed I was forcing a shower on him every time he turned around.

It could have easily spiraled into "I don't need a bath" and "Yes, you do." At first I managed to avoid this by playing a game of good cop vs. bad cop. I was the good cop, and Grandma was unwittingly the bad cop. When Grandpa needed to wash I would suggest that he take a shower and Grandpa would indignantly deny that he needed one. Grandma would then get impatient and say, "Yes, you do. Go take a shower!" He would then bluster and fume at Grandma, and I would tell him we would give him a shower, "Just to make Grandma happy." He would rail about how unfair and demanding Grandma was, and I would go on about how we needed to keep her happy. He would grumblingly agree with that, so it all became a matter of keeping Grandma happy instead of an argument over whether he *really* needed a bath or not.

That was a dicey strategy because there was no guarantee he would always be amenable to such persuasion. He only had to decide he was sick of taking a bath "every day" just to make Grandma happy and then I would be in real trouble. I realized we needed a more fixed schedule which Grandpa would find agreeable and which I could use to persuade him. As a result, Saturday became "bath day." It was only on Saturday that he had to take a bath or shower. When he would say, "Didn't I just take a bath?" I could say, "No, Grandpa, that was last Saturday. You only take a bath on Saturday, remember?" Then he would have to grudgingly concede that it was only mandated for Saturdays, and if it was indeed Saturday then it must be time for his bath.

I discovered the method to get him to come the most agreeably was if I said, "It's Saturday, Grandpa. That means it's bath day. Do you want to take your shower now?" He would always say, "It is? I don't want to take it now. Let's wait until later." Then I would say, "Okay, we'll do it in a little while." He would then sit there, thinking about the prospect of a shower hanging over him and about a minute and a half later he would say, "Aaah, we might as well do it now and get it over with."

It's all in the psychology.

This particular trick worked well for a time, but I knew it wasn't a permanent solution. It became increasingly unpleasant and difficult for Grandpa to bathe and I realized there would eventually come a time that whenever asked—no matter what the stipulations or circumstances—he would simply refuse to take a bath or shower because he would find the prospect too overwhelming. Throughout my time of caring for him I always tried to give him as much dignity of choice as possible—but there came a time when he was no longer able to make choices. Knowing when to make the switch from asking to simply doing—when he wouldn't be terribly offended by, or fight, the lack of say in the matter—was a decision of gut instinct. It reached the point where I realized being *asked* whether he was ready for his shower only agitated him and he was forgetful enough that I could just take him to the shower as if *of course* this was what we were going to do. The fact that we hadn't discussed it could slip past his mind entirely.

I found a very "devious" method of getting him into the shower. Back when he was still using the toilet some of the time, shortly after breakfast he would need to go pee (the morning coffee coming through), and I would take him to the bathroom and set him on the toilet. As he was using the toilet I would start up the shower and get things ready. Then when he was ready to get off the toilet I would help him up, get him undressed, and guide him into the shower. He never thought to question it. All the cues were there: He was in the bathroom, the shower water was running, and he was in a partial state of undress having just used the toilet.

Once he began using the wheelchair, this method became even easier. I would start the shower, and when Grandpa finished eating breakfast I would wheel him to the bathroom door, help him up, and start getting him undressed. Any slight hesitation on his part would be met with "We're doing your shower. Here's your washcloth. Hop in." At this point there was nothing to do but hop in. It wasn't even a thing to be thought about—it simply *was*.

That worked for a while. Then we reached the stage where he had problems washing himself. Fairly early on I started washing Grandpa's hair. It was the first thing he forgot to clean for himself—his head being something he didn't see—and when I broached the idea of me washing his hair he readily agreed. It then progressed to where I washed his hair and his back, and prompted him on washing the rest of himself. The transition went smoothly this far.

Washing other parts of him beyond his back was a different matter. This became a problem as he began to forget to wash increasingly more of his body. When he couldn't remember what he had washed, or what he needed to wash, or even what he was *supposed* to be washing—well, it was very hard for him to wash. I started by helping him through the process verbally. "Okay, now wash your chest." I would say. "Don't forget to wash your legs," and so on. This worked for a time, but became a rapidly failing solution. Quickly following the problem of forgetting what he had washed or needed to wash was the problem of not understanding what someone was telling him to wash. We hit the end of this method when the instruction, "Okay, Grandpa, now it's time to wash your legs," was met with the response of, "Yep, I'm working on that," while he vigorously scrubbed the side of the tub.

When this happened, explaining was useless. If something was going to be done, I had to do it myself. Since I had acclimated Grandpa to my hands on his back, I simply progressed to wash the rest of him as the natural course of things—as quickly as I could—and he gave no objection. Except when it came to the matter of washing his genitals. That was the one catch—the point where we couldn't just ease out of his modesty and dignity. Grandpa would have to be practically comatose before he would willingly allow someone else to wash his genitals.

The situation was miserable for both of us. Grandpa was no longer able to do it for himself, he didn't want me to do it for him, and I didn't want to do it for him. But it had to be done. And he couldn't do it. So I had to do it.

It was terribly, exceedingly, awkward. Invariably, I would start and the reaction was something along the lines of "What the HELL are you doing?"

What kind of answer can you give to that? "Um...cleaning you," seemed completely inadequate. In fact, there wasn't a satisfactory explanation that could be given so long as he had a functioning brain cell in his body. He knew he didn't need someone else cleaning *that* place down there. I could give no explanation to get around that objection. My only solution was to pick my battles. Some weeks I let that particular area slide if I sensed he was feeling feisty. Otherwise, my general method was do it fast, and distract him.

My typical distraction method was to say, "Okay, Grandpa, it's time for you to wash your face." Then, while he was washing his face I quick wash the other end and by the time he realized what was going on I was all done. Thus a confrontation was (just) avoided.

In all of this Grandpa's trouble with bathing followed the same trajectory as the rest of his life since his Alzheimer's began. First he needed a little help, then he needed more, and finally he needed a lot. There came the time when he no longer could stand for his shower, and so I acquired a shower chair. Then he started having difficulty stepping in the tub. By the spring of 2009 we had nearly reached the end of the road with his bathing situation, and by the end of spring I was picking him up and putting him on the shower chair because he couldn't step into the tub. The only step left was switching to a sponge bath.

That final transition to a sponge bath came when I realized he no longer understood the bathing process. It had become meaningless to him. Carting him into the bathroom, stripping him naked, and sticking him on the shower chair under the running water was an alien and meaningless experience. Some dim part of his mind understood I was trying to help with *something*, but to his emotions and senses it felt like I was assaulting him. This meaningless sensory assault made him by degrees confused, panicked, and combative.

When I realized this I pondered what I could do to alleviate the problem and then realized that switching to a sponge bath was the best solution. I still gave him his bath right after breakfast on bath day, but I no longer made him get out of his wheel chair. Leaving him fully clothed, I first wash his head and face. Then I dried his head and face. Next I took off his shirt and washed his upper body, dried it, applied lotion, and put on his clean undershirt and shirt. Then I pulled up his pant legs and washed as much of his legs as I could, dried them, and applied lotion. Since Grandpa was still able to stand with support I had him stand up and grab the table to steady himself while I took off his pants and diaper, washed his bottom and manly parts, dried him, and put on a fresh diaper and pants.

Since only a portion of him was exposed at any one time, and only for the briefest amount of time, he was only vaguely aware of being washed. There were no loud noises, no moving between rooms, and no water raining down on his body to upset him. For the sponge bath he was calm, and it may even have been relaxing for him. My stress level over bathing went down, and it was a lot less work.

Understanding how to handle problems, and when to move on to new solutions, was always key when caring for Grandpa. Nothing ever stayed the same.

§§§

LAUGHTER

Some of the sweetest memories I have from the years of caring for Grandpa are what we shared in humor. Many people were not fully aware of Grandpa's sense of humor because for most of his life his strong sense of decorum kept his humor in check. His humor was not the type for mature or refined company, so as an adult it was often restrained, only occasionally slipping out.

There was a good deal of overlap between Grandpa's humor and mine, though I think I have less sense of propriety to restrain my impulses. As Grandpa's Alzheimer's grew worse, his sense of humor became increasingly uninhibited. Where mature conversation was lost we gained the ability to tease, joke, and laugh.

Grandpa never, never lost his sense of humor.

Conveying our banter, games, and jokes, is difficult. Partly this is because a huge amount of nuance, texture, intonation, and inside references went into the verbal teasing. This makes it difficult to relay the full humor of an exchange in a way that accurately conveys why it was funny. The old adage is true: "You had to be there." But also it is difficult to convey the humor because as a comedian I am extemporaneous, making it up as I go along, and forgetting it just about as quickly. So, if you weren't there, you missed it, and I forgot.

At the time I didn't really think about why I indulged in the humor. It was just something that spontaneously welled up inside me that I let bubble out. In reflection, I see that the teasing and the jokes did several important things. First, it was a way for me to communicate with Grandpa, to express my love and affection in a way he could understand, all the way up to the end. Second, it was a way for me to take Grandpa's mind off his troubles and misery. Introduced at the right moment, a bit of laughter could effectively defuse Grandpa's worry or agitation. Finally, the jokes were simply an expression of me finding laughter in life, an act which provided a bit of antidote to the hard times, and sad times. It helped me cope.

Since Grandpa was significantly impaired in his speech ability this meant any verbal joking was largely a one-sided act performed by me. The routine (with all its varieties) was also almost exclusively absurdist. The key was to keep the lines short enough, and absurd enough, that Grandpa could easily grasp that it was a joke. A bonus was if I could bait him into giving one word responses.

We would go like this:

"Are you poor?" I would say. (Grandpa always thought of himself as very poor, so the answer was easy.)

"Yes," was always Grandpa's answer.

"I think we should go rob a bank," came my sly suggestion.

"What?" Grandpa said.

"Don't you think it would be fun to rob a bank?" I goaded.

"No," Grandpa said. (At this point he hadn't caught on to the joke. If he did he would dryly say, "Sure, lots of fun.")

"But it's lots of fun," I teased. "You get to shoot guns and drive cars really fast, and have the police chase you with sirens. And if you're really lucky, you get thrown in jail."

By this time I had piled on enough very bad and not fun things that Grandpa gets the joke. So I add the last twist. "But don't worry," I said. "When they catch us, and we go on trial, I'll testify against you and get off Scott free while you go to jail for twenty years."

"Haha, yeah you will!" Grandpa said. "You bugger!"

The last line was Grandpa's favorite, not only because it adds a little twist to the story, but also because it reflected his view on life: The guilty were always getting out of their due punishment by blaming someone else.

Other times I teased Grandpa more directly, like this:

(I sit down next to Grandpa and give him a hug.)

"Boy, you are *so* strong and handsome," I said. "How did you get so strong?"

"Don't speak such nonsense," Grandpa said.

"You're *so* strong, I wish I was as strong as you," I said gleefully. "I bet all the girls like you."

"You think so, huh?" Grandpa doesn't hide how stupid he finds my comments.

"Yep," I add with gusto. "I think we need to get you a girlfriend."

Grandpa remained silent.

I continued with great false excitement, "So what we'll do is, we'll take you to the beach in California and have you walk up and down the beach in a tiny bathing suit and flex your *big* muscles for all the girls. Doesn't that sound like a good idea?"

"Don't be stupid," Grandpa said.

I did a lot of variations on the "You're Handsome" joke. Grandpa was never a big man, never was a man for the girls, and certainly never wanted to prance around in *any* type of bathing suit. It was probably not possible to come up with a more absurdly *stupid* joke, and Grandpa rarely found it funny. But I enjoyed it immensely because it was a great way to tease him since he found such jokes about his person slightly embarrassing, highly stupid, and vaguely inappropriate.

I had various other stock basic jokes which I would alter in infinite variations. There were the "When you were a little boy" jokes, usually centering around some supposed wickedness he had done as a child, or somehow involving how his mother had treated him (kisses, hugs, spankings, etc). When I came in from outside and he asked who it was at the door, I would tell him I was his conscience come back to haunt him for all the bad things he had done. Sometimes he would dead-pan a line back. Sometimes he would laugh.

Then there were the motorcycle jokes, the car jokes, and the traveling jokes, all things which Grandpa hated and all things I would suggest he engage in, by some elaborate and over-blown fashion.

Some of my verbal jokes didn't necessarily involve Grandpa directly but were my own little personal riff on life which he may or may not have gotten (depending), but he certainly gathered my general mood. As Grandpa took to calling me Gene I took to calling him George. It was a good humored tit-for-tat of mis-named calling. He would shout "Gene!" and I would shout "George!" We were the two buddies shouting for our friend/brother who wasn't there. I joined in on the shouting as a subtle acknowledgment of the ludicrousness of our entire situation—calling people by names that weren't theirs, shouting endlessly for people who weren't present.

As time went on I became increasingly convinced that, in some sense, Grandpa was on to that deeper subtext of the joke. The most clear example came one evening when Grandma was quizzing Grandpa about the names of people in his family. One of the first things Grandpa lost to Alzheimer's was his ability to recall faces and names together, much less dig names up from his memory. So when Grandma asked Grandpa for the name of his mother he glowered at her, not wanting to face the humiliation of admitting he couldn't remember. After a moments pause he told her very distinctly, and defiantly, "Georgie." Since he couldn't remember his mother's name, he very deliberately gave her the *obviously* wrong name. His (rather brilliant, given the circumstance) verbal riposte left Grandma nearly hysterical with laughter. She got the joke, too. He couldn't remember his mother's name, but he *could* remember that Georgie was the "wrong" name that everybody kept using for the unnamed *somebody* who wasn't around and so he deliberately used it to make his own point.

I could never be entirely certain how well Grandpa followed my humor. Some times it was evident that he was in on the joke. Other times I couldn't be sure, and so had to be satisfied with amusing myself and leaving Grandpa to get it as well, or not, depending.

Sometimes he surprised me.

One day, sometime during his last summer, Grandpa was hollering at the top of his lungs for nothing in particular. I was sitting next to him, trying to keep him company while I flipped through a magazine. He would shout "Hey!" with ever increasing volume, staring across the room as if *something* over there should answer. I would say, "Yep," or "I'm right here," or "I hear you," in response. Either my responses simply weren't registering in his mind, or he was truly trying to get the attention of the (non-existent) person on the other side of the room, because his volume kept increasing. Finally, after a bellowed "HEEEYYYY!" from Grandpa I tired of giving the same mundane responses. So instead I drolled out, "A little louder, Grandpa. The Chinese can't quite hear you yet."

There was silence. Then Grandpa said, "Was that a snide comment?"

And I had thought he wasn't paying attention. I had to laugh then.

The best times were when he did get my jokes, and then tried to take them one step further. It didn't matter if his Alzheimer's thwarted his intentions—the effort was all that counted. On another occasion he was once again calling out randomly. He shouted, "Gene!" so I shouted "George!" as per usual. Except this time he followed up by shouting, "George!" as I had done.

Since we were apparently varying our routine I shouted "Where are you?" He promptly (and with no hint of humor) mimicked me, shouting "Where are you?"

At this point I caught on that his mind had fallen into repeat mode, so I decided to have a little more fun. This time I shouted, "Give me all your money!"

Grandpa started to repeat me—but then caught himself. In that instant the Alzheimer's parted for just a moment and he realized what we were doing. "You want it all, huh?" he said, mischievously. "Well, hold out your hand, palm up, and I'll put a little—" but then the Alzheimer's struck again, and his words left him and he lost the rest of it. I couldn't decide if he had been attempting to say he would put something naughty or nasty in my hand or that "all his money" was a pittance, but I laughed for his attempt to best me, and Grandpa laughed too.

Perhaps we had the most fun with our physical humor. I had a running gag where when Grandpa called—for me, somebody, anybody, to do something, anything, not sure what—I would come to him and offer him a pinch, a poke, or a bite. Sometimes, I would even tell him they were on a special sale. This would distract him from whatever imagined problem he had, and it almost always provoked a good reaction from him. If I gave him pinches we might just devolve into a "pinching fight" where we would both try to pinch the other while chuckling with fake malevolence.

I constantly harassed Grandpa physically, playfully, partly because with him forever calling me over it became boring to come and simply ask him what he wanted, especially when he couldn't come up with any answer. Instead of following that dull routine it became more fun to come over and harass him whenever he called. It served the purpose Grandpa really wanted, which was for somebody to come and pay attention to him, and remind him that he was loved. Of course, not to be entirely outdone, he wasn't averse to sneaking his hand out, thumb sticking up threateningly from the cushion beside him when I began to sit down. He never quite dared let me sit on his thumb, but it was his way of saying, "I gotcha back."

As his Alzheimer's worsened and he became increasingly unaware of his surroundings I found this a great opportunity to surprise Grandpa. For someone else, I'm sure the game would have been cruel, but not with Grandpa. The routine consisted in me coming upon Grandpa when he was completely absorbed in his task—typically consisting in crawling about on the floor picking lint from the carpet. While he was thus utterly preoccupied I would leap upon his crouched form, snarling and biting like some ferocious lion descending on its prey. Without fail he would shout in surprise and jump out of his skin. I would then fall down beside him, laughing and crowing, "I got you! I got you! I got you!" He would laugh, and say, "Yeah, you sure did. You sure got me that time!" Sometimes he would vow that one day he would get me back.

One of my most favorite times was when I sneaked up on him, commando style, slithering around the couch so I could pop up and take a bite out of his knee while he sat there, blissfully folding pages out of a magazine. He jumped—oh, he really jumped! Afterward, in the midst of his laughter, he said, "Did you see me? Did you see how I jumped? It's a good thing I didn't have my mini-club then or I would have splattered you all over the place."

Yes, indeed, Grandpa knew how to appreciate the fine art of getting someone. His goal was to get me back.

My most favorite time was the time he did get me back.

It was completely unexpected. He was having a bad evening and spent I don't know how long down on his hands and knees, shouting incomprehensibly. Finally exhaustion overcame him and when I checked on him in the living room he was sprawled on the carpet like a dead man. He looked so sad, weary, and worn out as I bent down to check on his sleeping form—and at that moment Grandpa went "Bwhahahahaha!" and came up, grabbing for me. Oh, yes, I jumped. I really jumped. Who would have expected this worn out man to be plotting on me? I don't know how he did it.

"I got you! I got you!" Grandpa said, chuckling gleefully. And I was so proud of him. He had finally got me back.

I treasure all of those times. They are memories that can still make me laugh. I treasure them, because even in the midst of Alzheimer's—

even in spite of it—those times were times when we had fun together in our own personal, crazy, zany, way. It was the way we spoke the language of love, a language that knew no boundaries.

This last story is not exactly a joke, but it seems a fitting conclusion to illustrate our life together. Every night when I put Grandpa to bed I would tuck him in and give him a goodnight kiss. But I got bored with that. So when I tucked him in I started giving him "hundreds" of kisses all over his cheek. I was teasing him, a little, even while I expressed my love and affection. Then one night when I bent to kiss him he looked up seriously and said, "Just one kiss, now. Any more than that, and it's a little queer."

If you say so, Grandpa. Just one kiss.

§§§

WHAT PICTURES SAY

The old familiar saying goes, "A picture is worth a thousand words." The sentiment is only partly true. A picture of the Grand Canyon can convey its physical appearance far more clearly than a thousand words. But a picture does not tell you what someone thought about the Grand Canyon. If someone brings home a postcard of the Grand Canyon that picture on the postcard does not tell you whether they were elated or fearful at the sight.

To take the thought further, a picture is not good at conveying the details of complex ideas. A good picture of a person may hint at the complexities of the subject, but it cannot speak clearly about past sorrows, joys, or accomplishments. I could convey more detail about the life of a person I know in a thousand words than in a single picture. But a picture would give you a clearer understanding of their appearance than I could convey in a thousand words.

It is also said, "Pictures don't lie." This is not true. Anyone who understands photography knows you can present false information in a picture, whether by the physical altering of the photo (very easy with today's technology) or by simply altering the lighting, posing, or setting of a photo. Even the most simple photograph is not just conveying what **is**—it is conveying a certain *perspective*.

Words don't replace pictures, and pictures don't replace words. They simply tell different stories.

Why am I saying all of this? Because when I look at pictures of Grandpa from during the time I cared for him I am always struck by these realities. There is so much the photos don't show. But the reverse is also true. Sometimes a photo shows something I couldn't convey in words.

The memories, words, and photos I have of the time I cared for Grandpa balance each other. They each tell a slightly different story. In my memories, and often in my writing, what comes more readily are the bad times. Then I see photos—photos of things I lived through —and it gives me a different perspective.

In my mind the photos I have are divided into two categories. The first are sad pictures, which present an approximate chronicling of Grandpa's decline. Then there are the happy pictures, which remind me of things I need to never forget.

The photos I have give a slightly different picture than I could ever convey in my words.

In the early days Grandpa spent a lot of time sitting at the kitchen table. He would sit at the table with a cup of coffee, or an empty cup, and think (or not) while he muttered and moaned. I have that captured in a freeze-frame of life.

Later, when he was no longer able to walk well (or at all) he would often crawl around the house until he was exhausted. Then he lay down and slept wherever he happened to stop. I have snapshots of these times. There is a bit of fondness in the memories—if it hadn't been an old man I could say he looked cute lying there on the floor. But mostly the image cuts to the heart because in the picture I have captured Grandpa's exhaustion and misery. The pictures show poignantly what he was losing, and had lost.

He never wanted to be alone. I can say it again and again, but when I see the photo of Grandpa sitting in his wheelchair at the entrance to the sun room, staring out at the people gathered there, watching, I see the longing for company encapsulated in a frame. The picture of Grandpa staring out from his wheelchair was taken only two months before he died. He had lost so much awareness and ability, but still he hungered for company.

It is hard to describe my reaction to those photos. They are sad, and at the same time when I look at them I feel like they don't do justice to what happened. The living, and feeling, can't be distilled down to what the pictures show.

Grandpa liked hats. He was always happy to wear hats. When one of my younger brothers came over to mow the lawn Grandpa would envy his hat. Grandpa found it a very interesting hat and if provided with the opportunity he would put it on. He looked an odd mixture of silly and dignified with that hat on.

I have pictures from the last days of Grandpa's life. They are pictures that don't seem to capture what was happening, and yet perhaps capture enough. Would you know he was dying if I didn't tell you? There is no hospital room, and no strange doctors or nurses. Instead he lies there on the couch, sleeping quietly, perhaps peacefully. It was what Grandpa wanted. Showing that, maybe the picture doesn't need to say any more.

The pictures that say the most to me are those from the 4th of July, 2009. In one Grandpa and Frank sit on the couch, laughing. Seeing that picture, a stranger wouldn't know the old man with one pant leg oddly hiked up couldn't walk, could barely speak a few intelligent words, couldn't feed himself, and was hardly eating. Looking at it, a person wouldn't know that in a little over two months Grandpa would be dead. That picture can't tell you that he was more lost than you could ever imagine, and yet not so lost as you might think.

When I look at that picture I want to cry, and I don't know if it is from gladness or sorrow. The memories come, and they burst upon me like a flood. I don't know if the hurt and the loss that comes with that picture is a remembrance of mine, or his. Once I get past that feeling, the picture reminds me of something that is often drowned in the weight of my own memories. Somehow, the ugly moments stay with me more clearly, and the smiles and laughter become forgotten. It is good to be reminded of the better things which my own perspective sometimes forgets.

The bad memories, and the hurt they bring, can become the only window through which I look back on those last months. But the pictures show a different side. The vision is so different from what I remember in my feelings it is almost hard to believe it is true when I look through the pictures. A stranger looking at those pictures wouldn't think Grandpa in a dire situation. They wouldn't guess how after the party was over it was a battle with apathy and exhaustion to get him to eat a few mouthfuls. For that reason the pictures can feel like a lie to me. For a moment it can feel like those photos paint a false picture. But it isn't that they lie—it is that they only capture a small part of the story. It is a very small part, but a very important part. A part I must not forget.

There were many sad times, and many hard times, but there were happy times too. Even though Grandpa was in the last weeks of his life, and just about everything had fallen apart for him, when his children and grandchildren were around he could still be happy.

Perhaps even very happy.

In some small measure it says what I had labored to give. Sometimes what dwells most fresh in my memories is the pain and the ugliness, and I can have a hard time getting past that. It hurt so bad at the end and those memories cloud my thinking. The pictures remind me of something which is easy for me to forget—that I did give Grandpa something tangible, something real, even in the midst of his loss. And that is good to remember.

§§§

In the early days Grandpa spent a lot of time sitting at the kitchen table.

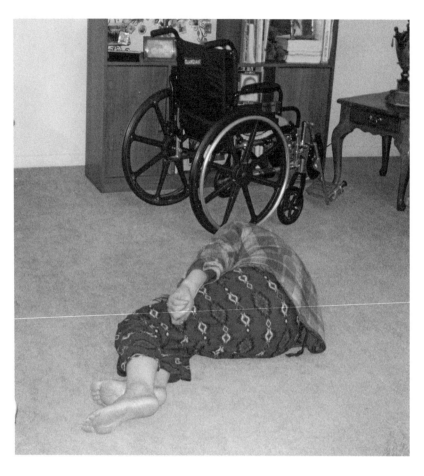

He would often crawl around the house until he was exhausted.

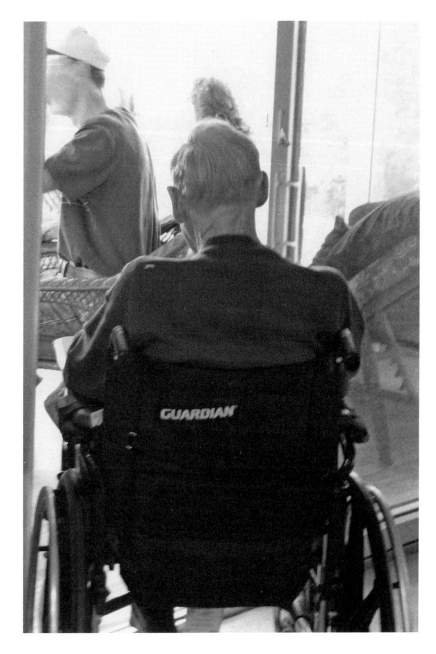

He never wanted to be alone.

Grandpa liked hats. He was always happy to wear hats.

He lies there on the couch, sleeping quietly, perhaps peacefully.

Grandpa and Frank sit on the couch, laughing.

What to remember.

§§§

THE COUCH

On the first of September 2009 I went for a walk along the creek. This was a beautiful time of year for a walk. The first hints of autumn were beginning to show in the greenery, and the water ran cool and quiet. It was soothing. Peaceful. A welcome rest from the reality of life.

There, down by the creek, I found an old discarded typewriter. Lying in the midst of bramble and brush, the Royal typewriter poked out from the weeds like an old wayfaring man from a different era. Long abandoned and forgotten, it was rusted beyond use. Keys which had once typed out poetry or philosophy were seized up with weather and age, never to type again.

This was the sort of rusted metal that one could walk past without a second look. But it caught my attention, and I stopped. I found some odd beauty in that old hunk of junk. It wasn't worth anything now, but it had been once. It couldn't do anything now, but it had done things before. In it were the memories of past accomplishments, and once remembered productivity. Somehow, even in its rusted and broken state some of the beauty from its once functioning life still shone through. It had never been a thing of elegance, but in its square solid frame and hefty weight it had been dependable. Hard working.

Reliable.

I brought the typewriter home and kept it on a shelf. There wasn't any sensible reason to do that—the typewriter couldn't do anything now and never would again. But it seemed like the thing to do. I could look at it, and think about life. Sometimes the worth of a thing is in what it gives without doing anything.

While on the walk I noticed some metal retaining walls had been built into the creek bed to slow the flow of the water. The creek pooled to dribble and splash over the barrier, then was free again to wander on among the boulders. On a whim, when I returned from the walk I asked Grandpa about the retaining walls.

"Oh yeah, they were put in some time ago," he said, once he understood my question. "I can't remember exactly when, but it was some time ago. They did it to help control the flooding," he added, showing that he really did understand what we were talking about. His ability to converse failed him then and he descended again into garbled nonsense.

For that brief moment he seemed like the man he had once been. Those flashes came, sometimes, though so much less often in the end. He had spoken so sensibly, if haltingly. How could this be the same person who had forgotten how to eat, and everything else besides?

At the very end, in the last weeks before he died, he had forgotten so much. He had forgotten how to walk, how to feed himself, and he had nearly forgotten how to talk. Seeing him sitting there on the couch, you would have been excused for thinking he remembered nothing at all.

He had forgotten so much, but not everything. He might not remember where he was, but he remembered where he had been, and what had happened then. He could remember the past, but he could barely remember how to live, and that was quickly fading.

And yet, he still remembered so much more than I could have imagined.

In the last weeks of Grandpa's life Grandma was preparing for a garage sale. In the process of gathering up stuff for the sale she came across a collection of small hand made arrows. The heads of the arrows had been made from stone, lashed to the arrow shafts with cord. Grandma thought Grandpa had made them years ago, but couldn't remember for sure, so she went to ask him.

Pause a moment to consider this irony: going to ask someone nearly completely lost in Alzheimer's whether they had made something. But, surprisingly, not only did he recognize the little arrows and understand Grandma's question, but he had an answer.

"Sure I made them," he said. "There was nothing to it. You just sit there and grind and grind," he explained, referring to the shaping and sharpening of the arrow heads.

His mind was being choked by Alzheimer's, but he was still there, up to the very end.

§§§

The days passed for him as a lonely vigil on the couch. Sometimes he slept a little, but more often he looked at his magazines, gazed at the pictures and wondered what they meant, read the words and wondered what they said, or else just sat on the couch lost in his own thoughts. I have a photo of Grandpa seated on the couch, looking at an over-sized cardboard picture book of the Cinderella fairytale. It is a nice photograph. The afternoon sunlight streams through the window, dappling the floor. Barefoot, Grandpa leans forward in his seat, studying the book with an intent seriousness. The old man is a scholar of the large picture book. It's funny, but poignant, too.

His world had shrunk so that if I was not right beside him, I was not there at all. He called out, only to sometimes startle when I answered, or appeared beside him. Still he called, and still I came. I would sit down beside him, wrap my arms completely around his scrawny middle, and squeeze him just as tightly as he could stand. I would gnaw on his back too, a few bites in fond memory of the days when he used to crawl about the floor and we had played our little games where I hunted him as a lion hunting the zebra. Then he knew he wasn't alone or forgotten.

We all grieve in different ways. Some people grieve loudly, others in silence. Some people take a long time to grieve, others finish grieving in a short time. Grandma told me she was grieving long before Grandpa actually died, and I think that was true for me also. But that doesn't mean I finished grieving before he died.

If grieving entails the acknowledgment of loss, sometimes absence speaks louder than words. For three years Grandpa was my life. My every waking and sleeping moment centered around him. What he needed, what he wanted, what his problems were, and what the solutions might be, were constantly on my mind. And if my life centered around Grandpa, the center of his life was the couch.

The couch was home base. The couch was the place where he always returned. It was the center of his domain. In the household, Grandpa was the constant fixture on the couch.

Grandpa liked the couch. It was a good couch, with good solid cushions. It was the place he was most comfortable. From there he could peer out the window, watch TV (back in the day when it meant something to him), and in general keep tabs on what was going on around the house as much as possible. On the couch he was there for me, always waiting. Sitting on the couch, sleeping on the couch—Grandpa and the couch were meant to be together.

So, it was no surprise that after Grandpa was gone I found the emptiness of the couch the most acute reminder of his absence. Its silence, and emptiness, were the loudest statement of the finality of his departure. The impulse of expecting him to be there was especially strong in the first days after his death. Before, for a man failing from Alzheimer's he could be remarkably sensitive to what was going on in the house. If a door opened or slammed, he wanted to know who it was. If someone was making noise in the kitchen, he wanted to know what was going on. If someone passed by, he wanted to know what they were doing. Grandpa wanted to be informed, and he didn't want to be forgotten. Often he would shout and call for somebody and often all he really wanted was somebody to come sit with him on the couch.

It's strange how habits become ingrained in your mind. In the first days after Grandpa's death I so much expected him on the couch that when I entered the living room it was almost as if I saw him from the corner of my eye—my mind so much anticipating his presence—and it was only when I turned to look that I registered his absence. When I came in from the outside, or shut a door, words would come to the tip of my lips, ready to answer Grandpa's shout from the couch. I would move about the house, and find in the back of my mind I was thinking about how what I was doing would reach Grandpa on the couch.

But when he was gone the couch became empty, and nobody was there to ask who was coming in the house, or what I was doing. The constant calling and questioning voice was gone, and the empty couch became a symbol of the hole in my life. It was a symbol for that which reached much further in my life, because the couch wasn't the only place I noticed his absence. For three years my life and Grandpa's life became so intertwined it was as if we had become conjoined. He always wanted me, and I was always thinking about him. When grocery shopping, I would always have an eye out for anything I thought he might like to eat—especially some dessert. Once he was gone I would go shopping and there was the flash of regretful remembrance when I stopped at the baked goods aisle and thought, "Grandpa would like that," to then in that instant know that I wouldn't be buying any more things for him.

He would almost always wake up early in the morning and get out of bed, determined to leave the bedroom even if he couldn't figure out how to open the door. He was determined to leave, even if he had to push a chair in front of him to walk, or had to crawl. And where would he end up once he finally escaped the bedroom? Seated on the couch.

There are all the memories of the morning coffee, and the daily routine, the little ways in which we both knew how things were supposed to go, and other people didn't, and didn't know why I could do it so much better than them. There are the hard memories of the many bathroom messes, and the bad nights, the irritating times when Grandpa would not stop calling no matter what. Then there are the good memories, the memories of how he liked my hugs, of how we would horse around, and how he would put up with my teasing.

Time is a double-edged sword. As the passage of time dulls the freshness of loss and hurt, so also time takes the freshness of what we once had. The expectation of Grandpa on the couch faded not long after he was gone, and what was, slipped into the past. I knew long before Grandpa died that he would be leaving soon, and I knew when I gave him my squeezing hug that soon I wouldn't be able to any more. So I hugged him, but not too tightly, because I knew that all things in this world must come to an end.

§§§

SAYING GOODBYE

I wish I could say it all ended nicely. I suppose it would make us all feel a little better if I told you a story of rose petals, dim lights, and softly playing music which ushered Grandpa so painlessly from this life. But that isn't what happened.

In the last months of Grandpa's life he began forgetting how to sit upright. He could manage it for a while, but eventually he would begin to list and he had no conception of righting himself. Left unattended, he would end up wherever gravity took him. It was worst when he was sitting in the wheelchair. I had bought a tray which could be attached to the wheelchair to make feeding him easier and this kept him from falling completely out of the wheelchair. Still he would end up flopped painfully over the side of the chair, drooling out of the side of his mouth and trying to support himself with one arm. To keep him in any semblance of an upright position I had to stuff pillows beside him in the chair. He was like a marionette cut from his strings.

The last unraveling had come upon us.

In those last months of Grandpa's life the great contradiction and dilemma I had agreed to take came upon me in full force. I could not escape it, and I was only beginning to know the price I would have to pay. I had agreed to give my all to care for a man I knew would die. So

I gave everything to have it all taken away. I knew it would hurt, but I couldn't really know that hurt until I started feeling it.

This journey had come with costs and contradictions I could not untangle. He was my grandfather; how did it come to be that he felt like my son, my child? I had come to help him through the long journey of dying, and yet I was trying to keep him alive. The contradictions were tearing me apart. It wasn't supposed to be this way.

And yet, it was. All I had done would be undone. All I had given, taken away. There are no easy answers to that reality, and no simple feelings.

I had known from day one that it would come to this. I can't say it took me by surprise, or that it was unexpected. And yet, somehow, in the end, the knowing didn't make it any easier. There are things I felt deep in myself in spite of everything I knew. I knew this was how things would go. I knew as spring waned to summer that I was losing him. Yet, it was as he slipped from my grasp that in losing him I felt I had lost. I told myself it wasn't true, but I couldn't make that feeling go away.

When Grandpa could no longer feed himself, I had to feed him. I was willing to do that. I would sit and take whatever time was required to feed him breakfast, lunch, and supper. In the days when I first started feeding him he often became mulish and snappish about me sticking food in his mouth, but with time and patience I made it work. Then it became worse. As the spring of 2009 marched toward summer, Grandpa's final moorings began to loosen. He lost comprehension of hunger, the meaning of food, and any desire to eat. We were entering terminal apathy. The battle was over, and still it went on every day. The ending was clear, but we had to live it out.

It didn't matter what I told myself. I could reason with words, but words became ashes when it *felt* like his impending death was the final defeat of my caregiving. When Grandpa would not eat, no matter how much I tried, I felt like a failure. It felt like Alzheimer's had won.

Every morning I got him up and brought him out for breakfast. Every morning I sat beside him, and coaxed him to eat.

"Here, have a bite, Grandpa. Have a bite." I would prompt him, bringing the spoon up to his lips.

"I don't want it," he would say.

"Just one more," I tried to cajole.

I could use all of my persuasion, all of my tricks, and still the time would come when he refused any more. "No more!" he loudly declared. "I don't want you to give me any more!" I would try to feed him, or give him something to drink, and he would refuse to open his mouth or else turn his head away.

It was hard, so very hard, for both of us. It felt like a great victory when he would let me feed him, and instinctively opened his mouth when I lifted the spoon and said, "Here, have a bite."

But those successes became less and less frequent. Life had become a succession of battles to get Grandpa to eat.

Supper was always the worst. By the end of the day his exhaustion and confusion were at their height. He was beyond pleading or persuasion then. Eating had no meaning. He would slump over the table and grab the edges to brace himself. Eyes half closed, in an almost semi-catatonic state, he yelled.

"Heeey! HEEEY!"

It could descend into a wordless bellow. It wasn't ceaseless—there was almost a rhythm to the noise. A yell would come after several breaths of silence, to repeat, and still repeat again.

In between the yells I would try to feed him.

This was no longer yelling for anyone or anything. It was yelling because he was lost, confused, and exhausted. Finally, when I could slip no more spoonfuls of food in his mouth, I would clean him up and take him from the table. Maybe I could get something in him for a bedtime snack, maybe not.

The next day we would start over again.

He was slipping beyond the point where I could do anything.

The feeling of futility and helplessness made me want to give up and walk away, but I felt compelled to go back the next meal and to try. There was nothing I could do. I couldn't pry his mouth open and force him to eat or drink. But to not even try was like giving up on Grandpa. So I would gently prompt him, and struggle with my own feelings of helplessness, and hopelessness. It was mentally and emotionally exhausting.

I fought the battle, but it felt like a thankless, pointless, task. I was losing, and it dragged out day after day. I would not give up. I wallowed in failure. My failure I saw in Grandpa's bone thin arms, felt it in his knobby knees. He was little more than a skeleton, and what could I do? All I could do was try.

How much longer? How much worse would it get? Those thoughts were dull in the back of my mind. I couldn't really think about them. All of my energy was focused on the next meal, the next day. Alzheimer's might have won, but I wasn't giving up. His life was winding down, and mine was flying to pieces.

What did I cling to in those days? What was left after every success and every effort from the past three years had become a failure before my eyes? What did I hold on to when there was nothing left I could heal, and nothing left I could give?

I could give different kinds of answers to that question, but one comes in the form of an exchange that happened before the last swells of Alzheimer's overtook us. This incident was back in the days when Grandpa still tried to go to the bathroom, a time which seemed so long ago.

It was the middle of the night, and I had just finished cleaning up another mess. There had been urine everywhere—a puddle spreading over the bathroom floor, more soaking Grandpa's clothes. The routine was all too familiar. I stripped him out of his filthy clothes, dressed him, put him to bed, and cleaned up the bathroom. Now back in bed myself, the darkness around me, I willed for sleep to come quickly.

"I'm sorry."

Grandpa's disembodied voice jerked me back to the present.

"What's that, Grandpa?" I asked.

"I...I've never said thank you," he said. "For all that you have done. It's not something anyone should have to do. And...It's not that I'm not. It's just that I...it's hard..."

"It's okay, Grandpa."

Sadness welled up inside sudden and strong, like a weight on my chest. It is hard to feel thankful and sorrowful so strongly at the same time.

"You don't have to say it," I said. "Don't think about it. I want to do this. I know. I understand."

"Yeah." he said quietly. "Well...it's just...that I am."

It would be dramatic, I suppose, but not true, to say I lay awake every night through those hard times remembering that moment. I didn't. In the exhaustion and grind of life my waking moments were consumed by the daily tasks. Still, it was the reality behind our words that night—a truth much bigger than either of us, and only dimly expressed in our small exchange—which kept me going and gave me strength though it seemed all strength would give out.

§§§

At the end of August I caught a mild cold, and at the beginning of September I passed it on to Grandpa. He became a little sick, and the cold made him more tired. Every sickness was a blow against his abilities, and so it was this time. Only this time his mind didn't have the strength to come back. His body recovered from the cold, but his mind decided it had finished the fight.

He was tired, so tired of living. He just wanted to close his eyes and rest. He slept, and didn't want to wake up. He woke up for ever more brief periods of time, increasingly unwilling to eat or drink. Then he slipped into a semi-comatose state. It felt sudden, but it wasn't, not really. The day was not for me to chose, only to meet. The battle I had been slowly losing was over.

I tried to keep up the fight. I tried to pull him through the gap one last time. But his last most coherent words were, "I don't want it! I don't want it! I don't want it!" which he snapped at me, his eyes only half open, when I tried to feed him some chocolate pudding.

What did he want to do? He wanted to rest quietly, and to not be troubled with the troubles of life anymore. He had gone beyond my reach. His ship was sailing, and he was leaving me behind.

When I took that walk down by the creek on the first of September I didn't know Grandpa had less than two weeks to live. He was already dying. I knew the end was drawing closer by the day, but I didn't know it was that close.

The end had come, and with it the last vigil.

At the end, there was a last time for everything. There were the last good-byes, but there were many more last things before that final farewell. The clock winds down, and the last days pass much as the last minutes do. There was the waiting, and the watching. Then there were the things I did. They might be the small things, and seem like meaningless things, but they can be poignant with meaning, too. They had been my life for the last three years.

I knew there were only so many more times I would have the chance to hug him. I knew soon, all too soon, I would not be able to tuck him into bed anymore, because he wouldn't be there to tuck in. I wouldn't be able to watch him lie in bed, sleeping the sleep of one exhausted by trying to live, and feel in my heart what I think a parent feels seeing their child sleep at night.

So I tried to remember the looming realities as the last days slid by, and tried to cherish those times I had to hug him, to answer his call, and to tuck him in at night with a kiss after all the struggle of the day was done. Even with the end near it was hard to value things as I ought. Or, at least, to know how much I valued them.

Preparing for Grandpa to pass in the winter, I didn't see how close the day had come until it was upon me. Perhaps it couldn't have been known, or maybe I didn't want to see. Perhaps it was best that it wasn't seen any more clearly.

I didn't know his last bath would be the last. I didn't know I would never comb his hair again. I tucked him in the last time in his own bed, only a few feet from mine, and I didn't know it was the last time. I brought him back to the bedroom in his wheelchair, moved him to bed, and tucked him in. I didn't know the next night he would be too exhausted, wouldn't want to leave the couch and I would have pity and let him sleep that night on the couch. Then every night remaining would be spent in the living room. Afterward the bedroom was mine alone. All those long nights suffering with Grandpa's struggles, and now I had it to myself in quietness.

As Grandpa began to slip more quickly, the nearness of the end grew clear. Then I knew with painful clarity that the "lasts" were piling up. It was a ritual of deeds, done so many times through all the long days before, now coming to the close of their final acts. I didn't want to think about that, and I didn't want to forget. The end could not bear careful thought. Death was there, and I could feel its closeness. I dared not feel too much.

He ate so little near the end he had hardly much at all to put out, but still there was the last time he soiled himself and I had to change him. Grandpa's strength gave out, and he could no longer stand at all. Up until the end he had always been able to stand long enough for me to change him, which made it easy. Now he was bed-ridden on the couch. I had to change him, and I had to change him where he lay. I had to do it alone.

After I finished changing him, he lay exhausted and hurting and our eyes met for the last time in understanding.

The hours passed, and he slept.

I would slip my hand into his and hold it for a little while. His hand lay still beside him, still and yet so very warm with life. I hadn't thought a dying man would feel so warm and alive.

I knew it would come to this, but that knowledge didn't make it easy. Grandpa had such a healthy body that if his mind had not been afflicted with Alzheimer's he might have lived to be a very old man. Now, even though his mind had shut down, still his body continued on.

It would not give up quickly.

The last time he ate or drank anything of substance was on Friday the 4th of September. He lived another full week.

He lay on the couch and I wondered if he was thirsty. The thought gnawed at me. He slept, but sometimes pain would seize him. Then his body shook, jerking and trembling from some unseen affliction, and he whimpered. I tried to still him, tried to comfort with touch and words, but there was little I could do.

The pain was difficult to watch. If we had him propped up carefully with pillows supporting various parts of his body he appeared comfortable most of the time. But whenever we had to move him to change his diaper, his frail body—and especially his lifelong problem with back pain—flared up and he spasmed and whimpered. I felt like we were putting him on the torture rack whenever we had to move him.

I felt helpless.

Unless the pain came he didn't look uncomfortable, but I couldn't help thinking about how it would feel to lie there, no longer able to communicate, slowly starving and thirsting to death. What if his throat was parched and he wanted a drink and was lying there silently wishing someone would give him a drink? I wanted to do something. I wanted to take care of him.

Over the course of the succeeding days I managed to coax a few dribbles of liquid down his throat—first with a spoon, then an eye-dropper. But then he began to choke because he could only swallow by reflex now and when he choked he felt like he was drowning and the scrunched struggling expression on his face made me sorry I had tried to give him something to drink.

Still his body kept going. He breathed regularly, quietly, his eyes closed, his body slowly consuming itself in a determined effort to keep living. One could call it a coma, but sometimes, for a brief moment, he opened his eyes a bit. If I was lucky he would drag them into focus to look at the world—and me—for an instant, before letting them drift shut again. He was still conscious of sounds and he recognized voices. When his daughter Daryl laughed in another room he smiled so wide I knew he had heard.

I took out his false teeth for the last time. There was nothing more to do. The end was very near, the sense of winding down palpable.

I played the audio Bible on headphones for him, because I knew he had enjoyed that from the early days. I tried to give him everything I could that I knew he had loved.

It was hard, and awful. But there are things no matter how terrible and painful they be, I want to live them. I can't explain it, I only knew I wanted to see this through. I needed to see it through.

Life never goes in the neat order I desire. I want to write about life and laughter, light and living. But sometimes the darker things break in, and I must face them. Sometimes I must say goodbye. I want it to be a long goodbye, but I don't always get what I wish. Goodbyes come so much sooner than expected.

This was our goodbye.

Except, I didn't know how to say goodbye.

Oh, cruel, cruel world.

In those few days when Grandpa was clearly dying, but not yet dead, I had time to ponder what it meant to say goodbye, and how exactly I would do it. I sat there and I stared at his sleeping face, and I wondered what I could do, what I should do. Somehow, however true "I love you" and "Goodbye" might be, they didn't feel like enough.

How can you distill a life down to a few words?

But as I sat there, I realized that I couldn't. There wasn't anything to do—not anything different. I realized that what I said was only as good as what I did. All my life I would be saying "Hello" and

"Goodbye" in whatever I did. The substance of my deeds toward each person would define whether I had given them a good "Hello" and "Goodbye." If my deeds toward others were deeds that spoke true love toward them then no better "Hello" or "Goodbye" could be said.

I said goodbye to Grandpa. I said those words, because it seemed like to not say them was some attempt to deny the reality. But mostly I realized that my best goodbye would be to do what I had been doing for the last three years—saying "I love you" all day, every day, by what I did for him. There could be no better goodbye.

So goodbye Grandpa. I love you. But you already knew that.

Alzheimer's takes many things, and there are days when it seems like nothing stands against the ravages of that disease. It can feel like Alzheimer's wins in the end. But there is one thing no sickness can take. When all understanding and ability is lost and the darkest nights have come, still nothing can take away love. Not even Alzheimer's.

I never became a good guitar player in all the months I had practiced with Grandpa as my audience of one. For him it had never mattered what I played, or how well I played. It only mattered that I was there. So I played the guitar for him and sang him hymns, one last time. I knew that if he could hear me, he would love it still. So with fumbling fingers I began to pick out the notes.

> *The sands of time are sinking,*
> *The dawn of heaven breaks;*
> *The summer morn I've sighed for—*
> *The fair, sweet morn awakes;*
>
> *Dark, dark hath been the midnight,*
> *But day-spring is at hand,*
> *And glory, glory dwelleth*
> *In Immanuel's Land...*

§§§

Grandpa died September 11th, 2009. In two more weeks I would have cared for him exactly three years. He was eighty-one.

§§§

The Sea is Wide

ABOUT THE AUTHOR

Rundy Purdy was born in November 1981 and homeschooled until graduation from high school. In September 2006 he began caring for his grandfather who suffered with Alzheimer's, and died in 2009. Afterward, Purdy cared for his ailing grandmother for an additional five years until her death in 2014. This experience gave Purdy a passion for helping other caregivers by sharing the lessons learned through his experience. He founded CaregivingReality.com as a place for all caregivers to find encouragement and support.